Care Work and Class

Care Work and Class

Domestic Workers' Struggle for Equal Rights in Latin America

MERIKE BLOFIELD

The Pennsylvania State University Press
University Park, Pennsylvania

Some of the material found in chapters 1, 2, 4, and 5 first appeared in Merike Blofield, "Feudal Enclaves and Political Reforms: Domestic Workers in Latin America," *Latin American Research Review* 44, no. 1 (2009): 158–90.

Library of Congress Cataloging-in-Publication Data

Blofield, Merike.
Care work and class : domestic workers' struggle for equal rights in Latin America / Merike Blofield.
p.   cm.
Includes bibliographical references and index.
Summary: "Examines the movement for labor reform among domestic workers in Latin America. Explores how domestic workers' mobilization, strategic alliances, and political windows of opportunity can lead to improved rights"—Provided by publisher.
ISBN 978-0-271-05327-1 (cloth : alk. paper)
ISBN 978-0-271-05328-8 (pbk.: alk. paper)
1. Household employees—Latin America—Social conditions.
2. Social classes—Latin America.
3. Equality—Latin America.
4. Industrial relations—Latin America.
5. Labor movement—Latin America—History—21st century.
I. Title.

HD8039.D52B56 2012
331.7'6164098—dc23
2011043058

Copyright © 2012
The Pennsylvania State University
All rights reserved
Printed in the United States of America
Published by
The Pennsylvania State University Press,
University Park, PA 16802-1003

The Pennsylvania State University Press is a member of the Association of American University Presses.

It is the policy of The Pennsylvania State University Press to use acid-free paper. Publications on uncoated stock satisfy the minimum requirements of American National Standard for Information Sciences—Permanence of Paper for Printed Library Material, ANSI Z39.48–1992.

Contents

List of Tables | vii
Preface and Acknowledgments | ix
List of Acronyms | xi

Introduction | 1

1
Domestic Workers in Latin America Today | 9

2
Overcoming Elite Resistance | 39

3
Working in Chronic Informality | 68

4
Bolivia and Costa Rica:
Social Mobilization and Reform from the Bottom Up | 83

5
Uruguay and Chile:
Basic Universalism Versus Top-Down Incrementalism | 106

Conclusion | 130

Notes | 143
References | 157
Index | 171

Tables

1.1 Percentage of economically active women employed in domestic service in Latin American countries (urban areas) | 24
1.2 Maximum work hours per week for workers in general and for domestic workers, 1980s and 2010, from each country's labor code | 29
1.3 Main characteristics of laws on domestic workers in South America, 2010 | 32–35
1.4 Main characteristics of laws on domestic workers in Central America, the Dominican Republic, and Mexico, 2010 | 36–38
2.1 Type and scope of reform in eight Latin American countries, 1990–2010 | 42
2.2 Year and scope of reform in the case studies | 48
2.3 Sociodemographic and political variables in Bolivia, Costa Rica, Uruguay, and Chile | 48
3.1 Percentage of female domestic workers with pension protections versus percentage of the total working population with pension protections | 71

Preface and Acknowledgments

The idea for this book was born during field research for my previous project. I visited the home of an upper-class conservative Catholic political activist in Chile for an interview. We sat in her sloping garden, where she rang a bell for the maid to bring coffee. She elaborated on the difficulties of balancing different interests in women's rights and used the example of domestic violence and the importance of family unity in poor families. Her maid, she told me, had a physically abusive husband. Were he prosecuted and jailed, the family's income would decline, and thus it was better to keep the offender at home. For the woman I was interviewing, the solution was not public involvement through services such as safe houses or even a personal responsibility on her part as the woman's employer, but rather to keep the violent offender in the home because of his financial contribution to the family household.

I was struck by this comment, juxtaposed with a gorgeous setting where the same victim of domestic violence served us coffee, and it made me keenly aware of the enormous social distance between the employer and her employee. Would she have advocated a similar solution to the women in her circles? Perhaps, but probably not.

Several years later, I began to look into the topic of domestic workers in Latin America and found that very little had been written on this sector of workers, especially from a social scientific perspective. On the other hand, as I would mention my emerging topic to friends, acquaintances, and students in or from the region, I was struck by how often people told me, "In Latin America, everyone has a maid." This comment intrigued me, as it quite clearly delineated the boundaries of "everyone" and reflected the simultaneous ubiquity and invisibility of the women who work in this occupation. I decided to investigate the laws, policies, and politics that surround this sector, and this book is the result. Even though the book is driven by normative concerns (of social equity), it is an empirical investigation into the political dynamics of domestic workers' rights. As it went to press, the ILO passed a convention on domestic workers' rights. This book examines the politics up to the convention and discusses the implications of the convention in the conclusion.

I would like to thank Sandy Thatcher for encouraging me to write this book. His enthusiasm convinced me that a book on this topic could and should be published. He brought me to Penn State University Press, and while he is no longer its director, I am grateful for his guidance and for the opportunity to publish with the press.

There are many others to thank. During my field research, many individuals were kind enough to open doors for me, to give me interviews, and to share their research with me. I would especially like to thank Betty Pinto in Bolivia, Pamela Farias in Chile, Juliana Martínez Franzoni in Costa Rica, and Fernando Filgueira in Uruguay. Institutionally, I would like to thank FLACSO-Chile and the University of Costa Rica. I am grateful to the Haas-Haesly family, who generously let me stay with them in Costa Rica, especially to Xavier, who, as a result, had to share a room with his baby sister for two weeks. Thank you also to the University of Miami's Research Support Award for funding a bulk of my field research trips.

I would like to thank the University of Miami political science colloquium participants for giving me several opportunities to share my research. For feedback on chapter drafts, I would like to thank Felipe Agüero, Louise Davidson-Schmich, Claudio Fuentes, Elise Giuliano, Liesl Haas, Kristen Hill Maher, Casey Klofstad, Gregory Koger, Juan Pablo Luna, Christopher Mann, Juliana Martínez Franzoni, Maria Victoria Murillo, Joseph Parent, Mari Peepre, and Bill Smith. Jennifer Pribble provided especially helpful comments on the final draft of the manuscript. In addition, Evelyne Huber has always been very generous with her professional and intellectual advice.

I would also like to thank the anonymous reviewers at Penn State University Press for their very helpful comments. The detailed and insightful feedback of "Reviewer #2" in particular helped me clarify my argument, and I express my gratitude to this anonymous person, if he or she picks up this book again. Alicia de Leon Bonilla, Susie Carballo, and Sivan Goobich provided able research assistance. Thank you to Drucilla Scribner for taking the photograph of the maid's uniform store in Buenos Aires for the book cover, and to Julie Schoelles at Penn State for being an efficient, meticulous, and friendly copyeditor.

Finally, I am grateful for the support of my family and close friends, and especially of my husband, Matthias Dietrich. He may not have realized what he was getting into by becoming involved with an academic but amazingly enough decided to stick with it and helps me put things into perspective.

Acronyms

ANECAP	Asociación Nacional de Empleadas de Casa Particular (National Association of Household Workers)
ASTRADOMES	Asociación de Trabajadoras Domésticas (Domestic Workers' Association)
FENATRAHOB	Federación Nacional de las Trabajadoras del Hogar de Bolivia (National Household Workers' Federation of Bolivia)
ILO	International Labour Organization
INAMU	Instituto Nacional de las Mujeres (Women's Executive Agency)
MAS	Movimiento al Socialismo (Movement Toward Socialism)
PIT-CNT	Plenario Intersindical de Trabajadores-Convención Nacional de Trabajadores (Inter-Trade Union Assembly–Workers' National Convention, or Central Trade Union)
PUSC	Partido Unidad Social Cristiana (Social Christian Unity Party)
SINTRACAP	Sindicato de Trabajadoras de Casas Particulares (Household Workers' Union)
SUTD	Sindicato Único de Trabajadoras Domésticas (Domestic Workers' Union)

INTRODUCTION

This book is about how class and gender interact with the state. It is about whether and how a group that is multiply disadvantaged gets political attention and recognition in a context of high socioeconomic inequalities. Often colloquially referred to as nannies, maids, and housekeepers—or in Spanish as *muchachas, nanas,* and *empleadas*—domestic workers come from poorer backgrounds and work in wealthier households. Often also from ethnic or visible minorities, they make up over 15 percent of the economically active female population in Latin America, or twelve million in absolute numbers, and their services enable the well-off to work outside the home and to engage in leisure-time activities that they consider more desirable than household work and the daily routine of child care. This dynamic is a by-product of highly unequal societies, which produce a demand for the outsourcing of domestic activities as well as a ready supply of inexpensive labor. Driven not only by class-based views but also by views of the appropriate status for what is traditionally considered "women's work," the state has—in Latin America as well as much of the rest of the world—mandated longer work hours and lower benefits for this sector, basically ensuring that the servant is always available, outside of sleep, to serve her employers. This has, in effect, subsidized a cheap labor force for higher-income families. Recently, these laws have begun, albeit slowly, to change.

The goal of this book is not to make a normative assessment of the desirability of paid domestic work as an occupation per se. What motivates the book, and what I consider *politically* compelling, is the role of the state in mediating this unequal relationship between the employers and the workers. The legal status of domestic workers exemplifies the tension between equal rights and class divisions and goes to the heart of the debate over what legal equality and social justice in a formal democracy entail. It also exemplifies the status that the state accords the reproductive activities of the household, which are overwhelmingly performed by women and traditionally undervalued. Often, it highlights racial and ethnic divides as well.

These dynamics apply not only to Latin America or to developing countries. Paid domestic work in advanced industrialized countries displays similar characteristics, although the vast majority of domestic workers are immigrants. It is estimated that the sector employs approximately 1.5 million workers across the United States, virtually all of whom are foreign born. Domestic workers in the United States are not covered by federal laws such as the Family and Medical Leave Act, employment discrimination laws, overtime laws, or occupational safety laws. Some states provide additional legal protections—most recently New York State in June 2010[1]—but many do not. In many other high-income countries as well, immigrant women work as domestics with lower legal protections.

What makes Latin America particularly interesting is that three trends come together: high inequalities, changing gender relations, and democratic politics. First, the region as a whole exhibits the highest income inequalities in the world. This inequality creates both the demand and the domestic supply for the occupation. Although immigration has increased in some of the more developed Latin American countries, the vast majority of domestic workers are nationals of the countries in which they work. While their status as citizens distinguishes the dynamics in this sector from many of the policy debates in advanced industrialized countries, this context of deep domestic inequalities places the workers in a particularly precarious position and makes overcoming collective action problems and competing with elites for political attention more difficult. Second, the significant increase of women in Latin American labor markets has likewise led to the demand for paid domestic work and its supply, explaining the continued prevalence of paid domestic work as an occupation in the region. This interaction of class and gender has led to the ostensible liberation of professional women but has shifted much of the burden not to men but to lower-class women.

Third, the region as a whole, with the exception of Cuba, is formally democratic, providing a context in which discrimination *can* be openly challenged. Indeed, transitions to democratic politics over the past two to three decades have provided an opportunity to contest explicit discrimination. Across the region, women's organizations, indigenous movements, labor unions, human rights groups, and others have organized and demanded equal rights and an end to discrimination, and many of the more egregious legal statutes condoning explicit discrimination have been overturned as a result. In many cases, historically disadvantaged groups have succeeded in at least gaining legal recognition and equality, even if proactive enforcement has been slower to come.

What is striking is that two decades after democratic transitions, legal reforms have been so slow to come for domestic workers. Four countries—Colombia, Bolivia, Uruguay, and Costa Rica—have recently equalized the rights of domestic workers with those of other workers (and Argentina may soon become the fifth). However, explicitly discriminatory legal statutes remained in place in fourteen Latin American countries in 2010. In most national labor codes, domestic workers are not granted the same rights as other workers (such as work hours, salary, or benefits), and in some countries the codes even maintain what could be considered feudal clauses (such as mandating the respect of the employee toward the employer but not the other way around). In Brazil, Guatemala, Honduras, Mexico, and Venezuela, domestic workers can be legally obligated to work fourteen hours or more a day, and in many countries, including Argentina and Venezuela, they are legally obligated to behave in a "subordinate" way. In Argentina—and Chile until 1998—they are explicitly excluded from maternity leave, a particularly powerful form of discrimination in an occupation made up overwhelmingly of lower-income women. In addition, enforcement of the rights that do exist is very inadequate, and domestic workers are much more likely than other workers to labor informally, without written contracts or social security. Hence, domestic workers suffer from a double discrimination: explicit legal discrimination and a lack of proactive enforcement of rights that do exist.

It is not substantive irrelevance that keeps this discrimination on the books. Even though some scholars predicted the demise of domestic service as an occupation with economic modernization, paid domestic work today shows no clear signs of decline. As noted above, the occupation employs over 15 percent of the economically active female population in Latin America and is hence the largest single source of employment for women.[2] Concomitantly, data from the late 1990s indicate that about 15 percent of households in the region employed more full-time domestic workers. Thus, if we also take into account part-time domestic workers, it is likely that at least 30 percent of all households in the region are intimately part of this economic exchange, either as employers or as workers.

Neither are the extant statutes due to simple oversight. In fact, when these laws have been contested, there has been considerable resistance among political elites to overturn them, as the status quo is natural to many of them and in their interests. This resistance is more than economic, however. It is also cultural; with this group, perhaps more starkly than with any other, race, gender, and class prejudices and discrimination are crystallized. Seventy-five years after the issue was first introduced, the International Labour Organization (ILO) passed an international convention on domestic workers' rights in 2011. This book addresses the politics of domestic workers' rights prior to the convention, and the conclusion discusses the approval of the convention and the implications in Latin American countries.

There are a variety of conceptual lenses through which to examine the dynamics of paid domestic work. First, a central question of this book is whether and how the political system addresses the demands of people who are socioeconomically most disadvantaged. However, the book is not just about "the poor" but also about the well-off, and how they see the world and their place in it. Legally and economically, the interests of domestic workers are opposed to the interests of their employers, who are drawn from the middle, upper middle, and upper classes.[3] How the state mediates this power relation—in terms of both laws and enforcement—is an indicator of how the state balances the interests of the rich versus the poor in a democracy.

Second, paid domestic work is also one component of the politics of care work and gender relations in contemporary societies. With urbanization and a shift to service sector economies, more women have entered the paid labor force and more families have sought to resolve their child care needs without full-time homemakers. This has specific gender and class implications in Latin America. On the one hand, care work—both paid and unpaid—is still predominantly performed by women. On the other hand, the options available to poor families versus well-off families are very different. In Latin America, wealthier families can afford private domestic workers, given the ready supply of cheap labor, while lower-income mothers leave their own children in informal care arrangements to work as nannies and maids themselves. Given the legal restrictions on employees in this sector, the state in effect provides a subsidy to the wealthy by allowing for a cheap labor force with extended work hours and few benefits. This has most likely also reduced demand for child care and elderly care centers among professionals. Such centers are the dominant mode of resolving dependent care needs of dual-earner couples in advanced industrialized countries.

Third, and relatedly, the politics surrounding this sector are not *only* about class and economic interests or about gender and the politics of care work; this is very much a case of the intersectionality of class, gender, and race or ethnicity. Domestic workers are overwhelmingly women and from poor backgrounds; they also tend to come from ethnic or racial minorities. Female domestic workers earn on average less than male domestic workers, and domestic workers from ethnic or racial minorities tend to earn less than white domestic workers, indicating that the low pay in domestic service is not only a function of the occupation per se. Finally, in some countries, many domestic workers are noncitizens. These multiple disadvantages place domestic workers in a particularly precarious and powerless position vis-à-vis society as a whole and even vis-à-vis potential advocacy coalitions (Strolovitch 2006). While domestic workers are women, laborers, and often from ethnic minorities, their needs have tended to remain invisible within labor unions, women's organizations, and indigenous movements. Indeed, Laurel Weldon (2008) recently stated that an excellent case study for intersectional analysis is that of paid domestic workers.[4]

Despite their substantive and theoretical importance, domestic workers have received surprisingly little attention in the scholarly literature to date. In 1989, Elsa Chaney and Mary Garcia Castro published a seminal edited volume on domestic workers in Latin America entitled *Muchachas No More: Household Workers in Latin America and the Caribbean*. In the introduction, they declared that "the scant attention paid to this important sector of working women is surprising" (3) and called for further research. While several excellent historical and anthropological works have since been published, the call has gone largely unanswered for studies from a sociopolitical perspective.[5] This book seeks to fill this gap by examining domestic workers from a specifically political and comparative perspective.

In chapter 1, I compare the politics of care work in advanced industrialized countries and Latin America, where inequalities are much higher. Paid domestic work is one component within the broader context of care work and gender relations, and its prevalence is also a function of the level of socioeconomic inequalities both domestically and globally. Within this context, paid domestic work embodies some unique characteristics, which I discuss, drawing on the extant literature. I then discuss the history of domestic service in Latin America and move on to describe domestic service in Latin America today, the prevalence of this form of employment, and the laws that surround it.

In chapter 2, I address the central question of the book whether and how the political system addresses the interests of groups that are multiply disadvantaged. Domestic workers exemplify such a group, as their specific shared identity is through the nature of their labor, which is poorly remunerated; in addition, virtually all are women and many are from ethnic or visible minorities that have been historically underrepresented and discriminated against. While domestic workers' organizations have demanded social attention and equal labor rights in many countries for decades, political actors in the region have been extremely reluctant to respond to their demands, given that increasing the position and rights of domestic workers involves some form of redistribution and that such changes conflict with the interests of political elites themselves and their better-organized middle- and upper-class constituents. The traditional undervaluation of household and care work, performed by women, also plays a role, and, finally, racism among some elites may make them less likely to view domestic workers who are darker skinned or from different ethnic groups as their social equals and deserving of the same rights. Resistance to extending rights—whether in the form of active opposition or indifference—is likely to be broad and steadfast, and most political elites will tend to either ignore such concerns or table legislative bills addressing them. Even ostensible allies such as feminists and labor unions are likely to focus on the interests of their more advantaged, organized members first (Strolovitch 2006).

Despite the weak position of domestic workers, however, there are instances of successful policy reform. Out of eighteen major Latin American countries, eight have substantially reformed domestic worker laws since democratization and as of 2010. Of these, four have achieved virtually equal rights (Bolivia, Colombia,[6] Costa Rica, and Uruguay) and four have to date enacted partial reforms (Argentina, Brazil, Chile, and Peru). I outline these reforms as well as reform attempts in countries where the attempts have not been successful. I then ask the question, how does equal rights reform make it onto the political agenda and get passed, and when it does not, why? Phrased another way, *when do domestic workers' interests win over those of their more powerful employers?*

While elite resistance to change can explain much of the overall lack of reform in the region, I argue that mobilization by domestic workers' organizations, a network of allies, and political "windows of opportunity," mostly linked to left-wing executive and legislative allies, can result in legal reform even in a region as unequal as Latin America. There is no single path to reform; smaller, piecemeal reforms require less mobilization and pressure than equal rights reform that includes work hours. The key struggle has been to make the issue visible and to get it onto the political agenda; once the issue gets to a plenary debate and goes up for a vote, it is very likely to be approved. With executive support, which to date has rarely been forthcoming, agenda setting and reform can be speedier and less obstacle ridden.

The enforcement of laws is, of course, as crucial an issue as are the laws themselves. Many of the legal rights of domestic workers—whatever they are—are not respected in practice. In chapter 3, I address enforcement and discuss two specific dimensions of it: access to social security protections and the prevalence of labor violations. I then discuss the key factors that explain variance in enforcement across the region. On implementation and enforcement, state capacity and executive ideology—particularly in the ministry of labor—are crucial.

In order to illustrate these dynamics, I process-trace the politics of legal reform and enforcement of domestic workers' rights in four countries: Bolivia, Costa Rica, Uruguay, and Chile. All four are unitary countries—making comparative analysis more feasible—and at the time of choosing the case studies, the four countries spanned the range of outcomes: full reform in Bolivia in 2003 and in Uruguay in 2006, partial reforms in Chile, and no reform in Costa Rica. Since then, in 2009, Costa Rica passed equal rights reform. However, the process of reform in that country remains illustrative of the political dynamics associated with domestic workers' rights.

This case selection also represents a pairing of "most-different" cases and "most-similar" cases (see table 2.3). With significant economic, sociodemographic, and political differences, Bolivia and Costa Rica are most-different countries with a similar outcome: equal rights reform. Uruguay and Chile, with more developed economies and more institutionalized democracies, are, on the other hand, most-similar countries with different outcomes: equal rights reform in the former and piecemeal reforms but not equal rights in the latter.

In chapter 4, I discuss Bolivia and Costa Rica, where the political process was long, arduous, and obstacle ridden. In Bolivia, the first country to achieve equal rights through Congress, the initial legislative bill to equalize rights was submitted in 1993. A revised version was approved in the House in 2000 and finally in the Senate in 2003. In Costa Rica, the initial reform bill was submitted in 1996, and after several attempts another bill made it through commission in 2003 and was finally brought to a legislative vote at the end of 2008, was approved, and became law in 2009. In both countries, reforms were the result of extensive mobilization and pressure from domestic workers' organizations and, over time, their social and political allies. The executive in neither country proactively supported reform, forcing advocates to go through slower legislative channels. There, resistance by political elites kept the bills from an open debate and vote for years, but finally advocates were able to take advantage of political windows of opportunity when they arose. On the other hand, in both countries but especially in Bolivia, enforcement efforts have lagged.

In chapter 5, I discuss Uruguay and Chile. In Uruguay, a legislative bill to equalize domestic workers' rights was submitted to Congress in 1990, and after a long wait it was approved in a plenary vote in the House in 1996. It was repeatedly postponed in the Senate and died in commission. In 2005, the newly elected left-wing government initiated equal rights reform, which was rapidly approved in 2006. In Chile, four piecemeal reforms over the past two decades, three of which were tagged onto broader labor reforms, have incrementally provided domestic workers with more labor rights (severance pay, maternity leave, minimum wage, and equal holidays). However, their legal workweek still remains significantly longer at seventy-two hours, compared to forty-five hours for wageworkers in general. While in both countries reforms were led by political elites, the differences between their reforms are reflective of more general political differences: Chile's narrower reforms were top-down, in the context of weak mobilization and strong conservative opposition, while Uruguay's comprehensive equal rights reform reflected the participatory, inclusive nature of the left-wing government (Pribble 2011). On the other hand, left or center-left governments in both countries have spearheaded improved enforcement efforts.

In the conclusion, I tie together the political dynamics that have characterized reform attempts toward this sector. I then discuss the process that led to the approval of the ILO convention on domestic workers' rights in June 2011 (as this book went to press) and its potential impact on the visibility of and agenda setting on this sector in the future. With the support of the ILO, advocates have received a boost in their reform efforts, and there may come a tipping point at which political elites decide that the political benefits of reform outweigh the costs. I draw on the current legal reform under consideration in Argentina—where the Chamber unanimously approved equal rights in March 2011 and where the bill now awaits Senate debate—to illustrate these changing dynamics. I then contrast domestic workers' rights with other claims to equal rights, highlighting the similarities and differences with other women's rights or gender equality issues, as well as with informal sector workers. Finally, I return to a broader discussion of the future of care work in Latin America and make some empirical predictions and policy recommendations.

1

DOMESTIC WORKERS IN LATIN AMERICA TODAY

Paid domestic work is one component within the broader context of care work and gender relations. I compare the politics of care work in advanced industrialized countries with those in Latin America, highlighting the distinct dynamics that deep socioeconomic inequalities have produced. Within this context, paid domestic work as an occupation has specific characteristics related to both the nature of the work and its setting that render it vulnerable to exploitation. I then move on to a discussion of the history of domestic service in Latin America and describe domestic service in the region today. I discuss the prevalence and characteristics of this form of employment and the laws that surround it.

The Global Politics of Care Work

In past decades many scholars assumed, and sometimes explicitly argued, that paid domestic work would gradually disappear with economic development and modernization (Boserup 1970; Coser 1973). This assumption may explain the relative lack of scholarly attention to the topic. In reality, however, paid domestic work as a source of employment on a global level may be increasing. In Latin America, it has declined only slightly from 19.2 percent of the urban economically active female population in 1995 to 16.8 percent in 2009 (see table 1.1) (Abramo and Valenzuela 2005; Hite and Viterna 2005; OIT 2010).

The continued importance of paid domestic work as an occupation for women on a global level should be understood in the interactive context of both gender and class inequalities. It is fueled by two key factors: first, by the incursion of women into the paid labor force outside the home, and second, by high levels of economic inequalities, both domestically and internationally, which enable the well-off to hire the services or labor power of the high numbers of lower-income individuals—in this case mostly women—for their personal use. These factors drive both demand for and the supply of domestic workers. In advanced industrialized countries, this is reflected in the increased numbers of immigrant women from developing countries crossing borders to be household workers. As a result, much of the literature on the topic has focused on immigration. This dynamic is maintained in a global cultural context where this occupation tends to be considered acceptable only for women. Indeed, in this study I focus on female domestic workers for two reasons. First, over 90 percent of domestic workers in Latin America are women. Second, most men who are classified as domestic workers have higher-paying and more professionalized jobs, such as chauffeurs and gardeners, and tend to be treated more like other wageworkers than their female counterparts in the house. Hence, many of the more unique, and exploitative, characteristics apply more specifically to the women and girls who work in this occupation inside the house, doing household and care work.

The first trend, increased women's labor force participation rates, situates paid domestic work within the broader dynamics of the politics of care work in societies (see Razavi and Staab 2010). Feminist theorists have paid a lot of attention to the traditional distinctions between the "private" sphere of the family and household and the public sphere of paid work and public life (see Pateman 1989, chap. 6). The private sphere of unremunerated care work, including daily household activities of cooking and cleaning, child rearing, and care of the elderly, has traditionally been relegated to women and often undervalued, while paid work outside the home has been considered the domain of men. With urbanization and the shift to service-dominated economies, more women have entered the paid labor force and fertility rates have declined, and this has changed the dynamics of child rearing and the reproductive activities of the household. Politically, democratic politics, combined with the rise of women's movements, has allowed feminists to question the traditional gender division of labor as well as the undervaluation of household and care work.

A great deal has been written about gender, welfare states, and the politics of care work in the advanced industrialized world, and I will not repeat it here.[1] In essence, families with young children have the following child care options: (1) one parent (usually the mother) stays at home with the children; (2) parents find informal care arrangements with relatives or friends; (3) parents send children to state-financed child care; (4) parents buy private provision of day care on the market; (5) parents hire a domestic worker.[2] There is also a sixth option, which is not really a choice but rather the default for parents who are unable to resolve their child care needs. With option six, the parent (most often the mother) either takes her children with her to work (e.g., street selling in the informal sector) or leaves them alone at home while she goes to work (Heymann 2006).

In many advanced industrialized countries, the government has taken on a significant role in providing free or subsidized early childhood education and care through general tax revenue. In some countries, most prominently the United States, this provision has largely been left to the market. The differences are reflected in the distinct "welfare regimes" of the advanced industrialized world: social democratic welfare states (mainly the Nordic countries) with stronger state roles in redistribution and in ensuring equality between the sexes; Christian democratic welfare states (e.g., continental European countries such as Germany) that have historically sought to maintain traditional family structures, including stay-at-home mothers, but are undergoing significant demographic transitions and are now finding the need to adapt to more liberal societies; liberal welfare states (the Anglophone world) that leave many services, including day care provision, largely to the market (Esping-Andersen 1990, 2002, 2009); and, finally, familial welfare regimes—to an extent a subcategory of the conservative welfare regimes but with less of a state role (found in Southern Europe)—that have historically assigned "a maximum of welfare obligations to the household" (Esping-Andersen 1999, 45).

Despite the differences across these welfare regimes, gender equality has become more of a policy concern in all of them. We can see feminist inroads into households, not just the "public realm"; there is evidence of a shift in gender roles in families in advanced industrialized countries. Men are, albeit slowly, taking on increased responsibilities in household and care work as their wives or partners have joined the paid labor force (Esping-Andersen 2009).

The second trend refers to continuing inequalities. In advanced industrialized democracies, the state has assumed an important role in redistributing income through taxation and regulation of labor markets and labor rights, providing more equality of opportunity and alleviating social risks. Income inequalities in the advanced industrialized countries are relatively low, ranging from a 22 percent after-tax income share of the top decile in Denmark to 30 percent in the United States (United Nations 2007–8). These lower inequalities are achieved through redistributive taxes and progressive social expenditures. In Europe, the Gini coefficient is reduced on average by 15 percent, from .46 to about .31 (Goñi, López, and Servén 2008, 5–6).[3] Overall, given lower levels of inequality—and hence higher relative labor costs—dual-earner families in advanced industrialized countries increasingly rely on the third (state-provided day care) and fourth (market-provided day care) options, while a smaller, wealthier minority hire private nannies. These nannies tend to be immigrants from less developed countries.[4]

In Latin America, inequalities are much higher and the role of the state in alleviating them much less pronounced. Latin America has the highest inequalities of any region in the world, with an average Gini coefficient of .52. The corresponding figure for East Asia is .4, and the only region that approximates Latin America is sub-Saharan Africa, with an average Gini coefficient of .5, hardly a propitious development comparison (Ferreira and Ravallion 2008). The share of the top decile ranges from 34 percent in Uruguay to 47.2 percent in Bolivia, with Colombia, Brazil, Chile, and Paraguay very close behind (United Nations, 2007–8). There has recently been a slight decline in inequalities in many Latin American countries (see CEPAL 2009; López-Calva and Lustig 2010[5]), but overall and compared to the rest of the world, income inequalities have remained high across the region during the last two decades (see Blofield 2011a, 2011b, 2011d). Moreover, measures of income inequality do not factor in wealth differences.

These inequalities are reflected in the class structures and divisions of Latin American countries. Portes and Hoffman divide the urban class structure in Latin America into capitalists, professionals and executives, petty entrepreneurs, formal workers, and informal workers. The size of the dominant classes (the capitalists, professionals, and executives) ranges from 5 percent of the population in El Salvador to 13.9 percent in Venezuela (Portes and Hoffman 2003, 52). While the combined size of the dominant classes is small, their share of the income and wealth in the region is high; Portes and Hoffman find that "all the excess income inequality of the region" is attributable to the combined income of this group (58–59). Informal workers—outside the reach of state regulation—are, on the other hand, the largest class in terms of population in all Latin American countries. The majority of these workers do not make enough income to surpass the poverty level, and this sector has increased in recent decades to encompass about 45 percent of the region's population (Centeno and Portes 2006; de Soto 2000; Filgueira 2011; Portes and Hoffman 2003). It is in this sector that the majority of domestic workers reside.

These class divisions have historically been reinforced by low levels of intergenerational mobility. Studies have shown that there has been little upward mobility and little downward mobility in Latin America; that is, the poor have tended to stay poor, and the rich have tended to stay rich (Gaviria 2007; IADB 2008). This lack of intergenerational mobility has fostered what Karl refers to as a "dualistic world" (2000, 153) and what others have referred to as "social distance" between individuals from different classes (Blofield 2011b; Blofield and Luna 2011; Fish 2006; Rollins 1985). This social distance is crystallized in the relationship between employer and household worker, or "master" and "servant," who, while sharing an intimate enclosed physical space, inhabit very different worlds and have very different life opportunities.

Government policies in the region as a whole tend to reinforce these inequalities. Taxes and transfers in Latin America reduce the Gini coefficient on average by only 2 percent (Goñi, López, and Servén 2008, 5–6). Tax burdens are low and rely more heavily on regressive value-added taxes than on progressive income and wealth taxes (Mahon 2011). When the tax burdens are higher, as in Brazil, the better-off try to find ways to evade them. While public education (except for higher education) and health expenditures tend to reach the poor better, the bulk of social transfer payments (e.g., pensions, unemployment insurance) are spent through contributory systems that privilege higher-income workers in the formal sector.[6] In six of the major Latin American countries, the top two income quintiles receive on average 70 percent of the social insurance expenditures, while the bottom quintile receives only 7 percent (Goñi, López, and Servén 2008, 18–19). While many states' implementation of conditional cash transfer programs (which give qualifying poor families small cash transfers in exchange for children's regular school attendance and health checkups) have improved the quality of life for numerous families over the past decade and a half, overall Latin American states tend to provide little risk protection for the lower-income quintiles and the vast informal sector.

In Latin America, immigration also feeds the supply of domestic workers. For example, Argentina, Chile, and Costa Rica receive immigrants from poorer neighboring countries as domestic workers. However, the prevalence of paid domestic labor in Latin America is primarily driven by the deep internal economic inequalities in each country, and the vast majority of domestic workers are national in origin.

It is in this context of deep inequalities that we need to examine the rise of women's labor force participation rates in Latin America. Women as a group have joined the workforce in Latin America in increasing numbers.[7] More than half—53 percent—of women in the region today work in the paid labor force, up from 32 percent in 1990. For women aged twenty to forty years, this figure reaches 70 percent, indicating that a clear generational shift is taking place (UNDP and ILO 2009).

At the same time, and more so than in many advanced industrialized countries, traditional gender roles in household work continue to predominate across the region. A large survey conducted by the United Nations Development Programme (UNDP) on time use in fourteen Latin American countries revealed a huge gender gap in time spent by women versus men on household and care work (UNDP and ILO 2009). Responsibility for family care continues to fall almost exclusively on women, even when they participate in the workforce, producing what many scholars refer to as the "double burden" for women. This burden differs by class as well as by sex. While both low- and high-income women increasingly work outside the home, their options for resolving this double burden are dramatically different.

The same child care options that exist in advanced industrialized countries are available in Latin America, but with different options predominating. Overall, care arrangements in Latin America are characterized by a high level of informality, without state support in service provision and often without state regulation of labor markets (see Filgueira et al. 2011; Martínez Franzoni 2008; Martínez Franzoni and Voorend 2009, 2011). The first option—having a stay-at-home mother—remains relatively common in Latin America. Just over 40 percent of women who have working male partners can afford to and opt to stay at home (Martínez Franzoni and Voorend 2009, 47). This option is not incompatible with hiring a domestic worker, and many families who can afford it have a stay-at-home mother as well as a domestic worker.

The fifth option listed above and the option that is the focus of this book—hiring a domestic worker—is the dominant choice among well-off dual-earner families in Latin America given the ready supply of cheap labor, and it accounts for the high levels of employment in this sector. It is also convenient for the families, as domestic workers not only care for dependents but come to the employer's residence, cook, clean, and work long hours. The majority of these workers remain in the informal sector, without social security or other benefits that come from formalization. Hence, the ostensible liberation of well-to-do women has taken place without the need to negotiate the sharing of household responsibilities with their male partners, but rather by outsourcing these responsibilities to women from lower socioeconomic classes (see de Santana Pinho and Silva 2010 on Brazil). Even when well-to-do couples do not have children, they often prefer to outsource household duties to a domestic worker. As noted earlier, data from the late 1990s indicate that around 15 percent of households in Latin America had one or more full-time domestic workers, and many more hire women part-time (Rodgers 2009, 92–93).

The second option listed above—relying on relatives and friends as caretakers—is common among the lower-income parents who work outside their homes. Those who can rely on extended families, often grandmothers, are lucky but increasingly less common. Many working families with low wages utilize low-cost informal networks that can often be unreliable and not provide the necessary care (CEPAL 2009; Heymann 2006). These trends are exacerbated among the growing number of single-parent families. Thirty percent of households in the region today are female headed, without the presence of an adult male—up from 23 percent two decades ago (UNDP and ILO 2009). While not all of these households are poor, the mothers in these families bear the burden of providing both income and care to their children. While the labor force participation rates of these women are higher than in other types of households given that they are the sole supporters of their dependents, they are also more likely to find themselves working as domestic workers or as street sellers and unable to meet basic needs of food, shelter, and care for dependents in a satisfactory way. It is these lower-income parents who are often forced to leave their children home alone (option six) or give up employment when they cannot bring their children with them and resort to street selling so that they can take the children along (Heymann 2006).

These informal care arrangements also tend to predominate among female immigrants with children, many of whom work in domestic service. Here we see what sociologists have referred to as "absent parenting" (Fish 2006, 88). When women migrate and leave their families behind in rural areas or in their home countries, children often lose their primary care provider, and as a result such migration can have more dislocating effects on families than male migration.

Day care centers are less common in Latin America than in advanced industrialized countries. While market-provided day care centers do exist, well-off families can afford to hire a domestic worker and tend to prefer this option to relying on day care given the conveniences it offers. (Many also enroll their children in early education programs.) State provision of day care remains very low in the region, and when it is provided, it tends to be an educational service for older preschoolers. This service is very important in its own right, but as a result services for zero- to three-year-olds are extremely limited, and opening hours for preschoolers are often narrow and do not correspond to work hours. In addition, even though some of the public services are targeted toward low-income families, wealthy children have more access to early childhood education than the poor through private services (see Filgueira 2011; Filgueira et al. 2011; UNESCO 2006, 2010).

Within this context, domestic workers with family responsibilities face particular difficulties in meeting care needs. They are more likely to have migrated and left their children in the care of others. Even if their children live with them, their longer work hours make it hard for these women to attend to them. Indeed, many put off having children of their own due to the difficulties of combining work and care. On a collective scale, the difficulties that low-income parents in general—and low-income mothers in particular—experience in attending to their children have significant effects on the physical and mental development of these children and contribute to intergenerational social exclusion and poverty (Heymann 2006).

The Dynamics of Paid Domestic Work as an Occupation

A domestic worker is a person who provides cooking, cleaning, child care, or other prescribed services at an employer's private residence. Sometimes the domestic worker also lives in the residence. Paid domestic work falls within the larger economy of care professions, where women dominate the workforce. However, it also embodies some unique characteristics that differentiate it from other wage employment within the care professions (such as early childhood education and care provision, nursing, and work in retirement homes) as well as from other wage labor more generally.

First, the realm of paid domestic work, as noted above, constitutes what is traditionally considered "women's work." Work in the household has tended to be performed without remuneration by female members of households. Because of this, household work has historically not been viewed as "real" or productive work, but is often considered unskilled and is not accorded the same status as paid work outside the home (Hondagneu-Sotelo 2001). As a Human Rights Watch report on Guatemala observes, "Paid domestic workers essentially perform for wages the tasks the woman of the house is socially expected to perform for free" (Human Rights Watch 2002, 20). Hence, even when such work is contracted out to a third party, it still tends to be viewed as less than "real work" by employers, by the laws, and sometimes even by the employees themselves, who may see their jobs as "helping out" another family.[8]

Second, and relatedly, paid domestic work involves working within a household, in an otherwise nonpublic, nonbusiness setting. Many employers do not perceive themselves as employers in the way they do outside the home, nor do they view their homes as sites of employment (Hondagneu-Sotelo 2001, chap. 1). Hence, the labor relation tends to be more informal. Contracts are often verbal, and boundaries regarding the rights and duties of employment are more fluid. In effect, the International Labour Organization (ILO) characterizes the employee status of domestic workers as "invisible because they work inside the household" (ILO 2010a, 2).

Third, in this work setting—and this characteristic does apply to care professions more broadly—human relations and affective ties are particularly important, especially when dealing with care of children or the elderly. The importance of this personal aspect of the relationship to both workers and employers is noted in studies of domestic work across the world, from the United States, to Europe, to South Africa, to East Asia, to Latin America. There is a widespread tendency among employers, across countries and continents, to claim that the employee is "like family" to the household (Bunster and Chaney 1985; Fish 2006; L. Gill 1994; Lan 2006, 19; Rollins 1985). Studies of labor relations between domestic workers and their employers use terms such as "personalism" and "asymmetry" (Lan 2006), and "deference" and "maternalism" (Rollins 1985), to capture the dynamics of the relationship. The behavior of employers can be paternalistic; for instance, employers sometimes refer to employees as "girls" or "my girl" and characterize them as childlike. Rollins, writing in the 1980s, recounts the practice in the United States of even calling servants by the employer's last name to denote belonging and ownership (1985, 177). These dynamics, combined with the perception that domestic workers do not do real work in a business setting, tend to obscure the labor relation.

Despite the informality and importance of affective ties, the relationship is fundamentally a labor relation, and a particularly unequal one at that. It is a source of employment for women in an unequal world, where wealthier families can afford to outsource their reproductive and household activities and low-income women will work for the wages offered. The subordinate socioeconomic position of domestic workers cuts across countries; they are economically less advantaged, and this has driven their choice of occupation, whether they are nationals of the countries in which they work or immigrants.

Given these global economic realities, the familial, informal relations within the household tend to produce effects that reinforce and exacerbate the inherent inequalities in this labor relation. While in many cases an intimate and affectionate relationship does develop between employer and employee, the mantra of "part of the family" often tends to obscure the very real labor and power relations between the two counterparts, to the detriment of the weaker person in the labor relation—the employee. This happens in a variety of ways.

First, in the majority of countries, the legal system does not view domestic work as equal to other forms of labor, and laws discriminate against domestic workers, according them lesser rights than other workers. As the ILO recently observed, "The same domestic services are treated differently when regulated outside the home and when performed within the household" (ILO 2010a, 11). Domestic workers are often legally required to work longer hours in a day and do not have full weekends off, and many have less vacation time, allowing them less private and leisure time than other members of society. They also tend to be entitled to lower severance pay, and in some countries they are legally entitled to lower social security benefits.

Second, neither employers nor the legal system tend to view the household as a site of employment, and in virtually all countries the mechanisms by which to enforce labor regulations and whatever rights domestic workers do have are inadequate. For example, in most countries, and in contrast to other sites of employment, labor inspectors are not allowed to enter a house without the permission of the employer. This weakens the already inadequate mechanisms for grievance procedures. In effect, workers end up being "subject to the idiosyncracies of employers" (Salazar Parreñas 2001, 164).

Third, and relatedly, as employers often do not view themselves *as* employers, they rarely register employees for social security (Bunster and Chaney 1985; Fish 2006; Hondagneu-Sotelo 2001; Rollins 1985). When pressed about it, employers often claim that they consider their workers "part of the family" and that they will take care of them in their old age. However, such claims or verbal promises, even if well intentioned, are unstable, aggravate the power relation, and, when they are (often) broken, are unenforceable. In addition, they only apply if the domestic worker has one employer over a long period of time. Another claim employers often make in defense of informality is that their workers prefer remuneration in cash instead of in social security contributions. This may be accurate in many cases, given the low wages received by this sector in general. This conflict, however, is no different from that in any other form of employment relation and is, indeed, why social security is mandated in so many countries and not based on a voluntary contribution. If all workers were given the choice, contributions to social security would be much lower, as many would opt for immediate consumption, and countries would face serious old-age poverty crises. The same obligation should equally apply to employers and employees in domestic work, especially given the particularly vulnerable economic situation of the latter and their otherwise high likelihood of poverty in old age.

Fourth, the closeness in employment relations can also be accompanied by social distance in two ways: first, as a "safe" intimacy, and second, as distancing practices in the allocation of space, food, and other goods. Rollins, discussing white employers and black employees in Baltimore in the 1980s, states that "using a domestic as a confidante may, in fact, be evidence of the distance in even the closest of these relationships" (1985, 167). Writing of South Africa, Fish finds that employers can maintain a higher level of intimacy with their servants partly *because* of the deep socioeconomic and racial divides between them, and the very different social circles they move in. In addition, she notes that "although these narratives acknowledge a level of personal intimacy as a result of the labor site in the private household, each employer also shared a level of social *distance* inherent to the nature of the friendship they shared with their worker" (2006, 92). Ultimately, the closeness that many employers refer to takes place on the terms of the employer. In general, there is a consensus in the literature that the perception of a domestic worker as "one of the family" can perpetuate, enforce, and aggravate unequal relations of power between domestic workers and their employers (Salazar Parreñas 2001, 179).

In addition, employers often discriminate against workers in the use of household space and amenities. In many countries, employers make employees use different plates and utensils to eat (Salazar Parreñas 2001, 165–66). (This is ironic given the nature of their work.) This practice is particularly common in countries where domestic workers tend to come from a different ethnic or racial group (or a different caste, as in India). Lesley Gill notes Bolivian employers' constant preoccupation with what they perceive as the "health threat posed by servants who must enter what they consider to be the aseptic confines of their homes" (1994, 115). Bunster and Chaney found through their research in Peru in the 1980s that many domestic workers were not allowed to use the furniture, had to sit on the floor, and were only allowed to use cold water for showers (1985, 5). Finally, in many cases, domestic workers are simply "invisible" to household members (Rollins 1985, 213). Thus, the politics of class, gender, and race are intertwined in highly personalized ways that make the dynamics, and challenges, of domestic service complex.

Much of the social scientific literature has focused on domestic workers as immigrants who move from less to more developed countries. Often domestic workers immigrate on short-term work contracts and are in a particularly precarious legal position (Kofman 2005, 455; Piper 2004). Salazar Parreñas documents the experiences of Filipina domestic workers in Los Angeles and Rome and refers to their "contradictory class mobility"—that is, the "decline in social status and increase in financial status" that result when higher-status immigrants from poor countries accept employment in lower-status jobs in order to earn money. Many of the immigrants had maids themselves in their home countries (2001, 150). Both Cheng (2006) and Lan (2006, 203–5) recount the experience of immigrant domestic workers in Taiwan, noting the desire for foreign workers who have a more deferential attitude than the locals. Lan identifies immigrant recruitment as a public policy strategy of Asian governments "to solve the care deficit ... and to push their female citizens into the labor market as part of national development" (2006, 248). Rollins notes that in the United States "foreign-born women, more vulnerable and less 'angry' (or, at least, less apt to show it), are attractive to employers ... because of their docility and more subservient manner" (1985, 130). Maher and Staab (2006) find similar dynamics among Peruvian domestics in Chile. Overall, many studies document the particular difficulties faced by immigrant domestic workers, who are, to differing degrees partly depending on national laws, "hostage" to employers and promises that may not be kept (B. Anderson 2000; Chang 2000; Cheng 2006; Constable 2007; Hondagneu-Sotelo 2001; Lan 2006; Piper 2004; Salazar Parreñas 2001, 167–71).

Some studies uncover, unsurprisingly, a degree of agency for domestic workers. Better economic conditions and relative scarcity of labor can provide domestic workers with more leverage. Support networks among workers and strategies such as hiring oneself out by the hour to many employers instead of working full-time for one family can also reduce dependency. However, as Fish notes, these acts "do not change the inherent power dynamics among women who are positioned in distinctly asymmetrical relations to one another through class and race privilege" (2006, 18). Indeed, as Lesley Gill has stated, "Domestic service is rooted in inequality, and its most enduring feature is that servants are drawn from groups considered inferior by those in power" (1994, 141).

Given these dynamics, many studies conclude that "paid domestic work is an inherently oppressive occupation" (Salazar Parreñas 2001, 163) and "an extreme and 'pure' example of a relationship of domination in close quarters" (Rollins 1985, 7–8). Writing of South Africa, Fish argues that domestic work is the "last bastion of apartheid" (2006, 81). Writing of Latin America, Rodgers argues that it is "a hybrid space between modernity and tradition" (2009, 80). Overall, given the unequal power relations and the attendant laws, policies, and dominant attitudes, domestic work tends to remain low paying, of low prestige, and, when not accompanied by adequate legal rights and enforcement, subject to exploitation.

The History of Domestic Service in Latin America

Domestic service has deep historical roots in Latin America and was an integral part of the patriarchal household unit in colonial Spanish and Portuguese

America. Kuznesof writes, "Everywhere in Latin America domestic service has been the most important form of female employment throughout history and has also been the least regulated of any employment" (1989, 31). As the hacienda system developed in colonial Latin America, it was regular practice for landowners to use women's labor power both in the fields and in the house (Bunster and Chaney 1985, 28). Indeed, servants became a part of even modest white or mestizo homes: "The servant throughout Latin American history—most often racially and/or culturally distinct from the master class—has subsidized the classes above her, permitting even modest Spanish households to live in a style which would be beyond their means if there were not a servant class" (26).

Graham, writing about domestic workers in nineteenth- and early twentieth-century Brazil, reflects on the nature of the employment relationship across the region: "The power exercised over [servants] within the domain of family and households by masters was private and personal. No public institutions could be appealed to by dependents that might, on their behalf, counter the weight of private power or temper the personal actions of masters" (1992, 3). Until the late nineteenth century and in many cases into the twentieth century, the domestic servant was "in a position of near absolute, unregulated subordination to the male head of household" (Kuznesof 1989, 28).[9] When domestic service became subject to government regulations from the late nineteenth to the mid-twentieth century, authorities did not tend to view it as real work compared to other occupations. Their preeminent focus was on minimal protections from abuse, on regulation of the behavior of domestic workers, and on containing the spread of potential diseases (Blum 2004; L. Gill 1994; Graham 1992; López, Soto, and Valiente 2005, 82–96).

The writing of the 1947 Guatemalan Labor Code during the brief democratic interlude between 1944 and 1954 illustrates some of the gendered, class-based, and racial views of political elites of the time. According to the Costa Rican author of the Guatemalan Labor Code, Oscar Barahona Streber, "It was necessary to include domestic service in the labor code because not to do so would have been unjustified, but to give them the same treatment as industrial or commercial workers would have constituted a bigger mistake, which would have created a general animosity toward the labor code among thousands of housewives. Remember that the domestic worker becomes a part of the family, which does not happen with any other type of workers" (Human Rights Watch 2002, 23). The former labor minister of Guatemala (from 1948 to 1950) maintained that "the fact that the vast majority of domestic workers were women decisively influenced the perception of domestic work and its regulation in the Labor Code" (22–23). Barahona Streber also implied that ethnic discrimination against indigenous women limited the rights he was able to grant to domestic workers: "Indigenous women were very looked down upon.... Indians ... were treated like animals" (23). The interactive effect of class and gender (and very likely ethnic) inequalities could reach brutal extremes: the former labor minister acknowledged that "there are cases of parents who want their son to have his first sexual experiences with the young woman employed as a domestic" (76).

In the twentieth century, and particularly after 1940, demand for domestic workers actually increased in the region as professional women entered the workforce in higher numbers (Kuznesof 1989, 29). Studies of domestic workers in the 1970s and 1980s found that for those who entered this occupation, there was little to no hope of upward mobility. It was a dead-end job, allowing for little occupational change and incompatible with marriage and child rearing (Jelin 1977, 137–38). Bunster and Chaney traced the patterns of migrants from rural areas arriving in Lima, Peru, in the 1980s—often young girls or adolescents of indigenous heritage—in search of jobs. In many cases, they found employment as live-in domestics and sometimes worked for no salary at all in their first years. If they got pregnant, they were often fired and had to resort to street selling (1985, 17–22).

In many countries, initial organizing efforts by domestic workers to improve their working conditions began in the 1930s and 1940s, but it was in the 1970s and particularly the 1980s that the organizations were able to more openly mobilize and demand equal rights (Chaney and Garcia Castro 1989; Orsatti 2011, 76–79). In most countries, these attempts initially focused on trying to overcome the deep difficulties in reaching domestic workers (Chaney and Garcia Castro 1989) and were met by either indifference or even outright hostility from the state and its respective organs (e.g., the ministry of labor). In addition, labor unions were not particularly interested or supportive. These initial organizations, if not autonomous grassroots organizations, were often linked to the Catholic Church, as were many other social organizations of the time. Within the latter, there were divisions reflective of the divisions in the church itself during the 1970s and 1980s.[10] In many cases, dependency on the church, while financially helpful, constrained the autonomy of the organizations in articulating their demands over time. More autonomous organizations, on the other hand, were likely to meet with hostility from the state. For example, despite an ostensibly reformist left (military) government in Peru in the 1970s, the Ministry of Labor refused to recognize the domestic workers' association in 1973.[11]

The 1980s was a tumultuous time for Latin America, as the debt crises at the beginning of the decade crushed the region's economies. The fallout was a massive economic contraction in virtually every country in the region, and the 1980s therefore came to be referred to as the "lost decade." The massive dislocations were particularly acutely felt by low-income families and women who struggled to support themselves and their families, and women's labor force participation rates increased as male unemployment surged (Martínez Franzoni and Voorend 2009, 43). Many women glutted the market for domestic service, as economic crises tend to reduce demand for domestic service but increase supply (Rodgers 2009, 78–79). Indeed, writing in the mid-1980s, Bunster and Chaney declared, "The major reason the situation [for domestic workers] does not improve is structural. A constant supply of young indigenous women, uneducated and untrained for any occupation, arrives from the sierra; the servant maid remains a readily available commodity purchasable for a very small price" (1985, 30–31).

By the end of the decade, most governments had dismantled much of import-substitution industrialization, reduced the role of the state in the economy, and ushered in market-oriented reforms. Writing in 1989, Kuznesof recounted the predominant attitude of the employing higher classes: "The patriarchal family favors a servant by allowing her into the household; she should indicate her gratitude by working as many hours as indicated and accepting whatever is offered without complaint" (30). Many had no choice but to do so given their limited resources, the lack of alternative employment with better conditions, and the lack of state regulation of labor rights in this sector.[12]

During the same decade, on the other hand, authoritarian governments gave way to elected civilian leaders across the region, and democratic politics provided an opportunity to voice criticism and demand equal labor rights. Since the 1980s, democratizations and more stable economic climates have allowed domestic workers more space to organize autonomously. However, deep class divisions, reinforced by divisions based on gender, ethnicity or race, and sometimes nationality, make it more challenging to demand equal labor rights for this sector, even in a democratic context. Indeed, while women have increased their years of formal education, in many countries surpassing men, and have entered the professional labor force at much higher numbers—and while improvements have been recorded over the last two decades in broad areas of women's rights, including political representation, equal employment policies, and family and domestic violence laws—legal discrimination against domestic workers has remained on the books in most countries.

Paid Domestic Work in Latin America Today

By the 1990s, the economies in most Latin American countries had stabilized and were growing, even if at moderate rates. Within this context, paid domestic work has remained an important source of employment for women in the region. Table 1.1 outlines the ILO data on the percentage of women occupied in domestic service in urban areas across the region since 1990.

As table 1.1 indicates, 16.8 percent of women were employed in domestic service in urban areas in the region in 2009, down slightly from 19.2 percent in 1995. In absolute numbers, there are about 1.8 million domestic workers in Mexico, just over 1 million in Argentina (Ministerio de Trabajo, Empleo y Seguridad Social 2005, 176), and more than 6 million in Brazil (Sanches 2009, 119). The percentages range from a low of 3.7 percent in Venezuela to a high of 18.2 percent in Brazil and Paraguay. The regional average is clearly pulled up by the share of domestic workers in Brazil, a country with almost 200 million people, while in Central America outside of Costa Rica and Panama the share is below 10 percent. There is, then, significant variation across countries but not by level of development. It should also be noted that the ILO statistics

Table 1.1 Percentage of economically active women employed in domestic service in Latin American countries (urban areas)

	1990	1995	2000	2005	2009
Latin America	—	19.2	18.6	17.4	16.8
Argentina	—	14.1	14.4	16.7	16.4
Bolivia	15.9	11.6	9.4	8.5	—
Brazil	16.4	20.2	20.0	18.7	18.2
Chile	18.5	16.3	16.2	12.9	10.8
Colombia	—	—	11.2	11.1	9.3
Costa Rica	12.0	9.4	11.4	12.0	10.0
Dominican Republic	—	—	9.9	12.1	12.9
Ecuador	11.6	11.4	11.1	11.6	9.3
El Salvador	13.0	9.1	8.2	7.2	8.9
Honduras	16.0	12.2	9.5	9.0	8.4
Mexico	11.9	12.5	10.2	10.3	9.4
Nicaragua	—	—	—	—	9.8
Panama	16.4	16.7	13.5	14.9	12.0
Paraguay	—	—	21.5	23.0	18.2
Peru	11.3	10.9	11.8	10.4	12.6
Uruguay	—	16.3	18.9	17.1	16.0
Venezuela	—	6.2	5.6	4.9	3.7

Source: For 1990 and 1995, see OIT 2007. For 2000–2009, see OIT 2010.

on domestic service tend not to include domestic workers who contract their services out to several households; they are classified as "independent workers." Very recent immigrants are likewise excluded in the data.[13] Given this, the ILO may undercount the actual percentage of domestic workers among the economically active population. Indeed, some national data (e.g., for Costa Rica) give higher percentages for domestic workers.[14] The benefit of the ILO data is that it provides more systematically comparative data for the region.

Immigration has increased between more and less developed countries in Latin America. According to the ILO, at the end of the 1990s domestic workers constituted close to 60 percent of internal and international migrants in the region (Rodgers 2009, 85). Chile receives domestic workers from Peru; Argentina receives domestic workers from Bolivia, Paraguay, and Peru; and Costa Rica receives domestic workers from Nicaragua. The share of domestic workers who are immigrants in these receiving countries ranges from an estimated 4 percent in Chile to about 17 percent in Costa Rica.[15] However, by far the largest source of domestic workers in all of these countries remains internal. While historically girls and women tended to migrate from rural areas and assume positions as servants in urban households, increasingly the supply of domestic workers comes from the urban poor (Rodgers 2009, 77–86).

In general, girls and women who work in domestic service tend to enter the occupation at an early age. This often impedes their ability to complete their education. It is estimated that around two million children in Latin America work in domestic service, the vast majority of them girls. Poverty is the driving factor behind child labor; families believe that they cannot feed and educate their girls and therefore send them to work in wealthier households.[16] The highest percentages of girls working as domestics are found in Central America; 14 percent of Guatemalan and 10 percent of Honduran and Nicaraguan girls between the ages of 10 and 14 were domestic workers in 2005.[17]

In Brazil, government statistics from 2002 indicate that a third of those working as domestics started doing so between the ages of 5 and 11 years old, despite laws that prohibit employment in general for those under 16 years old and only allow "apprentice" work for 14- to 16-year-olds.[18] In Mexico, one recent study found that the average age at which domestic workers enter the occupation is 14.[19] Moreover, 70 percent of Mexican domestic workers have only a grade school education or less.[20] In Guatemala, government statistics from 2006 show that of the domestic workers who are 15 years old and over, 59 percent have a primary education or less, and 32 percent have no formal education at all (COMMCA 2008, 36–40). Moreover, 71 percent of the domestic workers surveyed began work in this occupation before turning 18 years old (44). In Paraguay, more than half of domestic workers are between 15 and 29 years of age, while 4 percent are between 10 and 14 years of age (López, Soto, and Valiente 2005, 188). Over 70 percent of domestic workers have only a grade school education or less (189). In Peru, it appears that domestic workers have more formal education; according to one survey, half of domestic workers had finished high school, and one-third had a grade school education.[21] This is also reflected in the typically higher education levels of Peruvian immigrant domestic workers in Chile and Argentina (Ceriani et al. 2009; Stefoni 2009).

In addition, many of the women who work as domestics, regardless of whether they live with their employers, have their own family responsibilities. Data for Central America and the Dominican Republic indicate that 67 percent of the domestic workers surveyed have children of their own (COMMCA 2010, 223).

The average salaries for domestic workers are, unsurprisingly, lower than the average salaries for wageworkers in general in the region (Rodgers 2009, 85). CEPAL data indicate that the earnings of domestic workers were 41 percent of the average wage of the urban employed in 2008 (Tokman 2010, 5). Poverty rates among domestic workers tend to be higher than the national poverty rates overall and the average remuneration not much above the national poverty lines of each country (Loyo and Velásquez 2009, 29, 40). Moreover, CEPAL data indicate that, on average and across the region, the earnings of female domestic workers are 73 percent of those of male domestic workers (Tokman 2010, 5; Loyo and Velásquez 2009, 40). They also tend to be lower for workers of African descent or of indigenous heritage, both of whom tend to be overrepresented in domestic service (Rodgers 2009, 84; Sanches 2009, 124). These statistics indicate that while all domestics earn low wages on average, female domestics earn lower wages not only because of their class position but also because of their sex and—when they are from a visible minority—because of their ethnicity or race.

The definition of domestic service in the region's labor codes includes both household and caregiving activities. There is little systematic comparative data on the distribution of tasks of domestic workers—for example, the share of domestic workers who only do household tasks and the share of domestic workers who also engage in caregiving activities. A regional survey of Central America and the Dominican Republic in 2008 indicated that 65 percent of employer households had dependents in need of care. This figure ranged from a low of 53 percent in Costa Rica to a high of 76 percent in Panama (COMMCA 2010, 232).

There is also little systematic comparative data on the share of live-in and live-out domestic workers. A 1998 survey indicated that of the 15 percent of households in the region that employed one or more domestic workers full-time, 40 percent had one or more live-in domestic workers, while 60 percent had one or more live-out domestic workers. When examined by income, 22 percent of the richest decile of households had one or more live-in domestic workers, and an additional 24.7 percent had one or more live-out domestic workers. On the other hand, within the lowest 40 percent of households, 1.2 percent had a live-in domestic worker, and 2.2 percent had a live-out domestic worker (Rodgers 2009, 92–93). These figures do not take into account contractual workers who work for more than one employer at a time.

Overall, there appears to be a regional trend toward fewer live-in domestic workers and more live-out domestic workers. For example, in Chile, government data indicate that live-in domestic workers as a share of the total domestic service workforce declined from 39 percent in 1990 to 14 percent in 2006 (Ministerio del Trabajo y Previsión Social 2008). In Argentina, live-in domestic workers as a share of the total domestic service workforce declined from 29 percent in 1974 to 4 percent in 2010 (CEMyT 2010, 15; Rodgers 2009, 93). On the other hand, in Bolivia, a much poorer country, a survey of 129 domestic workers found that half of the women were live-in domestic workers.[22] In the wealthier countries, immigrant women have begun to fill the niche of live-in work while nationals have moved toward live-out and contractual domestic service (Valenzuela and Mora 2009b, 16).

While a share of domestic workers contract their services out to two or more employers, working for only one employer still appears to be the norm. Although systematic comparative regional data do not exist, in Argentina over 70 percent of domestic workers worked for only one employer (Esquirel 2010; Ministerio de Trabajo, Empleo y Seguridad Social 2005). The regional survey of Central America and the Dominican Republic found that in Costa Rica 80 percent of domestic workers worked for one employer; in Honduras, 62 percent; in Nicaragua, 85 percent; and in Panama, 92 percent (COMMCA 2010, 204).[23] It is also this group—domestic workers with one employer—that the ILO figures in table 1.1 tend to reflect.

Laws on Paid Domestic Work

The national labor codes of Latin American countries regulate both individual labor law, which governs the hiring, dismissal, and working conditions of workers, and collective labor law, which regulates the functioning of organized bodies of workers such as unions, federations, or confederations. Here I focus on individual labor law, as that is the focus of the labor code specifications on domestic workers.

Labor codes in the region in general regulate the workday of a worker at eight hours a day and their workweek at forty to forty-eight hours a week. Above this amount, labor codes specify an overtime that must be paid, which varies by country. Significant differences exist across countries in regulations regarding overtime, vacations, and maternity leave (see Carnes 2008, 41–42).

Carnes analyzes the development of the initial labor codes in Latin America during the mid-twentieth century and argues that they were influenced by structural factors—skill levels and the rate of unionization—and factors related to the political incorporation of labor (Carnes 2008, chaps. 2 and 3). By the mid-twentieth century, Latin America's labor laws were more similar to those of European countries than to those of other countries at similar levels of economic development (Carnes 2008, 26). All of them included specific chapters outlining the rights and duties of domestic workers, and all of them granted this group of workers fewer rights and benefits than other workers.[24]

What I examine here are not the differences between labor codes across Latin American countries but whether domestic workers have the *same* rights as other workers *within* each country's labor code. The tables at the end of this chapter provide the labor code specifications on legal work hours as well as other legal restrictions specific to domestic workers in South America (table 1.3) and in Central America, the Dominican Republic, and Mexico (table 1.4). They also provide the sources for the data and discussion below.

Table 1.2 summarizes the difference between the legal work hours of domestic workers and the legal limit for workers in general across countries and over time. This table, as well as tables 1.3 and 1.4, indicates that there are striking similarities in laws on domestic workers across the region. Until recently, the legal work hours of domestic workers were longer than those of other workers in all countries. In many countries, the labor code does not specify the maximum work hours of domestics but rather their minimum rest hours, which in effect delineate the maximum length of the workday as well, as domestic workers are expected to be available outside the mandatory rest hours. For example, Mexico and Brazil—and Peru and Bolivia until 2003—allow for up to sixteen-hour workdays. In Mexico, paid domestic work is characterized by a complete lack of regulation, simply stipulating that workers must have enough time to rest and to eat. This explicitly contradicts the Constitution, which grants all Mexicans an eight-hour workday.

In Brazil, domestic workers have received more rights over the years (such as the national minimum wage, maternity leave, and social security), but,

Table 1.2 Maximum work hours per week for workers in general and for domestic workers, 1980s and 2010, from each country's labor code

Country	Max. weekly hours for workers (1980s)	Max. weekly hours for domestic workers (1980s)	Difference (1980s)	Max. weekly hours for workers (2010)	Max. weekly hours for domestic workers (2010)	Difference (2010)
Argentina	48	72	24	48	72	24
Bolivia	48	104	56	48	48/60[a]	0/12
Brazil	48	(96)[d]	48	44	(96)	52
Chile	48	72	24	45	72	27
Colombia	48	(96)[b]	48	48	48/60[a]	0/12
Costa Rica	48	78	30	48	48	0
Dominican Republic	48	82.5	34.5	44	82.5	38.5
Ecuador	44	(104)[c]	60	40	(104)	64
El Salvador	44	72	28	44	72	28
Guatemala	48	96	48	48	96	48
Honduras	44	84	40	44	84	40
Mexico	48	(96)[d]	48	48	(96)	48
Nicaragua	48	72	24	48	72	24
Panama	48	90	42	48	90	42
Paraguay	48	72	24	48	72	24
Peru	48	96	48	48	48/?[a]	0/?
Uruguay	48	(96)[b]	48	48/44	44	0
Venezuela	48	84/48[a]	36/0	44	84/44[a]	36/0

Source: For general work hours, see Carnes 2008, 40, with two modifications. Brazil's work week in 2010 was 44 hours, and Uruguay's was 48 hours in industry and 44 hours in commerce. For domestic workers, see the sources for tables 1.3 and 1.4.

Note: Parentheses indicate that the length of the workday / hours of rest are not specified in hours but are implied.

[a] In Bolivia and Colombia, 60 hours applies to live-in domestic workers. In Peru, 48 hours explicitly applies only to live-in domestic workers, although the Ministry of Labor has interpreted it to apply to all domestic workers (see the sources for Peru in table 1.3). In Venezuela, 84 hours applies to live-in domestic workers.

[b] Regular work hours do not apply to domestic workers. In Uruguay, domestic workers have one day off per week.

[c] In Ecuador, domestic workers have one day off every two weeks. I calculate the maximum weekly work hours as 16 hours per day, minus half a workday per week.

[d] In Mexico, the Labor Code specifies "enough time off to rest and to eat," which has been interpreted to mean up to a 16-hour workday. In Brazil, the workday is likewise not limited, which in effect allows for up to a 16-hour workday.

importantly, daily work hours remain unregulated. The Dominican Republic allows for fifteen-hour workdays, and Guatemala, Honduras, and Venezuela allow for fourteen-hour workdays. In Argentina, the twelve-hour workday is not immutable; only nine hours of time off need to be continuous, and these can be interrupted (presumably for live-in domestics) for "serious or urgent cause."[25] Chile and Paraguay allow for twelve-hour workdays. Only in Bolivia, Colombia, Costa Rica, and Uruguay do domestic workers have the same hours as other workers, although in both Bolivia and Colombia the daily work hours of live-in domestics can be extended to ten hours. Furthermore, legally stipulated weekly rest is often less for domestic workers than for other workers. In many countries, as table 1.2 indicates, the legal weekly work hours are virtually doubled for domestic workers, making it very difficult for them to have a private life and to adequately attend to their own family responsibilities.

There is also discrimination with regard to annual vacation days. In South America, domestic workers in Bolivia, Brazil, Chile, Paraguay, and Uruguay are entitled to the same annual paid vacation days as other workers. In Peru, they are entitled to fifteen days, while other workers are entitled to thirty days. In Argentina, they are entitled to approximately two-thirds of the vacation days of other workers (specified by the number of years with the same employer). In Ecuador and Venezuela, while domestic workers receive the same fifteen-day annual vacation that other workers do, the vacation days for other workers increase with the number of years under the same employer but remain the same for domestic workers. In Colombia, the vacation days are not specified, but the assumption is that they also extend to domestic workers. In Mexico, as well, vacation for domestic workers is not specified.

In Central America, domestic workers in Costa Rica, Honduras, and Panama are legally explicitly entitled to the same annual vacation days. However, in El Salvador and Panama, domestic workers are legally obligated to work on national holidays if employers ask them to do so. Even though the countries' labor codes specify extra pay for this, it restricts domestic workers' right to rest and a private life. In Honduras, domestic workers do not have holidays off, as do other workers; their workday is simply reduced by six hours on a national holiday. In Guatemala, the Labor Code similarly reduces domestic workers' fourteen-hour workday by six hours on national holidays (as well as on Sundays), resulting in a de facto legal workday of eight hours. In essence, in Guatemala domestic workers never have a legal day off, since annual vacation is not specified either (Human Rights Watch 2002, 20).

In addition, in the countries where the minimum wage of domestic workers is legally specified, it is often set lower than the national minimum wage. It drops down to 40 percent in Paraguay (López, Soto, and Valiente 2005, 104). However, in Bolivia, Brazil, Colombia, Costa Rica (from 2009 on), and Chile (from 2011 on), domestic workers are legally entitled to the same national minimum wage as other workers. In Uruguay, since 2008 minimum wage has been established via tripartite negotiations, as are other sectoral salaries. In many other countries, such as Argentina and Mexico, it is established by executive decree; in these cases, the salary for domestic workers tends to be set at a lower level than the national minimum wage for workers in general. In-kind deductions are often allowed as well.

In Argentina to date (and Chile until 1998), domestic workers are explicitly excluded from maternity leave, a particularly powerful form of discrimination since this is the occupation with the highest proportion of women.[26] In many countries, written contracts between employer and employee are not required for domestic service, and notice periods for dismissal, severance pay, work injury protections, and collective bargaining rights are also circumscribed. Finally, in Argentina, Costa Rica (until 2009), El Salvador, Guatemala, Honduras, Mexico, Paraguay, and Venezuela, labor codes mandate the respect of employee toward employer but not vice versa.

Overall, it is not surprising that domestic work is not very well paid. What is more striking is the explicit legal discrimination against these workers, circumscribing their opportunities for a private life with freedom and dignity. It is also striking that this legal discrimination explicitly contradicts UN and ILO treaties prohibiting sex- or occupation-based discrimination—treaties that the vast majority of these countries have ratified. In addition, in many cases it explicitly contradicts national constitutions that prohibit sex-based discrimination and mandate equal labor rights, including eight-hour workdays. For example, as noted above, in Mexico the Constitution mandates an eight-hour workday. In some cases, legal discrimination against domestic workers explicitly contradicts other provisions of the labor codes themselves. In Guatemala, the Labor Code mandates an equitable minimum wage and prohibits sex-based discrimination, yet it does not accord domestic workers the minimum wage while making them work fourteen-hour days (COMMCA 2008, 82–84). Given the legal restrictions on the employees in this sector, the state in most Latin American countries in effect provides a subsidy to the well-to-do.

The ILO has sought to establish international standards for what is considered "decent work." The ILO defines "decent work" as work that is productive and secure, ensures respect for labor rights, allows adequate free time and rest, provides an adequate income, offers social protection, and includes social dialogue, union freedom, collective bargaining, and participation.[27] Paid domestic work as an occupation in Latin America today does not, overall and on average, come close to meeting these ILO standards.

Conclusion

The prevalence of paid domestic work as an occupation both globally and in Latin America should be understood in the interactive context of high economic inequalities and the changing role of women in society. As more women enter labor markets, families must find solutions to dependent care needs. Unlike in advanced industrialized countries, where more collective solutions such as day care or elderly care centers are more common, the ready supply of cheap labor in Latin America enables the well-off to hire full-time domestic workers who care for dependents as well as cook and clean.

The nature of the work within the household, its historical undervaluation as "women's work," and the deep class divides in Latin America have maintained the low status of this occupation. It is characterized by low wages and regulated by discriminatory laws. The next chapter examines when and how legal discrimination against this sector becomes politicized and is overturned. Chapter 3 discusses enforcement.

Table 1.3 Main characteristics of laws on domestic workers in South America, 2010

Country	Laws	Exclusions
Argentina	• 12-hour workday; 1 day (or 2 half-days) off per week • Can be fired for lack of respect or "injury to the honor" of employer without severance; have right to severance in case of employer "mistreatment" • Must present "good conduct" and "good health" certificates from corresponding authorities • Room and board can be included in salary but cannot be discounted from executive-decreed minimum wage for this sector (lower than for others)	• Right to severance pay • Granted about 2/3 the paid vacation of other workers • Excluded from maternity leave and family allowances **2005** • Social security obligatory and tax deductible

continued

Country	Laws	Exclusions
Bolivia	**Prior to 2003** • 16-hour workday; 6 hours off on Sundays **2003** • 8-hour workday, 10-hour workday for live-in workers; one day off per week • Right to national minimum wage	**Prior to 2003** • Half the severance pay and 1/6 the notice period of other workers • Granted 1/3 to 2/3 the paid vacation of other workers **2003** • No exclusions, but access to social security was not implemented as of 2010
Brazil	• No limits on workday **1988** • Right to 1 day off per week • Right to minimum wage **2006** • Employer cannot make in-kind discounts to salary • Right to double pay for work on holidays	• Excluded from family allowances • Lower severance pay (participation in the Fondo de Garantía de Tiempo de Servicio system optional) **1972** • Paid vacation • Right to social security **1988** • Right to maternity leave **2006** • Prohibition of pregnancy discrimination • Social security tax deductible
Chile	**Prior to 1990** • 12-hour workday; 1 day off per week for live-in domestics • 75% of national minimum wage **2009** • Right to vacation on national holidays for live-in domestics **2011** • Right to 100% of minimum wage	**Prior to 1990** • No severance pay or maternity leave **1990** • Right to severance pay **1998** • Right to maternity leave

continued

Table 1.3 *Continued*

Country	Laws	Exclusions
Colombia	**Prior to 1998** • Excluded from work-hour limits of other workers **Since 1998** • 8-hour workday, 10-hour workday for live-in domestics; Sundays off • Right to minimum wage **2007** • Prohibition of in-kind deductions for live-in domestics	**2007** • Affirmation of right to unemployment insurance **2007** • Affirmation of employers' social security obligations
Ecuador	• No work hours specified • 1 day off every 2 weeks • Not allowed to cease work with less than 15 days' notice if it causes "serious inconvenience" to employer	• No mention of vacations • Only salary in cash is to be counted for severance pay
Paraguay	• 12-hour workday; no weekend rest specified • Can work on national holidays • 40% of national minimum wage • Can be fired for "lack of honor or morality"; employer has obligation not to "mistreat" employee	• Receive paid vacation • Excluded from pensions and family allowances **Prior to 2009** • Those outside the capital city excluded from health care[a]
Peru	**Prior to 2003** • 16-hour workday **Since 2003** • 8-hour workday, 48-hour workweek for live-in domestics[b] • 1 day off per week for all domestic workers • No minimum salary	**Since 2003** • Receive half (15 days) the paid vacation of other workers • 15 days' severance pay per year • Right to social security
Uruguay	**Prior to 2006** • Excluded from 8-hour workday limit • Right to 1 day off per week **Since 2006** • 8-hour workday, 44-hour workweek • Equal rights	**Prior to 2006** • Excluded from unemployment insurance **Since 2006** • No exclusions allowed

Country	Laws	Exclusions
Venezuela	• 14-hour workday, 1 day off per week for live-in workers • Regular workday for live-out domestic workers • Live-in domestic workers not entitled to minimum wage or national holidays • Can be fired for "lack of honor, morality, or respect"	• Receive paid vacation • Half a month's severance pay per year

[a] The Social Security Institute lifted the exclusion of domestic workers outside of the capital from healthcare in 2009. Legislative reform is needed in order to include domestic workers more broadly in social security. See the sources for Paraguay.

[b] While the 2003 law specifies the work hours only for live-in domestics, the Ministry of Labor states on its website as of 2010 that these work hours apply to all domestic workers. See the sources for Peru.

Sources

Argentina: Ministerio de Trabajo, "Tribunal del Servicio Doméstico," May 15, 2008, http://www.trabajo.gov.ar/asesoramiento/domestico.htm. See also Decreto Ley 326/56; Decreto Reglamentario 7979/56; Ley 25.239, September 12, 2005. For social security, see Pereira and Valiente 2007, 46–59.

Bolivia: Ley 2450, April 9, 2003. For laws prior to 2003, see Fundación Solón 2001b, 26–29.

Brazil: Lei 10.208, March 23, 2001; Lei 11.324, July 19, 2006. See also Pereira and Valiente 2007, 35–37, 46–59.

Chile: Dirección del Trabajo, "Guía de empleadoras y trabajadoras de casa particular," available at http://dt.gob.cl/1601/articles-60059_recurso_1.doc. See also Biblioteca del Congreso Nacional de Chile, "Guía legal sobre: Trabajadores de casa particular," April 23, 2009, http://www.bcn.cl/guias/trabajadores-de-casas-particulares; Biblioteca del Congreso 1997, 1998, 2009.

Colombia: Corte Constitucional de Colombia, Sentencia C-372/1998; Sentencia C-310/2007; Tutela T-552/2008. See also Ministerio de la Protección Social, República de Colombia 2009.

Ecuador: Codificación del Código del Trabajo, 1997, Título III, Capítulo I, Artículos 268–76, available at http://www.ilo.org/dyn/natlex/docs/WEBTEXT/47812/68395/S97ECU01.htm.

Paraguay: Ley 213, Libro I, Título III, Capítulo IV, Artículos 148–56, available at http://www.ilo.org/dyn/natlex/docs/WEBTEXT/35443/64905/S93PRY01.htm. For social security, see Pereira and Valiente 2007, 45–69; Natalia Ruiz Díaz, "Paraguay: Seguro social para todas las trabajadoras domésticas," Inter-Press Service, September 15, 2009.

Peru: Ley 27986 (Ley de los Trabajadores del Hogar), June 3, 2003, available at http://www.mintra.gob.pe/contenidos/archivos/prodlab/LEY%20DE%20LOS%20TRABAJADORES%20DEL%20HOGAR%20Ley%20No.%2027986%20c2-06-03.pdf. See also Ministerio de Trabajo y Promoción del Empleo, "Preguntas frecuentes," http://www.mintra.gob.pe/mostrarContenido.php?id=365&tip=358.

Uruguay: Ley 18.065, November 27, 2006 available at http://www.parlamento.gub.uy/leyes/AccesoTextoLey.asp?Ley=18065&Anchor. See Trezza de Piñeyro 2001 for the law prior to 2006.

Venezuela: Ley Orgánica del Trabajo, Título V, Capítulo II, Artículos 274–81, available at http://www.tsj.gov.ve/legislacion/lot.html.

Table 1.4 Main characteristics of laws on domestic workers in Central America, the Dominican Republic, and Mexico, 2010

Country	Laws	Exclusions
Costa Rica	**Prior to 2009** • 12-hour workday; half a day off per week • Unilateral requirement for "respect" on the part of domestic workers • Employer can demand "good health" certificate • Room and board included in salary **Since 2009** • 8-hour workday, 48-hour workweek • Health certificate and unilateral respect removed • Minimum salary in cash	**Prior to 2009** • Receive paid vacation **Since 2009** • Equal rights
Dominican Republic	• 15-hour workday; 36 hours off on the weekend • Room and board included in salary, calculated as 50% of salary	• Receive paid vacation • Excluded from other general labor rights • No mention of social security
El Salvador	• 12-hour workday; 1 day off per week • Room and board included in salary • Must work on holidays (for extra pay) if employer requires it • Employer can demand "good health" certificate • Can be fired for "insubordination"	• No mention of vacation or severance pay • No mention of social security
Guatemala	• 14-hour workday; 6 hours off per week and on holidays • Room and board included in salary • Employer can demand "good health" certificate • Can be fired for "lack of respect"	• No mention of vacation or severance pay • No mention of social security; not obligatory in general for employers with fewer than three employees

continued

Country	Laws	Exclusions
Honduras	• 14-hour workday; 1 day off per week • 6 hours less on national holidays • Room and board included in salary • Employer can demand "good health" certificate • Can be fired for "lack of respect" or "sloth"	• 1 month's severance pay per year • No mention of vacation • No mention of social security
Mexico	• No specified hours ("domestic workers need to have enough time off to rest and to eat") • 50% of salary considered "room and board" • Executive decrees minimum salary for this sector • Must show "respect" to employers; employers must abstain from "mistreatment"	• 20 days' severance pay per year • No mention of vacation • Social security not obligatory
Nicaragua	• 12-hour workday; 1 day off per week • Room and board included in salary	• No mention of vacation or severance pay • Explicit right to social security
Panama	• 15-hour workday; 1 day off per week • Must work on holidays (for extra pay) if employer requests it • Room and board included in salary • Employer can demand "good health" certificate	• Receive paid vacation and severance pay • No mention of social security

Sources

Costa Rica: Ley 8726 (Reforma del Capítulo Octavo del Título Segundo de Código de Trabajo, Ley 2 del Trabajo Doméstico Remunerado), February 2, 2009. See also Código de Trabajo 2, Título 2, Capítulo 8, Artículos 101–8, available at http://www.leylaboral.com/costarica/Normas.aspx?bd=18&item=8754.

continued

Table 1.4 *Continued*

Dominican Republic: Código de Trabajo de la República Dominicana, Libro IV, Título IV, Capítulo I, Sección I, Artículos 258–65, available at http://www.leylaboral.com/dominicana/Normasdominicana.aspx?item=979&bd=54.

El Salvador: Código del Trabajo 15, Libro I, Título II, Capítulo III, Artículos 76–83, available at http://www.leylaboral.com/elsalvador/NormasElSalvador.aspx?item=17441&bd=27.

Guatemala: Código de Trabajo de la República de Guatemala, Título IV, Artículos 161–66, available at http://www.leylaboral.com/guatemala/Normasguatemala.aspx?item=1658&bd=41.

Honduras: Código de Trabajo de la República de Honduras, Título III, Capítulo II, Artículos 149–65, available at http://www.leylaboral.com/honduras/Normashonduras.aspx?item=193&bd=42.

Mexico: Ley Federal del Trabajo, Capítulo XIII, Artículos 331–43, available at http://leyco.org/mex/fed/125.html#t6.

Nicaragua: Código del Trabajo, Libro I, Título VIII, Capítulo I, Artículos 145–54, available at http://www.leylaboral.com/nicaragua/NormasNicaragua.aspx?bd=26&item=12602. See also Ley 666, September 22, 2008.

Panama: Código de Trabajo de la República de Panamá, Libro I, Título VII, Capítulo 1, Artículos 230–31, available at http://www.leylaboral.com/panama/Normaspanama.aspx?item=2948&bd=47.

2

OVERCOMING ELITE RESISTANCE

Demands for equal rights in Latin America today take place in a formally democratic political context and a broadly neoliberal, or market-oriented, economic context (aside from Cuba). On the one hand, democratization has allowed marginalized groups such as women's and indigenous movements to organize and demand more rights.[1] Indeed, the last two decades have seen impressive gains in women's and indigenous rights, especially on the legal level, even if proactive enforcement has been slower to come. On the other hand, as discussed in chapter 1, structural economic changes and neoliberal policies have changed the composition of the labor force. The informal sector has become more dominant, encompassing almost half of the economically active population in the region, with implications for the political power of organized labor (Barrett 2001; Carnes 2008; Centeno and Portes 2006; Cook 2007; Portes and Hoffmann 2003; Roberts 2002). These changes have taken place within the context of deep class differences and highly unequal opportunities and outcomes, despite some recent improvements in both inequality and poverty (see Blofield 2011a, 2011d; CEPAL 2009; López-Calva and Lustig 2010), and within the context of the shift to the left.[2]

These socioeconomic and political contexts pose both opportunities and constraints for disadvantaged groups. The central question here is whether and how the political system addresses the interests of groups that are multiply disadvantaged. Domestic workers exemplify such a group, as their specific shared identity is through the nature of their labor, which is poorly remunerated; in addition, virtually all are women and many are from ethnic or visible minorities that have been historically underrepresented and discriminated against.

While domestic workers' organizations have demanded social attention and equal labor rights in many countries for decades, political actors in the region have been extremely reluctant to respond to these demands. Increasing the position and rights of domestic workers involves a decline in the position of employers, and such a change goes against the interests of political elites themselves and their better-organized middle- and upper-class constituents. Moreover, the political participation of many legislators, especially female legislators given traditional gender roles, is based on having domestic workers at home. The workers, then, are not represented in Congress or in executive agencies, while their employers are. Hence, there is an inherent conflict of interest among politicians in extending more rights to the workers, and the political system is, as a point of departure, unlikely to be responsive to the concerns of domestic workers. In addition, as discussed in chapter 1, women's work within the household—whether paid or unpaid—has not historically been seen by elites or enshrined in the labor codes as "real work" deserving of the same rights as other forms of labor. Finally, racism among some elites may make them less likely to view domestic workers who are darker skinned or from different ethnic groups as their social equals and deserving of the same rights. This may be exacerbated if some of these workers are immigrants. Resistance to extending rights—whether in the form of active opposition or indifference—is likely to be broad and steadfast, and most political elites will tend to either ignore such concerns or table legislative bills addressing them. Even ostensible allies such as feminists and labor unions are likely to focus on the interests of their more advantaged, organized members first (Strolovitch 2006). Therefore, it is important to ask how such issues make it onto the political agenda and get passed, and when they do not achieve success, why. Put differently, *when do domestic workers' interests win over those of their more powerful employers?*

While elite resistance to change can explain much of the overall lack of reform in the region to date, I argue that mobilization by domestic workers' organizations, a network of social and political allies, and political "windows of opportunity," mostly linked to left-wing executive and legislative allies, can result in legal reform. There is no single path to reform; smaller, piecemeal reforms tend to require less mobilization and pressure than equal rights reform that includes work hours. The key struggle for advocates has been to make the issue visible and to get it onto the political agenda. Once the issue gets to a plenary debate and goes up for a vote, it is very likely to be approved. With executive support, which to date has rarely been forthcoming, agenda setting and reform can be speedier and less obstacle ridden.

The universe of my research is legal reforms on domestic workers' rights since democratic transitions in Latin America through 2010. A set of important factors is largely, and broadly, constant: high inequalities, formal democratic politics, and broadly similar histories and cultural heritages. On a global scale, socioeconomic factors such as the higher variance in the level of income inequalities, political factors such as regime type, and specific historical-cultural legacies (e.g., the caste system in India) may play a more determinant role in explaining political reforms or the lack thereof. Below, I first discuss these reforms—the dependent variable—since the democratic transitions in Latin America. I then explain the selection of my country case studies for the qualitative process-tracing in chapters 4 and 5. Finally, the bulk of this chapter lays out the theoretical framework in more detail.

Outcomes: Reforms and Reform Attempts Across Countries

There are three possible outcomes for domestic workers' legal rights: full, partial, or no reform. In the majority of countries, as discussed in chapter 1, there is no reform. In the countries where we see reform, the scope of reform may be a full equalization of labor rights or partial reform. Again, drawing on chapter 1, the key dimensions of legal discrimination include longer work hours, lower minimum wages, less vacation and severance pay, and explicit exclusions in social security. Given this, the scope of reform can be measured by whether rights are equalized in these dimensions. Some reforms equalize all dimensions of domestic workers' labor rights; others focus on a specific dimension, such as extending maternity leave to domestic workers. The scope of reform is also related, of course, to the extant legal restrictions and exclusions in any given country; for example, if vacation time is already equal, then it does not need to be reformed. On the other hand, in some cases the language of the labor code clauses on domestic workers is so vague that advocates feel the need to explicitly restate more general rights in the labor code to avoid confusion and to encourage compliance. It is worth noting that reform so far has been unidirectional; there have been no reforms or serious attempts in the last twenty years to reduce the extant rights of or further discriminate against domestic workers in Latin American labor codes, as there have been with some other gender equality policies, such as reproductive rights.[3]

Table 2.1 outlines the timing and scope of legal reforms in the region up to 2010. As the table indicates, only eight out of eighteen major Latin American countries have substantially reformed domestic worker laws since democratization. In four of these countries this has resulted in virtually equal rights (Bolivia, Colombia, Costa Rica, and Uruguay), and in the other four there have

Table 2.1 Type and scope of reform in eight Latin American countries, 1990–2010

Country and year of reform	Equal working hours	Equal minimum wage	Social security	Scope of reform
Colombia, 1998[a]	Yes[c]	Yes	Yes	FULL
Bolivia, 2003	Yes[c]	Yes	Yes	FULL
Uruguay, 2006	Yes	Yes[b]	Yes	FULL
Costa Rica, 2007[a]	Weekly day of rest	—	—	PARTIAL
Costa Rica, 2009	Yes	Yes	Yes	FULL
Argentina, 2005	—	—	Tax deductions	PARTIAL
Brazil, 2001	—	—	Optional unemployment insurance	PARTIAL
Brazil, 2006	—	Prohibition of in-kind deductions	Equal vacations, tax deductions	PARTIAL
Chile, 1990	—	—	Severance pay	PARTIAL
Chile, 1998	—	—	Maternity leave	PARTIAL
Chile, 2008	—	—	—	PARTIAL
Chile, 2009	Equal holidays for live-in domestics	—	—	PARTIAL
Peru, 2003	Partial	—	Health care and pensions	PARTIAL

[a] Constitutional Court rulings. In Colombia, I consider the 1998 court ruling to be a full reform, as it ruled that domestic workers could not be excluded from general labor rights. Two follow-up rulings in 2007 and 2008 affirmed that domestic workers cannot be excluded from general labor rights such as access to social security.
[b] Minimum wage to be decided through collective negotiations, as with other sectors.
[c] See endnote 4.

been partial, and in some cases multiple, reforms (Argentina, Brazil, Chile, and Peru). Bolivia, Uruguay, and most recently Costa Rica achieved full reform via congressional legislation, while in Colombia full reform was achieved through the Constitutional Court.[4] Finally, across the rest of Latin America, reformist bills have been proposed but have to date been buried in the legislative process and have not made it to plenary debate.

In countries where the option is available, advocates can go to the judiciary, given the explicit contradictions between ratified international treaties, national constitutions, and labor code clauses on domestic workers. Colombia's Constitutional Court was set up after the 1991 constitutional reform and has allowed rights-based claims to be heard via the judicial route much more effectively than in other countries. Its 1998 ruling extended the general rights in the Labor Code to domestic workers, with the declaration that "an excessive workday contradicts the principles of human dignity."[5] Another Constitutional Court ruling in 2007 affirmed the already implicit right of domestic workers to unemployment insurance and also prohibited salary discounts for in-kind benefits (e.g., food and lodging).[6] A third ruling in 2008 affirmed employers' obligation to register domestic workers for social security.[7] The judicial route, however, is less predictable in its outcome than the legislative route. In only one country—Colombia—have the court rulings unambiguously upheld equal rights. In other countries, discussed below, they have not.

In the cases of Bolivia, Costa Rica, and Uruguay, reform took place through Congress. In Bolivia and Costa Rica, the reform bills were initiated in the legislative branch, and in both countries the political process was long, arduous, and obstacle ridden. In Bolivia, the initial legislative bill to equalize rights was submitted in 1993; a revised version was approved in the House in 1996 and in the Senate in 2003. In Costa Rica, a bill was submitted in 1996, and a revised version was finally approved in 2009. Three court cases were also initiated and resulted in two rulings by Costa Rica's Constitutional Court prior to 2009, granting domestic workers a weekly full day of rest in 2007 but maintaining longer daily work hours.[8] In Uruguay, a legislative bill to equalize domestic workers' rights was submitted to Congress in 1990 and, after a long wait, was approved in a plenary vote in the House in 1996. It was repeatedly postponed in the Senate and died in commission. In 2005, the newly elected left-wing government initiated a new project to equalize rights, which, with executive backing, was rapidly approved in 2006.

In Argentina, paid domestic work was, at the end of 2010, still regulated by a decree from 1956 that mandates a twelve-hour workday for domestics, explicitly excludes them from maternity leave, and grants them less vacation. Periodic executive decrees have also granted them lower minimum wages. In 2005, in a broader bill on tax evasion, the executive included a clause to make domestic workers' salaries and social security contributions tax deductible for the employer in order to encourage social security contributions.[9] The law was passed in 2005 (Estévez and Esper 2009). Two separate legislative bills (one in 1999, one in 2007) sought to extend maternity leave to domestic workers but were not debated and died. On the other hand, in 2010 the president of Argentina, Cristina Fernández de Kirchner, submitted a project to Congress to equalize domestic workers' rights, including an eight-hour workday and a forty-eight-hour workweek, as well as inclusion in maternity leave.[10] With executive backing and the support of the president of the Labor Commission, a slightly revised bill was unanimously approved in the Chamber in March 2011.[11] It now awaits Senate debate. I will return to this developing case in the conclusion.

In Brazil, the 1943 Labor Code explicitly excluded domestic workers from general labor rights. However, in 1972, the military regime included domestic workers in the right to a paid vacation and social security. With democratization, the 1988 constitutional reform granted domestic workers maternity leave, the minimum wage, thirty days' notice, and a weekly day of rest. Contradictions between these constitutional rights and the Labor Code remained, and, after many legislative initiatives, two follow-up laws were approved—the first (in 2001) extending unemployment insurance to domestic workers on an optional basis and the second (in 2006) facilitating social security registration through tax deductions, equalizing domestic workers' vacation days with those of other workers, and prohibiting both in-kind deductions from their salaries and the firing of a pregnant domestic worker without due cause.[12] However, the legal daily work hours remain unregulated, and a change to this requires a constitutional amendment.

Chile has had four piecemeal reforms on domestic workers' legal rights since 1990. The two legal reforms of the 1990s were both initiated by legislators as clauses in broader labor reform bills. The 1990 reform provided domestic workers with severance pay, and the 1998 reform included them in maternity leave; they had been excluded from both. In 2008, when introducing the annual legal adjustment to the national minimum wage to Congress, the executive included a clause that would gradually equalize domestic workers' minimum wage from 75 percent to 100 percent of the national minimum wage over a three-year period. In 2009, a legislative bill with a small scope—granting live-in domestic workers equal holidays—was approved with executive support. The work hours of domestic workers, however, remain legally longer than those of other workers, at twelve hours a day and seventy-two hours a week.

In Peru, the first bill to reform domestic workers' rights was submitted to Congress in 1980 and went nowhere. A more recent version was submitted in 1994 and approved by Congress, but it was apparently rejected by then-president Alberto Fujimori.[13] After this, domestic workers' organizations arranged marches and campaigns, several bills were submitted to Congress, and in 2003 Congress opened debate on another bill.[14] Twenty-three years after the first bill was submitted, a watered-down legislative bill that partially equalized domestic workers' rights with those of other workers was finally approved in 2003.[15] This law extended the eight-hour workday and forty-eight-hour workweek to live-in domestic workers and affirmed their right to health care and pensions. However, domestic workers are not entitled to the national minimum wage, an eight-hour workday is not specified for live-out domestic workers, and while other workers receive thirty days of paid vacation a year, domestic workers only receive fifteen days a year. The law also does not explicitly grant maternity leave.[16] For these reasons, the final legislative reform has been criticized by advocates, and I consider it only partial equalization. In 2008, a group of legislators submitted a bill to eliminate the remaining inequalities; the project was archived in the Labor Commission in 2009.[17] On the other hand, while the law explicitly grants the forty-eight-hour workweek only to live-in domestic workers, the Ministry of Labor stated on its website (as of 2010) that it applies to all domestic workers.[18]

Finally, in Nicaragua, a bill on domestic workers was approved in 2008, but it did not substantially change any major aspects of discrimination (except improving some of the legal conditions of adolescent workers). Given this, and concurring with the views of country experts, I do not classify it as a case of substantive reform (see Palacios, Tinoco, and Centeno 2008).[19] To my knowledge, there have been no other reform bills in Latin America since democratic transitions that made it to a legislative vote and were voted down. Across the rest of the region, legal reforms aimed at domestic workers have not made it to plenary debate.

In Mexico, there have been attempts since 1997, spearheaded by the domestic workers' association, to reform the Labor Code clauses on domestic workers.[20] Sympathetic female deputies from the left-wing Partido de Revolución Democrática (PRD), together with domestic workers' organizations, produced a bill to equalize domestic workers' rights, including access to social security, which is extremely low in Mexico.[21] This group of deputies submitted the bill to the Commission on Gender and Equity in 2007, but it never made it to debate.[22] In March 2010, legislators from the governing right party, Partido Acción Nacional (PAN), presented a broader labor reform project. It included clauses to regulate domestic work, but these were quite weak and did not equalize work hours.[23] The PRD presented its counterproposal for labor reform and included more egalitarian reform clauses on domestic workers.[24] It was unclear which clauses were under consideration in the Labor Commission of the Chamber of Deputies as of December 2010.[25]

In Guatemala, attempts at reform have been numerous and fruitless. In 1996, the United Nations–brokered Social and Economic Agreement committed the government to enact "laws to protect the rights of women who work as household employees, especially in relation to fair wages, working hours, social security, and respect for their dignity."[26] This has not translated into Labor Code reforms, and the Guatemalan domestic workers' association has since been lobbying for an equalization of domestic workers' rights. In 1996, a legislator submitted a bill to extend social security to domestic workers, but it went nowhere.[27] With the participation of the domestic workers' association and more co-sponsors, the same legislator submitted three additional bills to Congress in 1999, 2005, and 2006, all without success (COMMCA 2008, 87; Human Rights Watch 2002, 25).[28] Appealing to the Guatemalan Constitution, these bills sought to equalize domestic workers' rights, including work hours. The Labor Commission rejected the 2005 bill, stating that the project "in no way provides the benefits it claims to provide."[29] The 2006 bill was not even discussed.

Frustrated by legislative inaction, the domestic workers' association, with the aid of lawyers supportive of the cause, took its case to the Guatemalan Constitutional Court in 2006, pointing out the inconsistencies between the Labor Code, articles in the Constitution, the Peace Accords, several ratified international treaties, and this discrimination. Despite clear evidence to the contrary, the court ruled in 2009 that the legal regime on paid domestic work was neither discriminatory nor unconstitutional. It also made the association's lawyers pay fines as a penalty for bringing the case to the court.[30] The Observatory on Gender and Justice gave this ruling the "silver award" for the worst ruling on women's rights in Latin America and Spain.[31]

In Panama, there are no records to date of legislative initiatives to end discrimination against domestic workers.[32] In 1994, Rafael Murgas Torraza filed a suit with the Panamanian Supreme Court, claiming that the Labor Code specification of nine hours of uninterrupted rest (from 9 P.M. to 6 A.M.) mandated a fifteen-hour workday and therefore conflicted with the Panamanian Labor Code, the Constitution, and international treaties. However, the court found that the Labor Code specifications were not unconstitutional and ruled against him.[33]

In El Salvador, a lawyer presented a legal reform project in 2004 to equalize domestic workers' rights, including work hours, but it is unclear whether it was ever submitted to a congressional commission (Bendeck 2004). In Paraguay, the domestic workers' association submitted a bill to Congress that sought to equalize the minimum wage and to gain access to social security coverage (explicitly excluded until 2009 for those who work outside of the capital), but it was archived (López, Soto, and Valiente 2005, 209). Similarly, in Ecuador, a bill proposed by a female legislator in the mid-2000s went nowhere. On the other hand, the current president, Rafael Correa, declared in 2009 that the general rights enshrined in the Labor Code, such as the forty-hour workweek, as well as other rights such as maternity leave and social security, should also apply to domestic workers.[34] While the clauses on domestic workers in the Ecuadoran Labor Code do not specify daily work hours, they explicitly stipulate one day off every two weeks. Given that this contradicts the general weekly work hours in the Labor Code, legal reform is needed for the executive's declarations to have staying power and to be implemented. An executive declaration is unstable and subject to a change in executive priorities as well as a change in government.

Curiously, the Bolivarian revolution in Venezuela has not extended to domestic workers, whose legal workdays remain much longer than those of other workers. In recent years, the Ministry of Labor requested an advisory opinion from the Venezuelan Supreme Court on the constitutionality of extant legal discrimination against domestic workers. The court's advisory, nonbinding opinion, emitted in April 2009, agreed with the claim that legal discrimination against domestic workers was unconstitutional.[35] It is still unclear whether this opinion will result in a legal reform bill in Venezuela.

In many countries across the region, constant calls by domestic workers' associations, and in some cases their advocates, for congressional attention to their concerns and for legal reform did not even result in legislative bills. What explains the lack of reform in most countries, and success in others? Before discussing the causal framework, I briefly explain the selection of my country case studies, which are discussed in chapters 4 and 5.

Case Selection of Bolivia, Costa Rica, Uruguay, and Chile

At the outset of my investigation, prior to field research, little research existed on the topic, and information about domestic workers, their organizations, and their coalitions was particularly scarce. Thus, in order to illuminate the causal processes involved, I chose to select cases that would provide maximum variance on the dependent variable—that is, on the political outcomes (Gerring 2007). I also restricted my cases to unitary countries in order to only focus on national-level politics. With this in mind, I chose Bolivia, Costa Rica, Uruguay, and Chile. At the time of choosing the case studies, they spanned the variation on the dependent variable: Uruguay and Bolivia were cases of full reform, Chile represented partial reforms, and Costa Rica represented no reform. The case studies also differ in levels of enforcement, as discussed in chapter 3. However, in 2009, Costa Rica approved equal rights for domestic workers; hence, I no longer have a case of no reform. While this complicates my research design, substantively it is, of course, an improvement for domestic workers in that country. In addition, the Costa Rican case remains illustrative of the dynamics of the political process, given that it took more than a decade to move from the initial bill to legislative approval.

This case selection also represents a pairing of "most-different" cases and "most-similar" cases. Bolivia and Costa Rica are most-different countries with a similar outcome: equal rights reform. I discuss them in chapter 4. Uruguay and Chile are most-similar countries with different outcomes: equal rights reform in the former and piecemeal reforms but not equal rights in the latter. I discuss Uruguay and Chile in chapter 5. Table 2.2 lays out the year and scope of reform in my case studies, and table 2.3 outlines sociodemographic and political variables on the four countries.

Table 2.2 Year and scope of reform in the case studies

Country and year	Scope of reform
Bolivia, 2003	Equal rights
Costa Rica, 2009	Equal rights
Uruguay, 2006	Equal rights
Chile, 1990	Severance pay
Chile, 1998	Maternity leave
Chile, 2008	National minimum wage
Chile, 2009	Holidays for live-in domestics

Table 2.3 Sociodemographic and political variables in Bolivia, Costa Rica, Uruguay, and Chile

Country	GDP per capita in PPP dollars (2000)	Year of democratic transition	% urban population	Inequality (Gini index, 2000)	Life expectancy (2005)	Literacy rate (1990s)
Bolivia	2,819	1982	64.2	.60	64.7	86.7
Costa Rica	10,180	1948	61.7	.50	78.5	94.9
Uruguay	9,962	1984	92.0	.45	75.9	96.8
Chile	12,027	1990	87.6	.55	78.3	95.7

Source: United Nations 2007–8.

As table 2.3 indicates, the GDP per capita of Costa Rica was more than triple that of Bolivia in 2000, prior to reform in both countries. Furthermore, while Costa Rica's Gini index is .5, Bolivia's is much higher at .6. Overall, life expectancy and literacy in Costa Rica are close, if not equivalent, to OECD levels, while literacy (at 87 percent) and especially life expectancy (at sixty-five years) in Bolivia are far behind. In addition, Costa Rica is a relatively homogeneous country, while Bolivia is ethnically diverse, with 60 percent of its population being of Aymara and Quechua heritage. The one similarity between the two countries is that, in both, just under two-thirds of the population lives in urban areas—below the regional average.

Bolivia and Costa Rica contrast politically as well. Costa Rica has been a peaceful, stable democracy since 1948, with relatively consolidated, programmatic political parties. Bolivia, on the other hand, has, since its transition to democracy in the early 1980s, been characterized by unstable and highly volatile political coalitions based more on clientelistic ties than on programmatic links, by weak political institutions, and by frequent breakdowns of constitutional rule. Given that both countries equalized the rights of domestic workers (in Bolivia, prior to the election of Evo Morales as president), specific values on these socioeconomic and political variables, at least on their own, are not necessary causes for reform; thus, we need to look beyond these variables for an answer.

Uruguay and Chile are similar in that they have high levels of GDP per capita for the region, life expectancies at over seventy-five years, and literacy rates at around 95 percent. Since their democratic transitions (Uruguay in 1985, Chile in 1990), both countries have had relatively programmatic political parties that tend to respect constitutional rules. And in both countries over 85 percent of the population is urban. However, one clear difference is that Uruguay has significantly lower levels of inequality than Chile; its Gini index is .45, while Chile's is .55.

In addition, both countries have relatively strong state capacity and have, in the 2000s, had left-wing or center-left governments with equity as a central programmatic goal. However, the process and outcomes differ: in Chile, clauses in three broader labor reform bills have resulted in partial reforms for domestic workers (severance pay, maternity leave, and minimum wage), and a minor issue-specific reform gave live-in domestics equal holidays. In Uruguay, one bill failed in the 1990s after repeated postponements, while executive-initiated equal rights reform was rapidly approved in 2006.

If we examine all four countries together in table 2.3, we can also see that specific values on none of the sociodemographic or political variables are, on their own, either necessary or sufficient causes for equal rights reform.

Context, Framing, and Alternative Explanations

The legal frameworks of labor rights and extant social security systems influence the context in which reform bills are proposed. As mentioned in chapter 1, while Latin American labor codes were overall quite well developed by the mid-twentieth century in comparison to other developing regions, there were also significant differences between less and more developed economies due to the economic and political effects of import-substitution industrialization (Carnes 2008, chaps. 1–3). One aspect was, however, common across the region: domestic workers had little political clout, and the labor codes specifying their working conditions did not reflect their demands and interests but rather those of their employers and the perceptions of male politicians. Indeed, the labor codes across Latin America had, by the mid-twentieth century, established regimes of patron dominance and servant subservience that basically ensured that the latter was always available, outside of sleep, to serve the former. With democratic transitions in the last quarter of the twentieth century, and the ostensible commitment among the governments of the region to equal rights, the opportunity to contest the discriminatory statutes arose.

The arguments in favor of equal rights for domestic workers in twenty-first-century democracies are powerful. They can draw on United Nations conventions such as the Convention to Eliminate All Forms of Discrimination Against Women (CEDAW) and numerous International Labour Organization (ILO) conventions that prohibit labor discrimination and that most countries in the region have ratified. Advocates can also often appeal to national constitutions that enshrine equal rights and prohibit sex-based discrimination. Furthermore, arguments in favor of equal rights tend to focus on the inherent importance of legal equality in a democracy, a powerful argument that is the basis for the extension of civil rights in general. Finally, advocates often argue that labor laws should focus on equal rights in principle, and in practice on protecting the weaker, more vulnerable party in a labor relation rather than discriminating against him or her. These arguments have been used repeatedly by advocates in the media, in legislative debates, and in court cases.

However, if convincing arguments were all it took, discriminatory laws would have been reformed soon after democratization, at the first mention of these contradictions. Instead, even into the early 2000s, not a single country in Latin America provided equal labor rights to domestic workers—with the exception of Colombia through its Constitutional Court ruling—making it clear that seemingly straightforward demands for equal rights confront entrenched opposition. This resistance consists of active opposition to reform as well as more passive resistance in the form of indifference to the issue and a reticence to prioritize it.[36]

While the preference of most of those opposed to reform is not to openly address and argue against it, there are instances in which opponents have been obliged to do so—for example, during committee meetings or congressional debates. In these cases, the framing tends to focus more on the practical effects of reform and is in some ways similar to broader neoliberal economic arguments on the effects of increased labor rights on labor market conditions.[37] The argument is that increased rights will produce unintended negative consequences for the intended beneficiaries of the bill by placing an unacceptable burden on the middle classes, who would become reluctant to hire domestic workers, thus encouraging informalization and unemployment. This argument was made repeatedly in congressional debates in Bolivia, Chile, Costa Rica, Peru, and Uruguay. In addition, and somewhat in contradiction to the previous argument, some politicians have argued against the need for legislative reform altogether. For example, a female legislator in Peru stated that "the era of abuse is already over because [domestic workers] also know how to defend their rights. Today abuses no longer exist."[38] Many others were concerned that legal reforms might disrupt domestic harmony and thereby negatively affect what domestic workers have informally been able to gain.

However, the arguments are unique in their patronizing tone, their underappreciation of the work done by domestic workers, and the personal experiences legislators often draw upon during debates. Opponents often appeal to what they consider to be the "exceptional" nature of domestic work. In Chile, during the debate on maternity leave, several male senators expressed discomfort at the idea of having a pregnant houseworker inside their own homes (Biblioteca del Congreso Nacional 1998, 153). Limits on work hours tend to elicit the strongest reactions. In Bolivia, a male senator argued that domestic workers, unlike other workers such as miners, who really needed to rest, were not in need of legislated vacation time.[39] In Costa Rica, a key female legislator argued that it was acceptable to retain a longer workday for domestic workers because they watched soap operas during the day.[40] A male senator in Uruguay, arguing against an eight-hour workday, stated that "the nature of domestic work is distinct to other kinds of work, such as in commerce or industry. . . . This is a type of work where rest, interruptions, moments of distraction . . . are totally different."[41] A Peruvian male legislator, also in reference to an eight-hour workday, pointed out that domestic work "can be discontinuous, with times of rest," and remarked that employers' houses "are not hotels."[42]

Several of the court rulings have followed the same framing or logic. The Panamanian Supreme Court argued that due to the "special characteristics" of this work, domestic workers "have breakfast, lunch, dinner, rest, and engage in personal activities" during their longer workdays, and longer legal work hours are therefore not unconstitutional.[43] The Guatemalan Constitutional Court stated in its ruling that because domestic work is performed inside the employer's house and is not "continuous work," it is not subject to the same rights as other occupations.[44] The Costa Rican Constitutional Court found that domestic workers were "an exceptional case" and therefore the general work hours did not apply to them.[45]

Supporters can and have countered with three points regarding the concern among political elites that domestic workers do not work hard enough during the day. The first point addresses the substantive contribution of domestic work and criticizes the tendency to undervalue this work, pointing to the significant effort, both physical and emotional, that goes into cooking, cleaning, and caring for dependents. The second and third points address the right of domestic workers to the same workday limits as any other workers. The second point compares domestic work to other dependent work relations. Wageworkers across occupations have downtime; for example, a cashier is not "off the clock" if he or she is not ringing someone up. The third point addresses the right of a worker to a life outside of work. Regardless of whether a domestic worker is on her feet all day, this point goes, she is obligated to be in the employer's residence during that time and therefore is not free to use her time as she wishes. Underlying the views of opponents of equal workdays is the notion that these workers do not have the same need for or right to a private life outside of work hours, for personal time and for their own family responsibilities.

Politicians across countries have also brought up what they consider to be the "special" and "delicate" relationship between employer and employee, which may be disrupted by increased legal rights. Their concern reveals the cultural and economic threats they perceive in equalizing the rights of domestic workers. This has deep historical roots in the region, where the relationship between servants and masters has long been seen by elites as private and paternal (Blum 2004; L. Gill 1994; Graham 1992; Rubbo and Taussig 1983).

How, then, do equal rights arguments win over continued discrimination? Interestingly, reform on domestic workers' rights does not parallel reform on more general labor rights. Carnes's 2008 study of labor codes and labor code reforms in Latin America provides a useful comparison. He finds that while Latin American countries dismantled other ISI-related economic policies in the 1980s and 1990s as they implemented neoliberal reforms, labor codes did not undergo the same sweeping reforms. In fact, when they changed, it was mostly in the direction of increasing labor protections rather than deregulating them, as we would intuitively have expected. Carnes finds that there has been a substantive increase in labor protections in eight countries; a decrease in labor protections has only occurred in Colombia and partly in Peru, where decreases in individual labor rights were partially offset by increases in collective labor rights. Overall, Carnes documents a "surprising resilience" in labor rights across the region (2008, chap. 1).

What is striking for our purposes is the lack of correlation between Carnes's findings on general labor code reforms and reforms on domestic workers' rights. In Carnes's cases of substantive increases in labor protections, the discriminatory clauses on domestic workers have not been reformed, with the exception of the two clauses on severance pay and maternity leave added to the broader labor reforms in Chile. Moreover, Carnes finds that four countries between the 1980s and 2004 actually decreased the maximum number of legal work hours per week (after which overtime kicks in): Ecuador went down to forty hours, Venezuela and the Dominican Republic to forty-eight hours, and Chile to forty-five hours (2008, 41). However, in all four countries the extended work hours of domestic workers remained intact. In addition, the two countries where there has been an overall decrease in individual labor protections— Colombia and Peru—are two of the countries where domestic workers' rights *have* been reformed, through judicial reform in the former and through legislative reform in the latter.

Carnes argues that the continued stability and increase in general labor code protections are the result of both policy legacies and the continued political influence of organized labor. The removal of protective labor legislation, Carnes contends, is more challenging, as a large number of insider workers have a vested interest in its continuance (2008, 112). This is consistent with power mobilization theory, which finds that labor unions and leftist parties promote workers' rights (Huber and Stephens 2001; Rueschemeyer, Stephens, and Stephens 1992). In Latin America, this has generally resulted in a focus on collective labor rights such as union rights, on the interests of predominantly male workers in traditional labor sectors (Carnes 2008; Shrank and Murillo 2005),[46] and on trade-related labor rights (Bartley 2003; Bellman 2004; Rodríguez-Garavito 2005; Schrank 2009).

These areas have not included domestic workers' legal rights. Clearly, what explains general changes in labor rights does not explain the equalization of rights for outsiders such as domestic workers. If anything, there might be an *inverse* relation between broader labor code reforms and reforms on domestic workers' rights, given the changes in Colombia and Peru. This contrast highlights the often weak relationship between organized labor and marginalized groups such as domestic workers, who are not part of the union membership base and are mostly outside of the formal sector.

Labor rights "outsiders" can be excluded in two ways: first, by legal discrimination, as in the case of domestic workers, and second, by de facto exclusion through employment in the informal sector. The general increase in informal sector jobs across Latin America during the 1980s and 1990s has eroded access to labor rights as well as labor organizing within the large unincorporated informal sector, and it poses a challenge for the future of workers' rights and social security in the region more broadly (Centeno and Portes 2006; Cook 2007; Filgueira 2011; I. Gill, Montenegro, and Dömeland 2002; Martínez Franzoni and Voorend 2011; Portes and Hoffmann 2003; Roberts 2002). Both types of exclusion apply to the majority of domestic workers.

Thus, the strength of organized labor per se, an important predictor of general labor code reforms, does not, at least on its own, explain labor reform that benefits outsiders. Other explanatory factors are involved.

The past decade has seen a wave of left-wing governments with declared commitments to pursuing social equity and justice come into office.[47] While left governments may be more amenable to the issue, left government, at least on its own, does not explain reform on domestic workers' rights either. While in Uruguay reform was propelled by a left government and in Argentina executive-initiated reform by a left government awaits Senate approval, left or center-left governments in Ecuador, El Salvador, Guatemala, Nicaragua, Paraguay, and Venezuela have not to date legally equalized domestic workers' rights. In Chile and Brazil, center-left or left governments passed some reforms, but work hours in both countries remain unequal. In Bolivia and Costa Rica, legal reform took place under center-right governments, although it was initiated and forced into debate by more left-leaning politicians.

Several scholars have found that having more women in politics has led to more feminist policy initiatives and reforms in the region (Franceschet and Piscopo 2008; Jones 1997; V. Rodríguez 2003; Schwindt-Bayer 2006, 2010). At the same time, the relationship between women and feminism is problematic; not all women are feminists, and other scholars have found little relationship between women in Congress and feminist policy reforms (Weldon 2002a). Indeed, having more women in Congress, at least as such, has also not been a predictor of reform on domestic workers' rights. In both Bolivia and Uruguay, women's representation in Congress was minimal at the time of reform, indicating that a critical mass of female legislators is not a necessary cause. In Bolivia there was only one female senator when the Senate passed equal rights reform in 2003, and in Uruguay only 11.1 percent of legislators were female during equal rights reform in 2006. In Argentina, a quota law that has been in place for twenty years has resulted in a solid one-third female presence in Congress since the late 1990s, but this has not brought about legal reform on domestic workers' rights, likewise indicating that a critical mass of female legislators is not a sufficient cause. While Costa Rica's quota law of 1997 granted at least one-third of congressional seats to women, it took another twelve years for reform to take place in that country. On the other hand, whether female executives make a difference remains to be seen, as the number of female executives has recently dramatically increased. In South America, three female executives from the left have taken a more proactive stance on the issue of domestic workers' rights. Cristina Fernández de Kirchner is currently spearheading legal reform in Argentina, and Michelle Bachelet promoted smaller, piecemeal reforms in Chile. Brazil's Dilma Roussef, at the beginning of her term in 2011, has promised to pay more attention to the needs of this sector.

Feminist movements in civil society have often been the most important actors in promoting women's rights in general.[48] Within this context, as will be discussed below, domestic workers' rights have largely remained invisible and passed below the radar of most feminist movements as well. What factors, then, help make the issue visible and propel reform onto the political agenda?

Explaining Reform: Coalition Building, Visibility, and Agenda Setting

The available frames—equal rights versus the "exceptional" nature of domestic work—provide advocates and opponents with different strategies for their goals. In the case of domestic workers, the equal rights frame for advocates is clear-cut, while the opposition lacks an equally effective frame in post-transition democracies. Indeed, the problem for opponents is that no broadly accepted morally legitimating discourse that upholds "exceptionalism" and denies equal rights to this group exists in this day and age. This distinguishes it from some women's rights issues, such as reproductive health and abortion, where opponents of liberalizing reform are backed by the Catholic Church and other religious organizations and can claim a moral high ground with more confidence (Blofield 2006, 2008; Blofield and Haas 2005, 2011; Haas 1999, 2010; Htun 2003; L. M. Morgan 2011). On the other hand, it is similar to other women's rights issues such as violence against women, where opponents are similarly hampered by a lack of legitimating arguments supporting violence (Htun and Weldon 2010b; Weisberg 1996a, 1996b; Weldon 2002a, 2002b).

Given these dynamics, the key strategy for advocates is to organize, recruit allies, and gain visibility for the issue and force it onto the political agenda. On a social level, domestic workers must organize autonomously to promote their cause, gain allies, and make the cause visible. Allies and visibility are particularly important when seeking full reform, including work hours. Advocates' biggest challenge is convincing potential allies of the importance of their cause and forging support among them, specifically labor, feminist, human rights, and indigenous organizations.

On a political level, advocates must gain political allies to push reform onto the political agenda. By agenda setting, I specifically mean getting a reformist bill to a plenary debate and vote. Even when elected officials oppose reform and state so in private, they are still hesitant to actually cast a vote against a reformist bill given the endorsement of explicit discrimination that such a vote implies. The more visible the issue becomes in public discourse and the communications media, the more embarrassing it is to maintain oppositional arguments. Once a bill makes it to a plenary debate, most legislators will not find it comfortable to openly oppose equal rights on principle or by resorting to arguments with sexist, racist, or classist undertones. At this point, the arguments in favor of equal rights tend to carry the day. Indeed, to my knowledge, no domestic worker bills that have made it to a plenary vote have to date been voted down.

Relatedly, the opposition, even if quite strong privately, is not particularly organized on a social or political level. It cannot count on an open support base to mobilize against reform (there is one known instance of a housewives' mobilization against reform in Bolivia in 2000). In addition, given Latin America's class structure, more constituents are likely to come from the classes that provide domestic workers than from the classes that employ them. Thus, numbers are not on opponents' side. The strategy of those opposed to reform has therefore been, in most countries effectively, not to directly confront arguments based on equal rights but rather to keep the issue of domestic workers' rights off the political agenda. More active opponents have drawn on more informal, less visible veto points such as postponing and tabling bills in commission, and they can often rely on general indifference to the issue among the bulk of legislators. Advocates, then, must "find" a political window of opportunity to break through that resistance and to push a reform bill to be voted on (Kingdon 1995; McAdam, McCarthy, and Zald 1996). The speediest strategy is to gain executive support, as was the case in Uruguay and is now in Argentina. In the vast majority of cases, however, the executive has not been supportive, and advocates have had to find sympathetic legislative allies and often wait for years for a political opening, as in Bolivia and Costa Rica. It can take years of social pressure for advocates to find that opening, get the bill to a vote, and achieve reform. In most cases to date, such openings have not emerged. Below, I discuss the social and political dynamics in more detail.

The Social Level: Domestic Workers' Organizations and Their Allies

Social movements propel social and political change across the world and have become important players during and following democratization in Latin American countries (Alvarez 1990; Alvarez, Dagnino, and Escobar 1998; Escobar and Alvarez 1992). They differ from more institutionalized interest groups and lobbyists, however: social movements tend to ebb and flow in "cycles of protest" and lack stable access to resources (Tarrow 1994, 4). This is especially the case with poor peoples' mobilization and advocacy organizations. Economically disadvantaged people do not have the resources, networks, time, or skills to participate in the political system at the same level as do more advantaged groups, nor do they tend to have representatives who promote their interests in politics (Bachrach and Baratz 1970; Piven and Cloward 1977; Strolovitch 2006; Tarrow 1994).

These disadvantages are particularly acute in the case of domestic workers in Latin America. While democratic and more stable economic climates have allowed domestic workers more space to organize, they face multiple barriers in trying to do so, particularly those who are live-in domestics. The daily work hours of domestics are legally—and in practice tend to be—longer than those of other workers, and they often have very few days off each month. For those who have their own families, the little time they do have off is often spent with them. In addition, they tend to have lower levels of education and their wages are low.[49] Given this, the time available for meetings, resources for campaigns, and skills for understanding the political system and social networks to access it are scarce. Those who are noncitizens are, of course, further restrained from political participation. Finally, unlike industrial workers and many service workers, by the nature of their work domestics are socially isolated and hard to reach.[50] Consequently, organizational affiliations of any kind tend to be extremely low among domestic workers (Chaney and Garcia Castro 1989; CONLACTRAHO 2004; L. Gill 1994; López, Soto, and Valiente 2005, 208; Valenzuela and Mora 2009a). Even if they manage to create organizations, unionization as an option is more complicated, because domestic workers negotiate with individual employers and do not have an organized employers' association to contend and bargain with. Given the difficulties related to unionization, many of the organizations that do advocate for domestic workers' rights and concerns tend to be associations or nongovernmental organizations. Striking, for instance, is virtually inconceivable. Domestic workers must go through political channels and lobby the state to extend equal labor rights to them and to enforce the ones that exist.

These structural and organizational problems are, to an extent, a constant across Latin American countries and have kept the overall membership of domestic workers' organizations at low levels. Nevertheless, such organizations exist in virtually every country in the region, even if some are barely surviving, and they serve important social and political functions. Aside from advocating for equal rights and better enforcement, these organizations can provide social services. They can offer women and girls spaces to gather and socialize on their rare days off, and they often also provide training courses and support services more broadly. Many seek to facilitate evening or weekend education classes for adolescents who have dropped out of school to work as domestics. Such spaces can be particularly important for girls and women who are far from home and their own families.

Politically, which is the focus here, these organizations and their leaders can play very important strategic roles in advocating for domestic workers' rights and in promoting visibility for the cause. Since the 1970s and 1980s, when many were linked to the Catholic Church (Chaney and Garcia Castro 1989), these organizations have become more autonomous. Gaining access to resources has been challenging, and some are now dependent on donations from international organizations. In 1988, leaders of national-level domestic workers' organizations from eight countries came together at a meeting in Bogotá, Colombia, and created a regional confederation called the Confederación Latinoamericana y del Caribe de Trabajadoras del Hogar (Latin American and Caribbean Confederation of Domestic Workers, CONLACTRAHO) (see CONLACTRAHO 2003). After more frequent initial meetings, the confederation was less active during the 2000s. However, a regional meeting in September 2009, with help from the ILO and with the participation of organizations from eleven Latin American countries, revitalized CONLACTRAHO and national domestic workers' organizations.

The political opportunity structure that these organizations confront varies by country and influences the ability of domestic workers' organizations to promote their demands and to forge social and political allies. However, factors endogenous to the organizations are also important; foremost among them is leadership. Given that the structural and organizational constraints faced by domestic workers' organizations can be overwhelming, in those countries where the organizations have managed to become politically more visible, strong and persistent leadership has been essential. Due to the significant constraints on their time, some of the most visible leaders have forgone child rearing and a private family life (after all, they tend not to have access to paid domestic workers) and have dedicated themselves to organizing efforts. In Bolivia, Casimira Rodríguez and Basilia Catari, two prominent leaders, dedicated their personal time to domestic workers' rights from the 1980s up to legal reform in 2003. In Costa Rica, many political allies give credit for keeping the issue of domestic workers' rights alive for more than a decade to Rosita Acosta, the tireless leader of the Costa Rican domestic workers' organization. In Uruguay, the domestic workers' union received a huge boost in 2005 when leadership was taken over by two former textile factory workers and organizers, who brought their militancy and know-how to an otherwise basically defunct organization. In Chile, Aida Moreno spearheaded organizing efforts, marches, and political lobbying on behalf of domestic workers through the 1980s and 1990s; during the 2000s, leadership has been weaker, divided, and demoralized, affecting their strategies and visibility.

In addition to strong leadership, being able to tap into a more broadly framed cause is an essential component of gaining social and political allies (Stetson and Mazur 1995; Tarrow 1994). For disadvantaged groups seeking equal rights, the "injustice frame" (Gamson 1992) and solidarity-based appeals are likely to be the most resonant. Moreover, given domestic workers' particularly vulnerable positions and their need to focus on generating solidarity among the broader population, they are likely to be better off using "legitimate" forms of protest rather than risking a loss of sympathy by engaging in violent or overly disruptive actions (Tarrow 1994).

Potential social allies for domestic workers' organizations are labor unions and feminist, human rights, and indigenous organizations. International organizations, such as Human Rights Watch (2002, 2006) and the ILO (discussed below), can also provide financial and strategic support and help make the issue visible. To get the attention of these potential allies, domestic workers have had to organize autonomously to push for their cause.

While labor unions as political actors have been around for a longer time, women's rights groups and indigenous movements have increased in visibility since countries emerged from authoritarian rule. As noted earlier, however, these potential allies for domestic workers are certainly not automatic ones. Considering the marginalized status of domestic workers in three dimensions (class, gender, ethnicity/citizenship), organizations dedicated to the rights of labor, of women, or of indigenous people broadly may not, as a point of departure, prioritize them. That is, domestic workers are sub-disadvantaged within each of these groups, and the priorities of more advantaged members of the groups tend to come first (Strolovitch 2006).

The issue is particularly complicated with gender. While indigenous people and workers as a group tend to be economically disadvantaged, women cut across class lines (Blofield 2006; Blofield and Haas 2011; Htun 2004). Given the deep class divisions, the majority of professional and elite women in Latin America employ domestic workers in their households, and their preferences can be quite different from those of their employees. Opposition to legal reforms has also come from female politicians and from conservative women's groups such as housewives' organizations.

Even for feminists, the issue of domestic workers' working conditions and rights has in general not been a priority (Chaney and Garcia Castro 1989). Because the entrenched traditional household division of labor in the region places the responsibility of housework on women, the ostensible liberation of most professional women, as discussed in chapter 1, is based on the availability of cheap domestic workers, and many feminists rely on domestic workers as well (for Brazil, see Alvarez 1990, 53–54; de Santana Pinho and Silva 2010). While they are unlikely to publicly oppose extending rights, this does affect their priorities. In Argentina and Chile, for example, feminists have remained strikingly silent on domestic workers' rights. In Ecuador, the president of the domestic workers' organization complained of a lack of support from women's groups.[51] Overall, feminist organizations across the region have been slow to take up this issue, although in some countries individual feminists have adopted the cause. For example, in Costa Rica and especially in Bolivia, several outspoken feminists became vocal supporters of reform over the arduously long process of converting a bill on domestic workers' rights into law. At the same time, in both countries, women were also some of the strongest opponents of reform.

Labor unions, as discussed earlier, have rarely proactively sought to promote the labor rights of domestic workers. Unions have often denigrated domestic service as "women's work" and worthy of less attention (L. Gill 1994) and have tended to sidestep or ignore domestic workers' organizations (C. Rodríguez and Moreno 2005, 102). Of the case studies of reform, only in Uruguay did the labor union confederation take a proactive role in supporting domestic workers' rights. In some cases, labor unions may do the exact opposite: a government official in Mexico City pointed out, in reference to domestic workers' rights, that labor unions in Mexico have opposed any changes to the Labor Code, as they fear that any reforms may open the door to a reduction of their extant rights.[52] This point exemplifies the gulf between insiders and outsiders.

Ethnic identity has often been a more powerful organizing principle than class (Tarrow 1994, 5). Indeed, during the last two decades, countries with indigenous majorities or significant minorities have witnessed a substantial increase in indigenous mobilization and the politicization of ethnicity (Brysk 2000; Madrid 2005; Postero and Zamosc 2004; Sieder 2002; Van Cott 2005; Warren and Jackson 2002; Yashar 2005). Indigenous movements have been conceptualized as a "new social movement based on identity and consciousness" (Brysk 2000, 34; see also Alvarez, Dagnino, and Escobar 1998). While much of the focus has been on land rights and cultural autonomy, Yashar highlights how, in the context of democratic politics, "second-generation" indigenous groups have strategically framed specific social and political issues as *indigenous* issues—that is, drawing on the politicization of the indigenous cleavage to promote their demands (2005, 72–81). This context can enable domestic workers' organizations in countries with significant indigenous populations to frame the issue of domestics' legal rights as one of indigenous oppression; this has the potential to resonate with a broader populace and indeed did so in Bolivia.

None of these potential social allies is automatic, as evidenced by the generally weak position and isolation of domestic workers' organizations. Successful framing and coalition-building strategies will vary across countries and be influenced by the leadership strategies of the organizations themselves as well as the political salience of the different cleavages in each country. In Bolivia, which has a historically oppressed indigenous majority, the politicization of ethnicity enabled advocates to frame domestic workers' rights as an issue of indigenous justice, broadening its coalitional appeal and finally making it impossible for political elites to vote against reform in a highly charged political atmosphere (but prior to the victory of Evo Morales). In Costa Rica, advocates' framing of the issue by the late 2000s as a human rights issue, in the context of the country's reputation as a leader in human rights, made it harder for political elites to oppose it, as this reputation is a central element of political identity there. In Uruguay, inclusive labor unions' rise to political power and their support enabled advocates to frame the issue as labor-based discrimination. The availability of allies and the effectiveness of these frames depend on the political opportunity structure and conjunctures in each country; leaders can seek to strategically use the available frames to promote their causes. Advocates are also constrained by their national context. In Guatemala, another country with an indigenous majority, multiple reform attempts have been fruitless. In the context of its history of wide-scale repression, the lack of a cohesive indigenous rights movement with political resonance or representation, and a particularly intransigent elite and unaccountable political system, this issue has not gained any visibility or traction.[53]

Interestingly, citizenship as a cleavage does not appear to be salient in the direction that we would intuitively expect. We may theoretically expect that if a visible sector of domestic workers are noncitizens, this may hamper both mobilizing potential and social receptivity to the cause.[54] Because of their status as noncitizens, we would expect that they are less likely to condemn labor abuses and demand rights and that there may be more resistance to granting them or the entire sector equal rights. While there is some evidence that noncitizens are less likely to complain of labor abuses,[55] legal reform appears not to be correlated with the citizenship status of the domestic worker labor force. In Argentina, Chile, and Costa Rica, three of the richer economies in South and Central America, a growing share of domestic workers are Andean and Nicaraguan, respectively. While this may have hampered social receptivity to equal rights, it is not a determinant factor, as can be seen from equal rights reform in Costa Rica and likely in Argentina, as well as at least piecemeal reforms in Chile.

A key labor rights advocate that has recently emerged in favor of reform for domestic workers is an international actor—the ILO. The ILO has played an important role in promoting international conventions on labor rights as well as in providing technical and financial assistance to governments and ministries of labor seeking to improve working conditions in general in their countries. It operates at the invitation of the government, however, and hence the relationship tends to be most productive when the government and the ILO are in agreement about goals and strategies.

While the issue of domestic workers' rights—or lack thereof—has been present in the ILO for a long time (the need to legislate on this group of workers was first brought up in 1936), it was shunted aside for three-quarters of a century (Valenzuela and Mora 2009a, 290–94). Momentum began to build up in recent years from within the ILO and through pressure by domestic workers' organizations and advocacy networks around the world to address the issue and push for an international convention. In 2006, a group of advocates organized a meeting in the Netherlands, with the participation of domestic workers' organizations from around the world and with funding and strategic help from trade unions, nongovernmental organizations, and advocacy networks in advanced industrialized countries. This network, supported by the ILO's Bureau for Workers' Activities (ACTRAV) and with expertise from other ILO officials, lobbied for a convention.[56] In 2010, the ILO voted affirmatively on whether to establish a convention, and it approved this convention in 2011 (ILO 2010a, 2010b). This process of lobbying and negotiation has given an important boost to domestic workers' organizations in many countries, enabling their representatives to attend the ILO negotiations in Geneva, Switzerland.[57] As a result, the international level as a variable—via the ILO—may change the dynamics of reform from 2010 on by giving reformers a boost and additional visibility. I will return to this topic in the conclusion.

Political Allies and Windows of Opportunity

How have advocates of domestic workers' rights gained political allies? While left-wing politicians and parties, as well as parties with a popular support base, have, as a point of departure, been more likely to be sympathetic to the rights of disadvantaged groups than other parties (Huber and Stephens 2001; Rueschemeyer, Stephens, and Stephens 1992), these allies have been far from automatic. The issue of labor discrimination against domestic workers has not featured in the party platforms of any major parties except the Uruguayan Frente Amplio in 2005.

A tight relationship between the left and multiply disadvantaged groups is, indeed, more complicated. Many ostensibly leftist governments shift away from their more redistributive electoral platforms once in power due to global financial pressures and general economic and political constraints (Campello 2011; O'Donnell 1994), and even if they do not completely do so, they face pressures to serve the needs of their more advantaged and organized constituents first. This explains the resilience of and increase in general labor protections documented by Carnes (2008). Even well-organized labor and other advocacy groups can have difficulties gaining policy input, and scholars have in general pointed to the lack of consistently programmatic leftist parties in the region (Kitschelt et al. 2010; Levitsky 2003; Roberts 2002).

For domestic workers, who do not form part of the traditional, organized support base of any party, finding sympathetic individuals within the political system who are willing to take up the cause without programmatic party backing has been vital. Indeed, while political advocates of reform on domestic workers' rights have tended to come from the left, they have also tended to act as individuals and without party backing. Such allies have often been pioneering advocates of the rights of the disadvantaged more broadly and have added this issue to their docket of causes. Together with domestic workers' organizations and their social allies, these advocates can pursue different strategies to get reform onto the political agenda.

In all attempts at reform, advocates have faced an uphill battle, as evidenced by the few reforms that have taken place. Within this general context, executive support, in the few cases that it has been forthcoming, has been an important predictor of success, given the formal and informal agenda-setting powers of the executive in Latin American countries.[58] There have also been more instances of success with partial reforms. It has been easier for domestic workers' organizations to gain allies for smaller, piecemeal reforms that do not seek to equalize work hours, and these are also easier to pass.[59] Such reforms can be issue specific, or advocates can seek to tag them onto broader labor reforms. Sometimes, well-placed political allies have been willing to pursue such reforms out of personal commitment and ideological conviction and without consistent pressure from domestic workers' organizations. This has happened in Chile, where such "top-down" reforms seem to be more common. One senator forced maternity leave for domestic workers into a broader labor reform on gender equality in the workplace despite strong opposition, and threatened opponents with public exposure of their comments. It was also the case when the executive introduced a gradual equalization of the minimum wage of domestic workers with that of other workers and when a legislative bill sought to equalize live-in domestics' holidays. In these cases, well-placed political officials acted without widespread social pressure from below. In rare instances, personal histories of otherwise unlikely politicians may also play a role, as was the case in Costa Rica when a right-wing legislator joined the cause for labor reform for this group because his mother had been a domestic worker and had suffered discrimination. More commonly, politicians do not tend to engage in such "principled" acts when an organized support base and perceived benefits are low and implicit opposition is strong.

Full reforms that equalize work hours tend to confront more opposition and have required more allies and more pressure over time. Attempts to tag clauses onto broader labor reforms have to date not worked. It is noteworthy that in the instances of broader labor reforms where the workweek has been reduced (see Carnes 2008), the longer workdays and workweeks of domestic workers were not changed, including in Chile, where a 2001 labor reform reduced the general workweek to forty-five hours but retained the seventy-two-hour workweek of domestics. Rather, advocates have had to forge a broader support base and pursue issue-specific reform bills; indeed, all three full reforms through the legislature (in Bolivia, Costa Rica, and Uruguay) resulted from issue-specific bills. In these instances, given that the bills dealt specifically with domestic workers, public debate focused fully on them, giving them visibility.

Especially when pursuing full reform, domestic workers' organizations and their social allies have faced a long, uphill battle in the legislature. In many countries, individual or small groups of legislators have proposed equal rights reform bills since the 1990s. These bills have tended to be derailed by opponents through procedural mechanisms that delay a bill's progress (e.g., by postponing discussions and a vote in commission, or simply by archiving the bill). Under these circumstances, the only option for advocates has been to keep up the pressure in civil society, to build coalitions, and to attract attention, often over many years—and to remind and keep the support of sympathetic politicians on the inside who can then force the issue onto the political agenda when a window of opportunity arises. Without this constant pressure, even ostensibly sympathetic politicians have been likely to table such issues in the face of other issues they consider more pressing and of higher priority.

Gaining executive support for legal reform can break through such resistance or indifference. Until recently, however, the executives in Latin American countries—whether on the left or the right—have been uninterested in lending their weight to legal reform attempts. The full reforms in Bolivia in 2003 and in Costa Rica in 2009 were achieved without active executive support. The Peruvian reform of 2003 was also a legislative-initiated reform. In these cases, advocates mobilized for years, waiting for political windows of opportunity. In Bolivia it took ten years for legal reform to take place, in Costa Rica it took fourteen years (and multiple iterations), and in Peru it took twenty-four years from the introduction of the first bill. The more common result of such reform attempts across the region has been failure, as advocates have not been able to get bills to political debate and the bills have simply languished.

In the cases where equal rights bills have made it to debate, advocates were able to take advantage of political openings by having a reform bill ready for debate at the opportune moment and by pushing for it. In Bolivia, Evo Morales's left-wing party, the Movimiento al Socialismo (Movement Toward Socialism, MAS), gained 20 percent of the seats in Congress in 2002. Despite being in opposition, the party was able, in a highly charged political atmosphere where the right-wing government was on the defensive, to force the domestic worker bill to a vote and approval in the recalcitrant Senate in 2003 (where it had sat for three years after Chamber approval in 2000). In Costa Rica, an institutional reform implemented in 2008 to deal with a broader legislative stalemate streamlined legislative bills to three "mini-plenaries," each with lawmaking authority; this allowed supporters of the domestic worker bill to pressure the president of just one of the mini-plenaries to finally put the bill to a vote in November 2008, right before ceding the plenary to the center-right executive, who was uninterested in having a vote on the bill. In Peru, opposition from President Alberto Fujimori stalled the domestic worker bill through the 1990s. Years of marches and campaigns led by domestic workers' organizations, as well as a more sympathetic executive (President Alejandro Toledo), finally allowed the bill to be debated, approved, and signed into law in 2003.[60]

While most left-wing executives have not pursued reform, in the cases where we do see executive-initiated reforms, they have come from left or center-left executives. However, although several of the smaller, piecemeal reforms were initiated or supported by left or center-left executives, the only country to date with equal rights where the executive lent its full support was Uruguay in 2006. (Argentina may follow in its footsteps in the near future.) In Uruguay, attempts at legal reform dragged on through the 1990s and went nowhere until the left-wing Frente Amplio coalition took office in 2005 with an absolute majority in Congress and a broad mandate to promote social equity. The government took up the cause of domestic workers and drafted a law, which was approved by Congress, to grant domestic workers equal rights in 2006. On the other hand, as this book goes to press, there are signs that the executive in several Latin American countries has begun to pay more attention to this sector, related to the ILO convention. Again, I will return to this in the conclusion.

Finally, advocates can attempt to seek a court ruling through the judicial system on the grounds of unconstitutionality, given the explicit contradictions between ratified international treaties, national constitutions, and labor code clauses on domestic workers. This option is available only in countries with judicial systems that allow for constitutional review by a judicial organ, and with accessible mechanisms to bring suits to such an organ. However, these courts have been less hesitant to explicitly rule against equal rights, as the rulings in Costa Rica, Guatemala, and Panama have demonstrated.[61]

Conclusion

Achieving full reform on domestic workers' rights has to date required significant mobilization and coalition building on the part of domestic workers' organizations. The biggest challenge for advocates has been to break through elite resistance and indifference. Most reform bills have died as a result of this resistance and indifference before making it to a plenary debate. Advocates must gain social and political visibility for domestic workers' rights in order to get them onto the political agenda. If the executive is willing to lend its support to such efforts, reform is likely to be speedier and less obstacle ridden. If not, achieving equal rights can involve years of persistent leadership by domestic workers' organizations themselves and require building up networks of allies in both civil society and politics. Once the issue is on the agenda and politicians are forced to publicly take positions, they will find it hard to openly advocate for continued discrimination. When advocates can get a bill to debate, it is virtually guaranteed to pass.

3

WORKING IN CHRONIC INFORMALITY

For equal rights, legal equality is necessary but not sufficient. The enforcement of laws is just as critical as the laws themselves. Many of the legal rights granted to domestic workers—full or partial—are not respected in practice. Hence, we can identify a double discrimination against domestic workers across the region: first, explicit legal discrimination, and second, weak enforcement of the rights that do exist. This directs our attention to the enforcement mechanisms of the state. Governments can take proactive measures to implement new laws or better enforce extant laws. Below, I discuss two indicators of the effectiveness of enforcement: access to social security protections, and the prevalence of labor violations and the mechanisms to address them. I then discuss the key factors that explain variance in enforcement across the region.

There are two key dimensions to enforcement. The first is the integration of domestic workers into the formal economy, in particular the registration of these workers in social security systems. This can be assessed by examining the proportion of domestic workers included in social security, as well as by measuring the gap between the registration of the total economically occupied population and domestic workers in a social security regime. The second dimension is mechanisms to promote compliance with the labor code, specifically the inspection mechanisms and complaint procedures established by the ministry of labor to respond to reports of labor violations. In both cases, the key agency in enforcement is the ministry of labor (and its social security offices), although women's state agencies may also be involved, especially in government campaigns. The judiciary is also involved if cases go to court.

Overall, there is a lack of systematic, comparative data on the working conditions of domestic workers and on the prevalence of labor violations. This dearth of information can be seen as a reflection of the low priority that governments have tended to give this sector. In general, ministries of labor pay little attention to domestic workers. To systematically assess working conditions and government mechanisms to enforce laws would require significant resources and systematic, comparative investigations of the processing and resolution of labor complaints, which have to date not been conducted. My discussion here draws on the limited extant data and field research from my case studies.

Social Security Protections and the Prevalence of Labor Violations

With regard to the first dimension, social security protections, there is more comparative data to draw on. While the overall rate for the total working population measures state capacity and a country's developmental trajectory more broadly, the gap between the rate for the total working population and the rate for domestic workers reflects more specifically the political effort of state agencies to reach the marginalized. The International Labour Organization (ILO) collects data on access to pensions and health care through employment. Given that some countries have stronger public health care systems, access through employment may not be a determinative factor of whether an individual has access to health care. In addition, family members may receive health care indirectly through the employment of the head of household. Thus, a lack of direct health care access through employment may not reflect a lack of access altogether. Pensions, on the other hand, represent a direct, individual-based safeguard for old age. Given this, I use access to pensions as a proxy for the extent of formalization and risk management of the domestic worker labor force. The ILO has data on pension protections for Argentina, Brazil, Chile, Colombia, Mexico, Paraguay, Peru, and Uruguay. For several other countries, the data do not separate access to pensions and/or health care, making it more difficult to concretely assess the formalization of domestic workers, and I do not include those countries here. Table 3.1 shows the percentage of female domestic workers with pension protections compared to the total working population for the included countries over time.

The table indicates that pension protections for the total working population—at just over half of the workforce—fall far below full coverage, despite legally mandated access to social security in most Latin American countries. There has been a very slight increase in access to pensions in these eight Latin American countries since 2000; pension protections for the total working population went from 50.1 percent in 2000 to 52.8 percent in 2008. In the case of domestic workers, coverage went from 23.4 percent in 2000 to 24 percent in 2008.

Overall, domestic workers lag far behind other workers at less than half of the coverage rate for the total working population. Only just under one-quarter of domestic workers had pension coverage in 2008, leaving just over three-quarters of domestic workers without coverage. Were the remaining Latin American countries included in the data, the share would probably decline further. The vast majority of domestic workers in the region live in what Estévez and Esper refer to as "chronic informality" (2009, 14).

This average hides significant country differences, both in total pension protections and in pension protections for domestic workers. The countries included in table 3.1 fall broadly into three groups. Brazil, Chile, and Uruguay have the highest rates of both overall pension protections and pension protections for domestic workers. Colombia, Mexico, and Argentina cover between one-third and one-half of their total working populations, but the figures for domestic workers are much lower. Finally, Paraguay and Peru cover between one-fifth and one-third of their total populations but less than 5 percent of domestic workers.

One observation stands out immediately. The countries that perform better on social security are not the same countries that have achieved legal equality. The only country that has achieved legal equality and performs well on social security by regional standards is Uruguay. Both Peru, which has had "partial" equality since 2003, and Colombia, which achieved legal equality through the Constitutional Court in 1998, perform weakly on social security for domestic workers.[1] While Bolivia and Costa Rica, which have had legal equality since 2003 and 2009, respectively, are not included in the ILO data, in Bolivia social security for domestic workers was virtually nonexistent as of 2010, as this sector was still waiting for regulatory decrees from the executive to implement the gains from the 2003 law. In Costa Rica, 23.9 percent of domestic workers had pension protections in 2004, while the figure for the total working population was 45.1 percent (Martínez Franzoni, Mora, and Voorend 2010, 44). Costa Rica therefore falls between the first and second groups. Clearly, at least partially different factors explain social security access versus legal equality for domestic workers.

A second observation likewise stands out. The three groupings that emerge from table 3.1 broadly correlate with Filgueira's classifications of welfare state typologies (1998, 2011): stratified universal regimes, dual protection regimes, and exclusive protection regimes. In stratified universal countries, the majority of the population was covered by health care and social security protection systems by the 1970s. However, protection was stratified, and the most

Table 3.1 Percentage of female domestic workers with pension protections versus percentage of the total working population with pension protections

	1995		2000		2005		2008	
	Domestics	Total	Domestics	Total	Domestics	Total	Domestics	Total
Latin America	—	—	23.4	50.1	21.8	49.7	24.0	52.8
Argentina[a,b]	—	—	—	—	6.3	42.6	10.6	45.4
Brazil[c]	25.4	57.3	34.5	57.9	35.8	59.9	37.5	63.3
Chile[b]	—	—	47.9	66.7	49.8	67.6	42.3	66.5
Colombia	—	—	14.4	34.3	13.1	33.4	14.5	38.9
Mexico	0.3	35.5	1.0	44.9	0.7	42.4	1.3	42.1
Paraguay	3.6	21.5	0.2	19.2	1.3	19.6	0.3	21.7
Peru[a]	8.8	34.8	5.3	27.0	3.0	27.0	3.7	31.4
Uruguay[c]	—	—	31.1	65.0	26.5	61.9	40.2	67.5

Source: OIT 2007 (1995 data) and 2009.

[a] Urban areas for Argentina; metropolitan Lima for Peru.

[b] 2008 data is actually for 2006.

[c] 2000 data is actually for 2001.

powerful and organized sectors received the best benefits, often through the male head of household. Since the neoliberal shift, these countries have differentially adjusted their social protection systems (Filgueira 2011; Pribble 2011). In Filgueira's dual protection regimes, approximately half of the population is covered by modern social protection systems, whereas the other half has no access to them. Finally, in exclusive social protection systems, a small minority accedes to benefits and the vast majority are excluded (Filgueira 1998, 2011).

As table 3.1 indicates, Brazil, Chile, and Uruguay fit roughly into Filgueira's stratified universal regime. Pension protections in 2008 (in Chile, 2006) for these countries' total working populations were between 60 and 70 percent. Pension protections for domestic workers substantially increased in Brazil from 25.4 percent in 1995 to 37.5 percent in 2006, and in Uruguay from 31.1 percent in 2000 to 40.2 percent in 2006. Government data for Uruguay indicate that this figure further rose to around 50 percent in 2009.[2] Pension protections for domestic workers in Chile actually declined, however, from 47.9 percent in 2000 to 42.3 percent in 2006. While in Brazil pension protections for the total working population increased from 57.3 percent in 1995 to 63.3 percent in 2008, in the other two countries they have, despite some fluctuations, largely remained the same. In Brazil and Uruguay, then, there has been a decrease in the gap between pension protections for all workers and pension protections for domestic workers, reflecting state efforts to include the marginalized.

In Argentina, Colombia, and Mexico, pension protections for the total working population in 2008 (in Argentina, 2006) were 45.4 percent, 38.9 percent, and 42.1 percent, respectively, falling roughly into Filgueira's dual protection regimes. The only available ILO data for Argentina are from 2005 and 2006, and they show a marked one-year increase in pension protections for domestic workers from 6.3 to 10.6 percent, while the percentage for the total working population increased from 42.6 to 45.4 percent. Since then, the Argentine minister of labor has reported in the media that 350,000 domestic workers (out of just over one million) were registered by 2010,[3] but an internal government document put the figure for 2009 at a much more modest 14.3 percent of the domestic worker labor force (Ministerio de Trabajo, Empleo y Seguridad Social 2010, 6).

In Colombia, pension protections for the total working population increased from 34.3 percent in 2000 to 38.9 percent in 2008, while the figure for domestic workers stagnated at 14.4 percent in 2000 and 14.5 percent in 2008. In Mexico, the figure for the total working population improved by 6.6 percentage points from 35.5 percent in 1995 to 42.1 percent in 2008, while the figure for domestic workers increased by 1 percentage point from 0.3 percent in 1995 to a dismal 1.3

percent in 2008. Although coverage in Argentina seems to be improving for domestic workers, albeit from a very low point of departure, in Colombia and in Mexico the state has actually reduced its commitment to this sector over time and in comparison to the total working population. The figures for Mexico are particularly dramatic: only one out of every hundred domestic workers in that country has old-age security.

As seen in table 3.1, Peru and Paraguay fall into Filgueira's exclusive social protection regimes. Pension protections for domestic workers in both countries declined—in Peru from 8.8 percent in 1995 to 3.7 percent in 2008, and in Paraguay from 3.6 percent in 1995 to an even more dismal 0.3 percent in 2008. Pension protections for the total working population in Peru slightly declined from 34.8 percent in 1995 to 31.4 percent in 2008, while in Paraguay this figure remained stable, at 21.5 percent in 1995 and 21.7 percent in 2008. Both countries, then, perform weakly with regard to the total working population and outright miserably with regard to domestic workers. In Peru, the decline in pension protections took place while the 2003 law on reforming domestic workers' rights was approved, indicating a clear lack of executive commitment to follow-up.

Country-specific data from Guatemala, Honduras, Nicaragua, and El Salvador indicate a dearth of social security protections for domestic workers. In Guatemala, a 2010 article reported that only 87 domestic workers were registered for social security, far below 1 percent of the total domestic worker labor force.[4] Employers in this country are not legally obligated to register workers for social security or health care if they have fewer than three employees, hence, in effect, denying coverage to most domestic workers. In Honduras, only 134 domestic workers out of a total of 74,000 were registered for social security in 2007.[5] In Nicaragua, the number of domestic workers registered for social security increased from 42 in 1998 to 3,252 in 2008, which still represents less than 3 percent of the 114,000 domestic workers in the country.[6] In El Salvador, the numbers of domestic workers covered by social security are not available, but it appears that they are either very low or nonexistent, as concrete mechanisms by which to register domestic workers did not exist until 2010.[7] Data from a regional survey of Central America and the Dominican Republic indicate that around 90 percent of full-time domestic workers do not have social security of any kind, including health care.[8] This masks country-specific differences: in Costa Rica, the figure is just over 40 percent; in Panama, between 50 and 60 percent; and in the rest of the countries, much closer to 100 percent (COMMCA 2010, 259).

The available data on the prevalence of labor violations across countries are less systematic, as many studies and newspaper reports rely on anecdotal examples or individual histories. A set of surveys conducted in 1995 (funded by the ILO and carried out by domestic workers' organizations) on the working conditions of domestic workers in six Latin American countries reveals highly exploitative conditions and weak enforcement of extant laws.[9] In the Dominican Republic, 91 percent of domestic workers surveyed did not know their labor rights, only 15 percent had a written contract, and 57 percent did not get the legally mandated paid vacation (CONLACTRAHO 2004, 22). In Peru, 41 percent of live-in domestics worked more than eighty hours a week in the mid-1990s (20). In Mexico, only 5 percent received the mandated vacation time established in the Labor Code (18). In Guatemala, 68 percent of domestic workers received less than the monthly minimum wage (16). In Costa Rica, only 22 percent had a work contract, and 39 percent received less than the minimum wage for domestic workers, which was about two-thirds the national minimum wage (15). In Brazil, 45 percent did not have a labor contract, and 27 percent did not get the eight hours of rest a night stipulated by the law (13). In Bolivia, the majority of domestic workers worked more than eighty hours a week in the mid-1990s, and very few got the (lower) vacation days they were entitled to (12).

Other, more recent studies corroborate low enforcement of the existing laws. In Argentina, only 15 percent of domestic workers in 2004 received the paid annual vacation they were entitled to, even though over 70 percent worked for only one employer (Ministerio de Trabajo, Empleo y Seguridad Social 2005, 182, 187). Moreover, while the executive-decreed minimum wage is lower than the national minimum wage for unskilled workers (18 percent lower in 2006, for example),[10] 60 percent of full-time domestic workers still earned less than even this minimum wage (191–92). In Mexico, 32 percent of domestic workers earn less than the minimum wage, while for the whole labor force the figure is 13 percent.[11] In Peru, four years after the 2003 legal reform that mandated a 48-hour workweek for live-in domestic workers, 61 percent of domestic workers still worked more than 48 hours a week.[12] A Human Rights Watch report on domestic workers in Guatemala City in 2000, based on eighteen interviews of domestic workers, found pervasive abuse of not only labor rights but also the human dignity of the workers. Employers and their family members often treated workers with disrespect, refusing to use their names and referring to them as *muchachas* or *indias*. Many workers did not receive enough food and were not given time to eat. One fourteen-year-old domestic worker was given only ten minutes to eat lunch and dinner during her 17-hour workday (Human

Rights Watch 2002, 63). Another worked for a household for five years and during that time had only one day off. Furthermore, employers would sometimes lock workers in the house and not provide them with keys, ensuring that they were unable to leave (70). The average workday of these workers was 14.5 hours long (68).

Surveys from a regional project on Central America and the Dominican Republic in 2008 indicate that 78 percent of live-in domestic workers worked more than 48 hours a week, and 32 percent worked more than 72 hours a week. In Panama, Costa Rica, and the Dominican Republic, 6 percent, 17 percent, and 21 percent, respectively, worked more than 72 hours a week, while in El Salvador, Nicaragua, and Guatemala, between 45 and 50 percent worked more than 72 hours a week. Among domestic workers who did not live with their employers, 52 percent worked more than 48 hours a week and 6 percent worked more than 72 hours a week (COMMCA 2010, 251). Of live-in domestics, 75 percent received one day off per week, 7 percent did not receive a day off, and 18 percent received more than one day off per week. Of live-out domestics, 70 percent received one day off per week, 2 percent did not receive a day off, and 28 percent received more than one day off per week (254).

In Guatemala, the survey found that the average workweek for domestic workers was 68 hours, and those who lived in their employer's house worked on average 77 hours a week (COMMCA 2008, 16–17). This is actually lower than the legally allowed 92-hour workweek, but it is still much longer than the legal workweek for others. While domestic workers are legally entitled to only 6 hours off per week, in practice 74 percent of those surveyed received at least one day off per week (10). While domestic workers in Guatemala are not legally excluded from maternity leave, in practice they are fired when they become pregnant (82).

The general reality across the region is that most domestic workers who become pregnant lose their jobs, regardless of whether the law permits dismissal (Rodgers 2009, 99). Sexual harassment is also a severe problem. Domestic workers often experience unwanted sexual advances as well as sexual assault on the job. While there is little systematic evidence of its prevalence, individual histories of domestic workers often reveal that they have had to put up with unwanted advances and assault at some point during their working lives.

Domestic workers are also often hesitant to denounce labor violations to the authorities. For example, in a survey of 169 domestic workers in Nicaragua, of those who said that their labor rights had been violated (62 percent of the survey total), only 3 had made denunciations to the corresponding authorities

(Palacios, Tinoco, and Centeno 2008, 56). This tendency is related to the perception that the authorities will not respond and is often based on reality.

Systematic violations such as those described above reflect a lack of state efforts to enforce the labor rights of this sector. Within its ministry of labor, each Latin American country has an office of labor inspections with the broad mandate of enforcing the labor code in general.[13] An important characteristic of paid domestic work, as mentioned in chapter 1, is that the work takes place within a private household, which is often legally or even constitutionally protected from inspection by public officials. While the hiring of a domestic worker does transform the household into a site of employment, most Latin American legal systems have not made adequate provisions for investigating potential violations of the labor code in these specific cases. In virtually all countries, the laws specify that "inspections are restricted by the inviolability of the home" (see Pereira and Valiente 2007, 63–67). In some countries—for example, Peru, Uruguay, and Venezuela—laws specify that a judicial order can override this.

What is most important is how these laws and norms are actually applied and implemented. The capacity of the labor inspectors varies dramatically by country.[14] Overall, Chile has by far the highest number of labor inspectors per worker in Latin America (see Schrank and Piore 2007, 22). There is little systematic information with regard to domestic workers in particular, but it appears that some of the strongest mechanisms for investigating and resolving the labor complaints of domestic workers are in Chile, Uruguay, and the city of Buenos Aires. I discuss the cases of Bolivia, Costa Rica, Uruguay, and Chile in the country-specific chapters.

One important factor is whether ministries of labor have provided officers or personnel to specifically process labor complaints from this sector. Domestic workers are not lawyers and face particular difficulties in accessing avenues for labor complaints without technical advice and support mechanisms. To my knowledge, the only systematic study on this topic is Birgin's (2009) investigation of labor complaints from domestic workers in the city of Buenos Aires in Argentina, where the Ministry of Labor for that city has a specific office dedicated to processing the labor complaints of these workers and their employers. Birgin found that even with free legal support, the processing and resolution of complaints—which in the mid-2000s were averaging slightly more than two thousand per year—take on average four years (2009, 274–75).[15] While the processing time may be long, the existence of a specific office for this purpose does show an effort on the part of the Ministry of Labor to address complaints related to this sector.

This effort can be contrasted with Ministry of Labor officials in El Salvador, where—as outlined by a Human Rights Watch investigation of child domestic labor—it is estimated that tens of thousands of girls are employed in domestic work and where low wages, long hours, and exploitation have been documented (Human Rights Watch 2004). In the early 2000s, Ministry of Labor officials consistently denied that domestic work among girls was widespread. The director-general of labor, in an interview with Human Rights Watch, claimed that "really the work of minors in domestic service is very little. . . . The work of those under fourteen is practically zero" (26). A labor inspector in El Salvador was not even aware of the minimum age for employment of domestic workers but explained, "It's that girls are almost never working" (28). The director-general of inspection at the Ministry of Labor told Human Rights Watch that "we never find cases of kids working as domestics" (30). These comments reveal that child domestic workers are completely invisible to the political officials who are ostensibly responsible for ensuring their rights. Acknowledgement that a problem actually exists is a precondition for even beginning to address the issue.

In general, many ministries pay little attention to domestic workers, and there is a dearth of information on and public policies toward this sector in most countries.[16] This results in weak mechanisms to ensure the rights of domestic workers.

Explaining Government Efforts to Protect Domestic Workers' Labor Rights

Variation in the enforcement of labor protections and rights for domestic workers is partly explained by broader political dynamics, specifically the factors identified in the welfare state literature more broadly, including industrialization and development trajectories, state capacity, years of democracy, and the influence of labor unions and left-wing government.[17] More specifically, enforcement of labor protections and social security, on the one hand, and of labor rights via mechanisms for processing violations, on the other hand, may not necessarily correlate. However, the available empirical evidence, spotty as it is, does indicate that the countries that do well in the first area seem to also do well in the second area. Chile and Uruguay—discussed in chapter 5—stand out here.

With regard to enforcement, the key agency is, of course, the executive, given its control over implementation of government policies. State capacity matters:

a capable civil service willing and able to implement laws is crucial to enforcement, as is the agency responsible for social security. Social security agencies can put varying amounts of effort into encouraging registration and formalization of the workforce. Many ministries of labor in the region are under-resourced and lack both the capacity to reach out to informal sector workers and enough capable staff members to process complaints of labor violations. In addition, corruption among officials may be a problem. Corruption benefits those with the resources to engage in it; they are rarely domestic workers who seek to file a complaint and are more likely their better-off employers who want to see the complaint go away.

As with legal reform, we would theoretically expect left-wing governments in general to be more proactive about enforcement. A left-wing executive is ideologically more predisposed to promote the enforcement of labor laws and the formalization of the labor force than a right-wing executive, whose priority tends to be to allow for flexible labor markets as an incentive for investment and economic growth. The ideological position of the executive is likely to interact with state capacity—specifically, a capable civil service willing and able to implement policies.

When it comes to domestic workers in particular, variation in the enforcement of labor protections and rights cannot be explained by these broader trends alone, however. Enforcement is also a result of efforts—or the lack thereof—directed specifically toward domestic workers. In Latin America, there has been a nearly ubiquitous legacy of indifference or outright hostility on the part of state organs with regard to protecting this group of workers. The key factor in the enforcement of protections and rights for domestic workers is whether governments have sought to overcome this history of indifference through proactive measures. Hence, as with the dynamics of legal reform, enforcement is strongly influenced by the efforts of well-placed political allies—in this case in the executive—with a commitment to reach the marginalized, first by making them visible and then by incorporating them into programs and public policies. Such a commitment tends to involve proactive measures such as government campaigns to promote knowledge of rights and obligations, mechanisms to process complaints, social security registration, and professionalization of the sector.

In cases where legal reform has taken place, the reform path has also influenced enforcement efforts. When the executive initiates legal reform, it is more likely to take ownership of it and implement it. In addition, governments that have been open to advice from ILO officials in recent years have become more sensitive to focusing on this sector. Finally, stronger domestic workers' organizations in civil society, when they have policy access, can help with these campaigns and make them more effective. A left-wing executive with strong state capacity, advisors from the ILO, and strong domestic workers' organizations are likely to result in more effective enforcement of labor protections and rights for this sector.[18]

Indeed, improvement in the rate of pension protections for domestic workers took place under left governments in Uruguay and Argentina. In Brazil, on the other hand, the most significant increase occurred under the centrist government of Fernando Enrique Cardoso, while the increase under left-wing president Luiz Inácio Lula da Silva was slower.

Uruguay is discussed in detail in chapter 5. To summarize, comprehensive legal reform as well as the enforcement campaign took place under the left-wing presidency of Tabaré Vázquez. After legal reform in 2006, the Social Security Bank launched a massive registration campaign directed at domestic workers, including door-to-door visits, fliers, and television ad campaigns. These efforts paid off, and Uruguay is now the only country in Latin America where around half of the domestic worker labor force is covered by social security.

In both Argentina and Brazil, the left-wing executive initiated and Congress approved laws that allowed domestic workers' salaries and social security contributions to be tax deductible, thus providing an incentive for employers to formalize these workers. In Argentina, the social security rate of domestic workers was only 6 percent in 2005; in a broader bill on tax evasion that year, the executive included a clause that would make domestic workers' salaries and social security contributions tax deductible for the employer in order to encourage social security contributions (Ministerio de Trabajo, Empleo y Seguridad Social 2005, 193).[19] Since then, the Ministry of Labor has proactively engaged in public campaigns to increase the number of domestic workers enrolled in social security (Estévez and Esper 2009). These have involved sending letters to hundreds of thousands of middle-class households to inform them of the law and to request compliance.[20] While government figures on actual registration rates are not clear, access to social security among domestic workers has increased at least modestly and may further increase if the current legal reform under consideration, initiated by the executive, is approved and enforced.

In Brazil, the most substantial increase in domestic workers with pension protections took place between 1995 and 2000, during the presidency of Fernando Enrique Cardoso. Since 2000, the increases have been slower. To encourage more registration, the executive, under left-wing president Luiz Inácio Lula da Silva (2002–10), passed a law in 2006 that, among other things, facilitated social security registration of domestic workers by making contributions tax deductible.[21] Data from 2007 indicate that the law did not immediately result in appreciable increases in social security registration rates among domestic workers (Madalozzo and Bortoluzzo 2010). However, in 2003, soon after Lula assumed power, the Ministry of Labor held a series of meetings with domestic workers' organizations. This resulted in a set of ambitious programs launched in 2005, with the participation of domestic workers' organizations, to enforce the rights and promote the professionalization of domestic workers more broadly (Sanches 2009, 129–36).

In Chile, the decline in pension protections between 2000 and 2006 actually took place under center-left governments. This may be related to the specific nature of Chilean social security inherited from the Pinochet regime: it is privatized, with high administrative costs and high minimum contribution years, and payments are the responsibility of the employee, creating disincentives for regular contributions from low-paid employees. However, the center-left government of Michelle Bachelet (2006–10) passed a 2008 pension reform to incentivize low-income working women in particular to join and benefit from the system, and it may be that enrollment in social security has increased since then. This was also accompanied, as will be discussed in chapter 5, by an executive campaign in 2008 to enforce the rights and promote the professionalization of domestic workers.

These examples show that proactive efforts can make a clear difference in pension coverage and likely in a general respect for the labor rights of this sector. On the other hand, a left-wing executive per se is not a sufficient cause for proactive enforcement. In Bolivia, a left-wing executive—under Evo Morales since 2006—has not resulted in effective implementation of social security protections, despite its rhetorical commitment to the cause of social justice for domestic workers. Weak state capacity, excessive politicization of the civil service, and the weak capacity of the domestic workers' organizations to consistently pressure the executive for enforcement have resulted in little concrete progress, as will be discussed in chapter 4.

In Ecuador, left-wing president Rafael Correa increased the minimum wage for domestic workers above the national minimum wage in 2010[22] and threatened employers who do not register their domestic workers for social security with prison sentences.[23] Yet it remains to be seen whether such rhetorical flourishes as the latter are accompanied by more positive incentives to promote long-term formalization of domestic workers.

Center and right-wing governments, and less ideological, clientelistic governments, have been slower to promote enforcement of domestic workers' labor rights. In Peru, after the 2003 legislative-initiated legal reform, the executive did not follow up with effective implementation. Two barriers continue to impede social security registration in that country. First, the language on social security in the law itself is ambiguous, and as of 2010 there are no concrete mechanisms by which to register domestic workers and by which to obligate employers to register them.[24] Second, the regulatory decree to implement the law mandates the minimum contribution for both health care (paid by employer) and pension payments (paid by employee) on the basis of the national minimum wage, yet it does not grant domestic workers this minimum wage, thus elevating the percentage cost for them.[25] In the absence of government efforts to facilitate access to social security protections, take-up rates are likely to remain very low. General disregard for the law appears to be the norm: as mentioned earlier in this chapter, 61 percent of domestic workers surveyed worked more than forty-eight hours a week in 2007, four years after the legal reform that mandated a forty-eight-hour workweek for live-in domestics.[26] Consequently, domestic workers' organizations have mobilized to pressure the executive. A labor union was created in Peru in 2006 to defend domestic workers' rights, and it has called for the Ministry of Labor to work with it on awareness and enforcement campaigns.[27]

In Costa Rica, Congress approved equal rights in 2009, but the executive was not behind the reform. Hence, despite stronger state capacity in Costa Rica, the lack of explicit executive support has reduced implementation efforts. The Ministry of Labor's stance on the legal reform is ambiguous, and by the end of 2010 it had not proactively sought to reach domestic workers through special offices or programs. This will be discussed in chapter 4.

In Colombia, it is the Constitutional Court, rather than the executive or Congress, that has expanded domestic workers' rights, as well as the rights of marginalized groups more broadly. Not only was equal rights instituted via court ruling in 1998, but the right to social security for domestic workers was affirmed in a Constitutional Court ruling in 2008. This ruling affirmed the employee's right to a pension and the employer's responsibility to provide it, sending a clear signal to employers about their legal obligations.[28] As table 3.1 indicates, pension protections for this group have reached less than 15 percent of domestic workers in Colombia, and it remains to be seen whether punitive sanctions such as this one will increase the rates or whether a concerted, proactive effort on the part of the Ministry of Labor is also required.

In Mexico, under the current law the employer has no obligation to register a domestic worker for social security. In addition to the country's dismal pension protections, government statistics indicate that 96 percent of domestic workers lack access to health care.[29] Under two consecutive right-wing governments—those of Vicente Fox and Felipe Calderón—there has been little effort from government ministries to reach this sector, and domestic workers have remained invisible. Proactive mechanisms to process domestic workers' labor complaints do not exist, resulting in extremely low levels of denunciations from this sector compared to other labor sectors, despite high levels of violations. It remains to be seen whether the current broader labor reform in the Labor Commission (as of 2010) includes the right to social security for domestic workers.[30]

In Central America, aside from Costa Rica, weak state capacity, clientelistic or outright repressive regimes, and a lack of committed public officials have produced dismal results with regard to protections for marginalized groups, as indicated by the Human Rights Watch report on El Salvador. For example, in response to ministerial denials of the prevalence of child domestic labor in that country, a local activist pointed out that "nobody [in the ministry] wants to get into that issue" and that there are no coordinated mechanisms for compliance (Human Rights Watch 2004, 28–29). On the other hand, on International Labor Day in 2010, El Salvador's first left-wing president, Mauricio Funes, announced a government campaign to register 25 percent of domestic workers for health care and maternity benefits in the country's Social Security Institute.[31]

Conclusion

Overall, enforcement of the labor rights of domestic workers has been weak, as evidenced by the low coverage of these workers in pension programs and their low visibility in most ministries of labor. The countries in which there has been improved enforcement are those with left-wing governments with stronger state capacity and a core of committed officials in the ministries of labor. Examples of such efforts can be seen in the governments of Uruguay, Argentina, Brazil, and Chile, which have, in the past decade, sought to more proactively reach out to domestic workers through enforcement campaigns.

4

BOLIVIA AND COSTA RICA

Social Mobilization and Reform from the Bottom Up

Bolivia and Costa Rica are in many ways opposites. The former is poor, heterogenenous, and highly unequal, and it has a history of political instability and exclusion. The latter is more developed and more homogeneous, with lower inequalities and a long history of democratic stability and higher respect for human rights. Both countries, however, achieved equal rights reform—in contrast to almost all of their regional counterparts—and did so through years of organizing, through legislative initiatives, and without executive support. In both cases, strong leadership by representatives of domestic workers played an important role, and leaders were able to recruit social and political allies, gain visibility for the cause, and take advantage of political opportunities. They did so by gaining the support of individual politicians in the legislature and without whole-scale executive support. On the other hand, in neither country has enforcement been strong—a problem related to the interactive effect of state capacity and executive commitment.

Bolivia: Equal Rights as Indigenous Justice

Bolivia is the poorest country in South America and the only one with an indigenous majority. As table 2.3 indicates, Bolivia's per capita income in 2000 was under US$3,000 in PPP dollars. With a Gini index of .6, it also has one of the most unequal distributions of income in the region and in the world. The indigenous majority has historically suffered from political, economic, and social exclusion, and most live in absolute poverty. The country has also been characterized by highly unstable politics. Yet Bolivia managed to be the first country in Latin America to equalize domestic workers' rights through Congress in

2003. Moreover, the reform took place prior to the historic victory of Evo Morales in 2005, with his left-wing platform of social justice for indigenous people.

Social and Legal Context

Out of a total population of 9 million people, Bolivia has approximately 144,000 domestic workers, 95 percent of whom are women (Fundación Solón 2001b). Ethnicity has been very salient in this workforce. A 1995 survey of domestic workers in La Paz found that the first language of 83 percent of live-in domestics and 72 percent of live-out domestics in the sample was Aymara (CONLACTRAHO 2003, 35). The divide between the oftentimes white employers and indigenous employees is not only economic but also social and cultural (L. Gill 1994). Prior to the 2003 law, the Labor Code discriminated explicitly against domestic workers. It established a maximum workday of eight hours for other workers, while separate articles for domestic workers allowed for a sixteen-hour workday with only six hours off per week on Sunday, in effect making Sunday's workday ten hours long. Domestic workers received only ten days of legal annual vacation, as opposed to fifteen to thirty days for all other workers. Moreover, employer notice for domestic workers was fifteen days, while it was ninety days for all other workers (Fundación Solón 2001b, 26–29).

The 1995 survey revealed highly exploitative conditions. Of seventeen- to twenty-five-year-old workers, 85 percent worked more than eighty hours a week. Some got an average of only three hours of sleep per night. Less than one-quarter actually received the legally mandated annual vacation. Many were not allowed by their employers to go see a doctor when ill (having to wait until time off on Sunday), and more than one-third complained of not receiving enough food (CONLACTRAHO 2003, 43–50). In addition, humiliating treatment and sexual abuse were common (CBDHDD and CDH 2005; CONLACTRAHO 2003; L. Gill 1994; Peñaranda Davezies, Arandia Davezies, and Castro 2005; Sindicato de Trabajadoras del Hogar 1982). Adolescents and girls were particularly vulnerable to exploitation (Defensa de Niñas y Niños Internacional 2004).

The Political Process

Bolivian politics was, until 2005, characterized by clientelism, elite-led politics, and the social and political exclusion of the indigenous people (Van Cott 2000, 2005). While suffrage was extended to indigenous people in 1952, politics was dominated by the white elite, and democratic politics broke down in 1964, leading to almost two decades of military rule. Since the democratic elections of 1982, Bolivia has continued to be characterized by high levels of political instability. Although three clientelistic parties—the historically leftist Movimiento Nacional Revolucionario (MNR) and Movimiento de la Izquierda Revolucionaria (MIR), and the right-wing Acción Democrática Nacional (ADN)—dominated the Bolivian political landscape in the 1980s, the 1990s witnessed new entrants to the party system. Two populist parties briefly rose and fell, while a more solid indigenous movement was gaining a social and political base (Albó 2002; Van Cott 2005; Yashar 2005). As a gesture to recognize this rising movement, presidential candidate Gonzalo Sánchez de Lozada appointed an indigenous activist, Victor Hugo Cárdenas, as his vice presidential candidate and won the elections in 1993.

The first bill on domestic workers' rights, submitted by an individual legislator to the Women's and Minors' Commission in the Chamber in 1993, was repeatedly postponed. Vice President Cárdenas did not end up backing the bill. However, the indigenous movement continued to mobilize through the 1990s, and a series of constitutional and political reforms opened up the political system to nontraditional parties, enabling the rise of programmatic indigenous-based parties—most prominently the Movimiento al Socialismo (Movement Toward Socialism, MAS) (Van Cott 2003; Yashar 2005).

After extensive pressure by the domestic workers' organization and its allies, from within and outside Congress, an updated version of the domestic worker bill was approved in the Chamber in 2000. This bill granted an eight-hour workday for live-out domestic workers, a ten-hour workday for live-in domestic workers, and the same rights as other workers in all other areas, and it mandated inclusion in social security. After Chamber approval, the bill entered the Senate, where it was stalled for three years. During this time, MAS continued to increase in popularity. Its leader, Evo Morales, finished second in the 2002 presidential elections (out of eleven candidates), and candidates from his party gained 22 percent of the seats in Congress. President Sánchez de Lozada, in power again, governed with just a fifth of the vote from 2002 until he was forced to resign in October 2003 amid increasing social protests and government repression. Carlos Mesa, his vice president, was installed as president.

In 2003, under severe pressure, the Senate finally approved the domestic worker bill—two and a half years prior to the presidential victory of Morales—thus equalizing the legal rights of domestic workers. The indigenous movement continued to gain momentum. Highly unpopular government policies toward natural gas reserves and privatizations, as well as the resignation of the acting president, resulted in early elections in 2005. Evo Morales was elected to the presidency and his party, MAS, to Congress, both with an absolute majority. The revindication of the rights of domestic workers culminated in Morales's appointment of Casimira Rodríguez, one of the leaders of the domestic workers' organization, as minister of justice in 2006, attracting worldwide attention. However, she was replaced a year later, and implementation and enforcement of the 2003 law have lagged.

Organizations, Coalition Building, and Agenda Setting

Domestic workers began to organize more openly during and after the transition to democracy. Over time, they built a relatively strong organization and gained social allies, due to both leadership and the growing political salience of the ethnic cleavage in Bolivia.

First, leadership has played an important role. A core group of women dedicated to the cause has, since the late 1970s and despite numerous obstacles, tirelessly sought to recruit domestic workers. With the democratic transition in the early 1980s, they were able to organize openly, although grassroots organizing was very difficult at first due to workers' fears of employer reprisals for participation. These committed individuals spent their time off on Sundays building a network among domestic workers in La Paz. The process was slow and required a lot of patience given their very limited free time, and the organizers faced hostility from employers if they were found out. Nevertheless, the group managed to organize marches to fight for social attention to the plight of domestic workers and for equal rights (CONLACTRAHO 2003). Because time outside of work was scarce, several of these leaders dedicated all of their free time to organizing efforts. Two of the key figures during this time were Casimira Rodríguez and Basilia Catari.[1]

The ethnic cleavage, on the other hand, created a political space and networks to foster organization. Rather than transnational immigrants (Bolivia is a labor exporter), migrants from rural to urban areas—virtually all of them Aymara or Quechua—form the majority of the domestic worker labor force. While they have been historically marginalized both socially and politically in La Paz, their large numbers and mutual isolation, as well as common cultural backgrounds, have fostered solidarity and social networks among them.[2] This created a more amenable social base for mobilization once ethnic discrimination became increasingly politicized and domestic workers could make demands as indigenous Bolivian citizens.

Despite the difficulties related to time, resources, and fears of employer reprisals, by 1992, growing small-scale organizations across the country were able to come together and create the National Household Workers' Federation of Bolivia (Federación Nacional de las Trabajadoras del Hogar de Bolivia, FENATRAHOB). They agreed to work on reforming the Labor Code on domestic workers. The first bill on domestic workers, written by FENATRAHOB with legal help, was introduced by a sympathetic legislator in the Women's and Minors' Commission in the Chamber in 1993 (CONLACTRAHO 2003). The broader indigenous movement was gaining political force by this time, and traditional politicians had begun paying attention to and courting it (Albó 2002; Laurie, Andolina, and Radcliffe 2002; Postero and Zamosc 2004; Van Cott 2005; Yashar 2005). Indeed, the executive appointment of Cárdenas to the vice presidency raised FENATRAHOB's expectations that this high-level ally would force a congressional debate on its bill. However, he ignored the federation's requests to open up debate on the bill, and it was buried (CONLACTRAHO 2003), showing that this group still remained marginalized within the indigenous movement as well.

From 1993 on, domestic workers staged marches and sought media attention to their cause. Although they were at first isolated and targets of police repression, their persistence paid off. Indigenous-based claims continued to gain political attention through the 1990s, and the organizers framed the issue of discrimination against domestic workers as one of indigenous oppression, and the equalization of their rights as an issue of indigenous vindication. This brought them allies, and after 1996 more organizations joined the effort to force a congressional debate on the domestic worker bill. International organizations provided funding, and domestic feminist, human rights, indigenous, and popular organizations came to support the cause.[3] The rights of domestic workers became entwined more broadly with indigenous rights and social justice, and their fight for rights became identified with a broader struggle against colonialism and racism. Indeed, the leader of a human rights organization stated in 1998, "This theme brings out a broader dimension, which is ... colonialism and racism."[4] A supportive female legislator declared, "In this colonialist society ... there is discrimination.... We need to consider domestic work as any other form of work and give it the same respect and the same rights."[5]

In 1998, FENATRAHOB and its allies formed an ad hoc committee, the Comité Impulsor, in order to force congressional debate on the bill (Fundación Solón 2001b, 37–38). This committee exerted pressure on Congress, where sympathetic legislators kept trying to put the issue on the agenda through different commissions. The Women's Commission in the Chamber organized a series of workshops with the Comité Impulsor, and the latter lobbied other commissions to counter the lack of political will (FENATRAHOB, TAHIPAMU, and Fundación Solón 1998; Fundación Solón 2001b, 44–45). The committee even took the cause to the international level and added a civil society report on domestic workers to Bolivia's first official report on the state of its human rights to the United Nations Economic and Social Council, which monitors human rights in each country. As a result, the UN council, in its 2001 report, noted "the deplorable de jure discrimination against domestic workers" in Bolivia (United Nations Economic and Social Council 2001).

While FENATRAHOB is affiliated with Bolivia's Central Labor Union (Central Obrera Boliviana, COB), the union initially paid little attention to the domestic workers' cause. It generally focused more on protecting the interests of the male support base than extending rights to women and to the informal sector.[6] However, once FENATRAHOB reached prominence and gained social allies, COB also sent representatives to its events (Choque 2003, 75).

This broad-based attention and pressure from so many social organizations, as well as political allies, finally forced the Chamber to open up debate on the bill. In Congress, positions on the bill did not coalesce along either party or gender lines.[7] In fact, the most public opposition to reform came from a woman, Mabel Cruz, a self-identified feminist legislator from the (ostensibly leftist) MIR. She argued that a lack of legal regulation in domestic service was positive; it was not a purely contractual labor relation but rather a process in which indigenous girls were educated and socialized into modern urban life by becoming domestic workers. According to Cruz, the relation was not one of abuse but one where "the girls form part of the family." The proposed bill, she argued, would destroy these nonmarket relations and make the situation worse for its intended beneficiaries.[8]

When Cruz's opposition was publicized, hundreds of middle-class women in La Paz came together and created a housewives' organization for the specific purpose of fighting the bill along with her. Many middle-class women felt that the bill was biased against them.[9] On a political level, many legislators privately confessed to Cruz that they agreed with her opposition. In fact, while Cruz said that she was not racist, she acknowledged that many of those who supported her in Congress were. However, due to what she referred to as the political power of the "indigenous anticolonial discourse," they were unwilling to publicly support her and oppose the bill.[10]

Because political advocates were able to force the issue onto the political agenda and to a vote, the bill passed in the House in 2000, with the Comité

Impulsor watching in attendance. However, once it entered the Senate, it was stonewalled. The only female (and self-identified feminist) senator, Erika Brockman, who was from the same party as Cruz, spearheaded support for the bill, revealing the lack of programmatic party positions on this issue. She engaged in intensive lobbying against what she called "feudal arguments" by senators (expressed in private) against the bill.[11] Resistance to openly debating the issue in the Senate was strong. Open debate would brand opponents of reform as racists, something that was not palatable in Bolivia in the early 2000s, given the political context.

Meanwhile, FENATRAHOB and the Comité Impulsor continued to fight from the outside. The following quotes from the committee members—a broad array of social and political allies—illustrate how the issue was framed as one of indigenous justice. Senator Brockman linked the issue to "colonial" relations of "brutal servitude."[12] The leader of another human rights organization stated that domestic workers suffer from "ethnic, racial, economic, and gender discrimination" and a "colonial relation."[13] Finally, the human rights ombudsman—a woman, actually—acknowledged "the cultural resistance to recognizing the equality and just pay for work that is not considered real work, because it is done by women who are not only poor but also from an indigenous background."[14]

During this time, Casimira Rodríguez, president of FENATRAHOB, delivered fourteen thousand signatures in support of equal rights to the president of the Senate (Choque 2003, 79). Nevertheless, the Senate decided to postpone dealing with the bill. Over the next two years, the Comité Impulsor organized regular marches, media events, and protests, in one of which police used teargas on the protestors (80).

What finally provided the window of opportunity was the rise of indigenous left-wing parties, especially MAS, to Congress following the 2002 elections. Severe pressure following the elections forced the bill onto the political agenda in the Senate. By this time, indigenous politicians had articulated a clear stance in favor of approving the domestic worker bill, which they viewed as an issue of indigenous rights. MAS had included in its 2002 electoral campaign a very effective video clip of the plight of domestic workers.[15] Once the indigenous legislators gained eight out of twenty-two seats in the Senate, they demanded a vote on the bill.

This rise in electoral representation of indigenous parties was accompanied by high levels of polarization and increased mobilization against the right-wing government of Gonzalo Sánchez de Lozada. In early 2003, the government responded to indigenous protests with repression in what came to be referred to as "Black February." The fallout and increased support for MAS drove the government to seek to shore up some legitimacy. One of its strategies was to give in to pent-up social demands such as the domestic worker bill. Under pressure from MAS legislators, the executive allowed for a plenary debate on the domestic worker bill during the executive-controlled extraordinary legislative sessions in early April, citing its need to respond to "social concerns." Most senators did not dare to publicly voice opposition any longer. The few who did focused on the economic difficulties the middle classes would have in meeting provisions such as the minimum wage and paid vacations.[16] One senator argued that unlike workers such as miners, who really required rest, domestic workers were not in need of legislated vacation time.[17] The majority of arguments supported equal rights and social justice for indigenous women, and a slightly modified version of the bill granting domestic workers equal rights was approved on April 2, 2003.

Enforcement

Since 2003, FENATRAHOB, along with such allies as the Ombudsman's Office, has sought to ensure adequate implementation of the law (CBDHDD and CDH 2005, 407–8; Defensoría del Pueblo 2004). While the enforcement of labor rights and mechanisms to process complaints through the Ministry of Labor have improved from prior to 2005, enforcement overall remains weak. With regard to social security, the law left regulation of access to an executive decree, which had yet to be passed in 2010.

Overall, the capacity of Bolivia's ministries is weak. As in the case of many of the less developed Latin American countries, Bolivia's bureaucracies suffer from low levels of technical expertise and professionalism, low levels of merit-oriented appointments and high politicization, and, finally, a lack of resources (IADB 2006). The weak state capacity is reflected in the Ministry of Labor. A lack of resources, low levels of training, and turnover are serious problems. For instance, there were only eight labor inspectors for all of the La Paz metropolitan area in 2008, which includes around one million people. In addition, there is little communication and coordination between ministries or even within ministries.[18]

The problems with a politicized bureaucracy have continued under Morales's tenure, with hirings of political sympathizers among its civil servants predominating over merit-oriented criteria.[19] While Morales's high-profile appointment of Casimira Rodríguez as the minister of justice in 2006 was viewed as a symbolic affirmation of what she and her struggle had represented, it is unclear whether this resulted in concrete progress for domestic workers. While internationally lauded, domestically her appointment was criticized, as she had little experience and no law degree. One year later, she was replaced by a new minister of justice.

The government's shifting priorities and political instability have also worked against effective implementation of the law. Highly polarized politics—the administration prioritized the nationalization of natural gas and the writing of a new constitution for Bolivia (approved by popular referendum in 2009)—made it difficult to achieve incremental progress on less visible issues in various areas of government. On the other hand, the government's ideological predisposition has also had favorable consequences for domestic workers in their quest for equal rights. The inspectors at the Ministry of Labor are a case in point. Since Morales assumed power, explicit discrimination and bias against domestic workers has lessened, labor inspectors are more sympathetic to denunciations by domestic workers than in the past, and channels for complaint in cases of egregious mismanagement by inspectors have increased.[20] Moreover, and partly as a result, domestic workers are more likely to make denunciations. However, weak training and high turnover mean that inspectors are often not cognizant of the new law on domestic workers and hence are less likely to effectively handle complaints. According to Miguelina Colque, the leader of FENATRAHOB from 2006 to 2008, the organization had to "repeat, repeat, repeat facts about the new law over and over again" to inspectors across the country.[21]

The Ministry of Labor has also taken more proactive steps to promote enforcement of labor rights. Well-meaning officials in the ministry have implemented some small programs to promote the professionalization of domestic workers by providing certificates for different skills.[22] In addition, the government created a unit within the Ministry of Labor in 2008 to focus on gender, coerced labor, and child labor, and the director indicated that domestic workers' rights were a priority for the unit.[23] In civil society, both the national and regional offices of FENATRAHOB have sought to diffuse information about the legal rights of domestic workers as well as provide regular training classes to promote professionalization However, one study from 2010 found that the average salaries of domestic workers in Oruro and Potosí were less than half of the minimum wage, inciting condemnation from the vice minister of labor.[24] Another study from the same year found that in Cochabamba many domestics worked more than twelve hours a day, despite the work hour limits in the law.[25]

Finally, institutional changes in FENATRAHOB itself have influenced leadership. Since 2003, it has maintained statutory limitations on leadership terms—two years for both the president and the leadership council, with only one member of the council allowed to stay on. This creates high turnover: in essence, a new set of council members and leaders are brought into La Paz every two years, often from the provinces, and only one person can be carried over from term to term. This keeps good leaders from being reelected and also prevents cumulative learning and continuity, as new leaders have to learn the ropes for themselves.

Yet FENATRAHOB is very dependent on the quality of its leadership, as the base has little time, resources, or skills to do much, especially regarding the more technical aspects of implementation. One of the major concerns for the organization has been to seek executive regulation of access to social security, both in health care and in pensions. In the context of executive inaction, constant turnover has led to each set of leaders having to learn how things operate all over again.[26] For example, Miguelina Colque did not even know of the existence of the ad hoc committee that had lobbied for congressional approval of the 2003 law until a year into her term. Upon learning of it, she reconvened the committee to help her in lobbying for the implementation of access to health care at the Social Security Institute. After months of negotiations, a draft of a regulatory decree was written in 2008 but as of 2010 had yet to be approved by the government.[27]

In sum, while the ideological predisposition of the executive has been broadly favorable, weak state capacity and shifting priorities have made it hard to achieve the kind of continuous, incremental change that is necessary to establish and then expand access to social security and to enforce labor rights. This has not been helped by constant turnover in the leadership within FENATRAHOB.

Costa Rica: Extending Human Rights

Costa Rica is regionally unique in its history of stable democratic rule through the entire post–World War II era, when other Latin American countries succumbed to military regimes. Costa Rica abolished its army in 1948 following a brief civil war and instituted a progressive constitution, laying out its development model. As shown in table 2.3, Costa Rica's per capita income in 2000 was quite high at just over US$10,000 in PPP dollars—and much higher than that of its Central American neighbors. As of 2005, Costa Rica boasted impressively high levels of life expectancy (78.5 years) and literacy (95 percent), despite its status as a middle-income country. At .5, the Gini coefficient in 2000 was one of the lowest in Latin America and reflects less deeply entrenched class divisions.

Moreover, several political factors make Costa Rica stand out. In addition to its democratic history, Costa Rica has a reputation as a leader in human rights and has ratified all international conventions relevant to human, labor, and women's rights. Costa Rica is known as an island of peace, democracy, and more equitable development in a sea of military regimes, repression, and high inequalities. Costa Rican president Óscar Arias (1986–90, 2006–10) won the Nobel Peace Prize in 1987 for his relentless pursuit of peace in Central America at a time when Costa Rica's neighbors were being devastated in U.S.-financed civil wars. The country has several institutions designed to safeguard human rights, including the Constitutional Court and an ombudsman as in Bolivia, and it is also home to the Inter-American Court of Human Rights. In addition, the Costa Rican Constitution guarantees workers an eight-hour workday and a forty-eight-hour workweek, as well as one day of rest after six days of work.

Domestic workers have been excluded from this constitutional right, and within this context, advocates have sought to promote equal rights through both the courts and the legislature since the mid-1990s. After an unfavorable Constitutional Court ruling in 1994 and congressional inattention, a Constitutional Court ruling in 2007 gave domestic workers a full day off on the weekend and on national holidays but kept the daily work hours intact. Finally, an institutional opening allowed advocates to push through legislative reform, which was unanimously approved, equalizing labor rights in 2009.

Social and Legal Context

In Costa Rica, a significant share of the female working population continues to be engaged in domestic service. Of female wageworkers, 17.2 percent were domestic workers in 1987 (Centro Nacional para el Desarrollo de la Mujer y la Familia 1997, 11), and this number increased to 18 percent in 2005 (Martínez Franzoni, Mora, and Voorend 2010, 24). The national figures are higher than the 10 percent given for 2009 by the International Labour Organization (ILO) (table 1.1), most likely because of differences in how domestic workers who are recent immigrants or who have more than one employer are classified. The absolute number of domestic workers in 2004 was just over 130,000 in a nation of 4.5 million people (31). Moreover, Costa Rica has Central America's most dynamic economy and thus receives immigrants, most prominently from neighboring Nicaragua, which has a much lower per capita income and where the salary of a domestic worker is about one-third of the salary in Costa Rica.[28] It is estimated that 17 percent of domestic workers in Costa Rica are of Nicaraguan origin, although this could be an underestimate (20).

The Costa Rican Labor Code was established in 1943. The clauses on domestic workers extended their work hours to fourteen hours a day, with no rights to weekly rest or vacation time. In 1948, the country's current constitution was approved, guaranteeing an eight-hour workday and a forty-eight-hour workweek. Despite this, the work hours of domestics remained unchanged in the Labor Code. In 1964, due to pressure from a domestic workers' organization, Congress reformed the code to limit domestic workers' daily work hours to twelve (with up to four "extra" hours allowed), to permit them half a day off per week, and to give them an annual vacation of fifteen days (Fundación Paniamor 2002, 50). Prior to 2009, executive decrees established their minimum wage at approximately two-thirds of the national minimum wage determined by the executive for "unqualified workers" (one-third of the salary was considered to be in kind—food, lodging, etc.). In addition, the Labor Code demanded "respect, care, and discretion" on the part of the employee but not the employer.

One study from 1996 found that almost 90 percent of domestic workers surveyed started working as domestics before nineteen years of age (ASTRADOMES 2004, 29).[29] Three-quarters said that they received good treatment overall, and 70 percent said that they received their yearly vacation. Just over one-third (37.5 percent) received severance pay, and 43 percent of those surveyed were registered for social security (39). The latter figure is actually almost double the percentage of total domestic workers with pension protections in 2004, as discussed in chapter 3, perhaps reflecting a sample bias (Martínez Franzoni, Mora, and Voorend 2010, 44).

Another study investigated forms of child and adolescent domestic work in Costa Rica in 2002 and found that 68 percent of surveyed adolescents over fifteen years of age worked more than legally permitted (Fundación Paniamor 2002, 100).[30] While it does not appear from either survey that a majority suffered from degrading and slave-like conditions, both indicate that a significant share of domestic workers did not enjoy the rights they were legally entitled to even prior to reform.

Finally, Martínez Franzoni, Mora, and Voorend, drawing on government statistics from 2007, found that about 30 percent of domestic workers had less than a grade school education (2010, 25). Furthermore, just over 50 percent of full-time domestic workers earned less than the minimum wage established for this sector, which was already about one-third lower than that of any other sector. Almost 20 percent of full-time workers earned less than half of this amount (41). Finally, the authors found that 85 percent of women who worked in domestic service had one or more children twelve years or younger in age, and a survey of just over four hundred domestic workers indicated that a large percentage of these workers found it difficult to both work and adequately attend to their own families and care responsibilities (29).

The Political Process

After the brief civil war in 1948, a democratic two-party system was consolidated in Costa Rica. The Partido de Liberación Nacional (National Liberation Party, PLN) had more of a left-leaning bent, while the Partido Unidad Social Cristiana (Social Christian Unity Party, PUSC) was more conservative. However, by the late 1980s, these programmatic differences had largely disappeared (Martínez Franzoni, Mora, and Voorend 2010, 53). The two parties dominated politics and alternated in power until 2002, when the two-party system broke down. A third party, the center/center-left Partido Acción Ciudadana (Citizen Action Party, PAC) broke onto the scene along with many other small parties.

As in other Latin American countries, the executive is constitutionally strong. Costa Rica, like Mexico, does not have immediate reelection of congressional legislators or the president, leading to the complete renewal of the Legislative Assembly every four years. Costa Rica imposed obligatory quotas on the representation of women in Congress in 1997 (the second country in the region to do so after Argentina), and by 2007, 38.6 percent of congressional representatives were female (United Nations 2007–8).

Costa Rica has two institutions created specifically to safeguard citizen rights. The Constitutional Court was formed in 1989 to enforce constitutional rights. Any citizen is allowed to bring cases before the court, and many of them are considered and ruled on by the court. Second, like Bolivia, Costa Rica has an independent public institution, the Defensoría del Pueblo (Ombudsman's Office), that is vested with the task of protecting citizen rights from the abuse of state power and providing ostensibly binding recommendations to the government. In addition, the Inter-American Court of Human Rights—the court of last appeal for the Organization of American States members who have ratified the court's jurisdiction—has its headquarters in San José, Costa Rica.

Given Costa Rica's institutional makeup, advocates of reform have sought to change the Labor Code clauses on domestic workers through the Constitutional Court as well as legislative channels. Despite the Labor Code's explicit violation of the Constitution, the Constitutional Court upheld elements of the code in two different rulings in 1994 and 2007 (a third motion of unconstitutionality was rejected for consideration by the court in 2008).[31]

In all, six legislative bills on domestic workers were submitted to Congress between 1995 and the early 2000s. Most were archived; one was debated in the Social Commission in 2000 but never left the commission. The bill that eventually became law was approved by a renewed Social Commission in 2003, after which it entered a five-year limbo in wait of a plenary debate. This bill equalized the rights of domestic workers, including daily and weekly work hours. Leadership by Rosita Acosta, the president of the Domestic Workers' Association (Asociación de Trabajadoras Domésticas, ASTRADOMES), which gained allies and increased visibility for the cause, combined with building pressure among a core group of legislators, forced a reform bill to a plenary vote at the end of November 2008. The group of legislators framed the issue as an embarrassment given Costa Rica's reputation as a leader in human rights, and an institutional opening allowed the bill to go to a vote. It was unanimously approved, equalizing labor rights and, most importantly, reducing the workday to the constitutional eight hours. The president at the time, Óscar Arias, from the now center-right PLN, did not lend the bill his support but did sign it into law in July 2009. Laura Chinchilla, also from the PLN, subsequently assumed the presidency (2010–14), and the executive has not, as of 2010, made a proactive effort to enforce the new law.

Organizations, Coalition Building, and Agenda Setting

Elite resistance to reform in Costa Rica, as elsewhere, was solid, although it became less open over time as the issue of domestic workers' rights gained visibility. Legal reform in 2009 was the result of the tireless efforts of Rosita Acosta, her recruitment of social and political allies in order to keep the issue alive and to give it visibility, the prioritization of the issue among a tight group of political allies when the opportunity finally arose in Congress, and these individuals' framing of the issue in the context of Costa Rica's international reputation as a leader in human rights.

The first domestic workers' organization was created in 1962 under the auspices of the Catholic Church. This organization pushed for the changes made to the Labor Code in 1964 (Fundación Paniamor 2002, 50) and functioned until 1972. ASTRADOMES was formed twenty years later, in 1991, by a group of women in the Costa Rican Women's Alliance (Alianza de Mujeres Costarricenses) with the explicit goal of seeking to equalize domestic workers' rights (ASTRADOMES 2004, 8). Since then, under Acosta's leadership, the association consistently pressured social actors and politicians to promote the labor rights of domestic workers. Its active membership included several hundred women in 2008; compared to many other countries, this number is quite high, even though it is a minimal fraction of the 130,000 domestic workers in Costa Rica. ASTRADOMES has also attracted international funding, which has allowed it to buy its own house, giving the members their own space to hold meetings and workshops.[32]

Acosta submitted the first motion of unconstitutionality of the Labor Code clauses on domestic workers to the Constitutional Court in 1994, soon after the formation of ASTRADOMES. In a ruling the same year, the court found that the Labor Code was not discriminatory, as domestic workers could be considered an "exceptional case" and hence the same rules did not apply to them. However, two dissenting judges found that this "exceptionalism" (which the Constitution allows for) applies specifically to more qualified and advantaged members of the workforce and is not meant to apply to the most vulnerable groups in society, such as domestic workers. The dissenters argued that the code clearly discriminated against women and was unacceptable in a modern society.[33]

Since then, six bills have been presented in Congress by legislators sympathetic to or with help from Acosta and ASTRADOMES. No political party—Costa Rica does not have a clear left party—took up the cause of reform. Neither did the executive proactively support reform, although officials in several executive agencies did. As Martínez Franzoni, Mora, and Voorend note, the bills were proposed by legislators as individuals, not as part of any party programs, by women as well as men, and by legislators from all of the main parties (2010, 54).

The first bill was presented in 1995, following the 1994 court ruling, by a female legislator from PUSC. It sought to equalize work hours and was archived on a technicality. Between 1998 and 1999, three other bills were submitted, one of which made it to the Social Commission to be studied. This project, presented by a group of legislators from different parties, was a cooperative effort involving the Women's Executive Agency (Instituto Nacional de las Mujeres, INAMU), the Ministry of Labor, and the Ombudsman's Office, as well as ASTRADOMES. It delineated a nine-hour workday, with one hour for lunch, and gave workers one day off per week. It also took out the unilateral "care and respect" clause and sought to provide state support for child care centers for the children of domestic workers.[34] The project was justified by appeals to equality, to the constitutional right to an eight-hour workday, and to international conventions of the ILO as well as the Convention to Eliminate All Forms of Discrimination Against Women (CEDAW), which Costa Rica had ratified.

The discussion that took place in the Social Commission in the following months, particularly regarding the workday, provides a window into support for and opposition to the bill among political elites. The main objections, raised by female deputies in the Social Commission, stemmed from concerns regarding the effects of equal work hours on middle-class women who worked outside the home. What is interesting is not only the substance of their arguments but also the patronizing tone of some of the debate.

In August 1999, Acosta was received in an audience with the Social Commission before the legislators had actually read over the legal project. A female deputy on the commission assured her, "You can trust us completely as we discuss this project. As women, we have a commitment to every one of you; we are people who also work a lot and know what it takes to do domestic work."[35] At this point, Deputy Abel Pacheco of PUSC (who went on to become president of Costa Rica from 2002 to 2006) intervened to say, "I would like to note that we men also know about domestic work: I am an excellent gardener [and] do carpentry. I do all sorts of things, and when my wife cannot cook, I do it pretty well."[36] Once the commission actually studied the project, however, it disagreed with the bill's nine-hour workday and modified it to ten hours. This elicited the immediate opposition of the executive agencies and of ASTRADOMES.

ASTRADOMES was granted another audience with the Social Commission in December 1999, following its vote to change the project's original workday. In defense of the extended workday, Rina Contreras, a member of PUSC and president of the Social Commission, cited the need to balance the interests of employers and employees and to make the project capable of passing the plenary. When a lawyer representing ASTRADOMES argued that this was unfair, given that all other workers had an eight-hour workday, Contreras noted that the workday for domestics was "not a consecutive workday," as they also spent "hours watching soap operas, resting, and having lunch, etc." When Acosta and the lawyer seemingly reacted to this statement, she told them "to calm down because if not, we will have to clear you out."[37] She went on to argue that equal rights would end up harming the intended beneficiaries by increasing their unemployment: "Here we are trying to legislate for the benefit of domestic workers and the labor relation, because it does not help you at all if we approve a law where afterwards you will not be hired, specifically because of the law."[38] She then stated, "We cannot keep making laws that are prejudicial to women."[39] When both the lawyer and Acosta argued that a ten-hour "regime of exception" goes against ILO conventions as well as Costa Rica's Constitution, Contreras responded, "If you want to go to the ILO, then let's not talk anymore! ... Since you do not want to be helped." She claimed that a "change in attitude is needed" and that "we cannot work together if we become hotheaded."[40] The project was tabled pending review.

When debate was reopened a few months later, the executive ministries continued to support the nine-hour workday.[41] The minister of labor argued that "there is an undervaluation of domestic work" and that the issue should be seen as one of gender equity, especially in a country like Costa Rica, which has a long-standing commitment to fully respect human rights and labor rights. He also cited the need to "depersonalize" the discussion (referring to the tendency of those opposed to reform to rely on personal experiences and examples) and stated that one group's rights should not be violated in favor of another group; rather, labor rights apply to all equally. The ombudswoman stated that one woman's liberation could not be based on the exploitation of another woman and that equal rights should be enshrined in the Labor Code.[42]

The female deputies on the Social Commission opposed the delimitation of work hours with the following arguments. One legislator argued that equalizing work hours assumed that all women who employed domestic workers were rich, which was not the case. She observed, "If domestic workers have to leave after exactly eight hours, what will happen? They will end up tying the children into their beds so they do not get out or have fires." She also noted that a lot of women, such as those in the banana industry, had it worse than domestic workers, and hence attention should be focused on them. In reference to equalizing work hours, she asked, "What would happen to the secretaries if they abandon their work for two hours to watch television?" Finally, she claimed, "I continue to love the woman who brought up my daughter ... but ... I cannot understand why I should legislate ... only for one group of women and leave the other 37 percent completely lacking."[43] Another deputy pointed out that a relationship of "trust" with "privileges" for the domestic workers could be lost with this new law.[44] The arguments of the legislators were clearly influenced by their personal positions as employers of domestic workers. They also did not take into account that over 85 percent of domestic workers had young children of their own.

A representative of a group of housewives who was invited to speak to the commission argued, "I think it is very important to clarify that domestic work is done by housewives and that servants help us in that work, because our husbands do not pay us for the work we do at home; despite this, we women have to pay the servants for the work that they do."[45] She argued that limiting work hours would make life extremely difficult for women like her and in the end would lead them to hire domestic workers by the hour instead of full-time or to put their children into day care instead; this would then hurt the intended beneficiaries of the bill, the domestic workers. Finally, she appealed to the special relationship between a domestic worker and her employer, as she was considered "part of the family." The commission voted to keep the workday at ten hours and omitted references to state support of child care centers from the bill.[46] However, the project never left the commission.

Some more attempts to submit reform bills were made, but these were either turned down or archived. In 2003, the project that eventually became law was presented by three recently elected female deputies from the three main parties (PUSC, PLN, and PAC). By this time, given the prohibition on consecutive reelection, Congress had a completely new set of legislators. The new project reduced the workday to eight hours (six hours if the shift was at night), although the workday could be extended to ten hours as long as the workweek did not exceed forty-eight hours. The bill also granted domestic workers the legal minimum wage for "unqualified workers" and changed the unilateral obligation of respect from employee toward employer, making it mutual. Finally, it explicitly obligated employers to register employees with the Social Security Institute, which had already been an implicit legal obligation since 1982.

The Social Commission was now composed of different legislators, and there was less open opposition (Martínez Franzoni, Mora, and Voorend 2010, 57). Statements from various executive agencies were fully supportive of the project. Even the Ministry of Economy, Industry, and Commerce declared that it had no objections to the project, and INAMU and the ombudsman once again strongly supported the project, citing the principle of equity, the Constitution, and international conventions such as CEDAW and those of the ILO. The president of INAMU, Esmeralda Britton González, even noted that CEDAW recommended—when Costa Rica submitted its 2004 report—that domestic workers' rights be promoted.[47] The project was approved 7 to 1 in the Social Commission. The dissenting vote came from a male politician from the small right-wing libertarian party Partido Movimiento Libertario (Libertarian

Movement) who stated that "no new law was needed" and that this project was unnecessary and "contrary to all criteria of rationality and proportionality."[48] Thereafter, the project spent five years being relegated to the end of the lineup for a plenary debate and vote.

In 2005, Acosta, frustrated with the legislative inaction and assisted by INAMU and the ombudsman, presented another motion of unconstitutionality to the Constitutional Court. This time, the court ruled unanimously on March 8, 2007 (not coincidentally, on International Women's Day) that domestic workers should receive a full day off each week as well as full-day holidays instead of the half-days stipulated in the Labor Code. However, on the daily work hours the court was divided. The majority, and final, ruling declared that the twelve-hour workday was not unconstitutional, although again the argument simply drew on "exceptionalism." This time, four of the nine justices dissented, claiming that the ruling was unconstitutional given the Constitution's explicit stipulation of an eight-hour workday and forty-eight-hour workweek.[49] The ruling was unsatisfactory to Acosta and others, and she filed a new motion with the help of a sympathetic legislator in 2008, which was rejected for consideration by the court.

Acosta continued to seek social allies in civil society among feminists and other reformists. Overall, labor unions in Costa Rica are quite weak and were not interested in actively mobilizing on behalf of an even weaker group of workers.[50] While Costa Rica has strong women's organizations in civil society, they did not make domestic workers' rights a priority. According to a prominent feminist and a supporter, they have focused on reproductive rights and domestic violence, issues that more easily transcend class divisions, while domestic workers' rights has remained invisible.[51] However, Acosta was able to gain the support of some notable feminists, who threw their full weight behind reform efforts.[52]

In 2006, some of these feminists, most notably Ana Helena Chacón and Patricia Romero, were elected to Congress (because of the prohibition on consecutive reelection, many political activists rotate between Congress and civil society). They gained the support of Carlos Gutiérrez, an "unlikely" ally from the right-wing Movimiento Libertario, whose mother and aunts had been domestic workers. In addition to arguments based on social justice and gender equality, these advocates framed the issue as a violation of human rights in a country that prides itself on its reputation as a leader in human rights.

These political allies—three core advocates in all—faced executive and legislative reticence. While executive agencies such as INAMU and the ombudsman had been consistently supportive of reform, no president proactively supported any of the reform projects or allowed them to be considered during the executive-controlled extraordinary legislative sessions. In fact, it appears that between 2006 and 2009 Arias's administration may have actually exerted some pressure not to deal with this bill specifically, due to his focus on implementing the Central American Free Trade Agreement (CAFTA), which involved making labor legislation more "flexible" rather than increasing rights.[53] President Arias also never answered a 2008 letter from Gutiérrez exhorting him to take action on this issue given Costa Rica's commitment to and reputation on human rights.[54] The bill was at the end of the lineup in the ordinary legislative sessions, and Arias was unwilling to allow it to be considered during the half-year extraordinary sessions. This meant that without some kind of intervention it was highly unlikely to come up for congressional debate.

The advocates also faced opposition due to antiforeign sentiment.[55] Although it appears that only roughly one-fifth of domestic workers are Nicaraguan, there is a widespread perception that half of them are. Supportive politicians claimed that, in private, the opposition frequently echoed the refrain "Why legislate for a bunch of Nicas who do not vote?"[56] These perceptions likely weakened support for legal reform, increased opposition, and allowed the bill to be repeatedly postponed.

Finally, a window of opportunity arose when Congress was divided into three "mini-plenaries" in 2008. This was a specifically Costa Rican strategy to move beyond some of the massive legislative stalemates that had characterized Congress in the previous years. After the two-party system broke down, political parties had become increasingly fragmented, and it became hard to pass any legislation, not just this bill. To deal with this stalemate, Congress voted to divide the Legislative Assembly into three legislative mini-plenaries, each of which had the authority to pass legislation.

The advocates specifically asked to be assigned to the plenary with the domestic worker bill in its docket. They then began lobbying the president of this plenary to move the bill up in order to give it a chance of being passed before the close of ordinary legislative sessions. All three core advocates agreed that forcing politicians to take a public stand on the bill, in the context of Costa Rica's reputation on human rights, would lead to its approval. In the words of PAC deputy Patricia Romero, "I think that at the time of voting for this type of project [the politicians] will not run the social risk of appearing as if politicians from the upper classes act only in their personal interest even though the majority agrees with the project. In Costa Rica this does not go over well."[57] The advocates' constant reminders to the plenary president about Costa Rica's reputation on human rights finally paid off, and he allowed for a vote on November 26, 2008—at the last moment before the executive took control of the agenda at the beginning of December.[58] At this point, legislators were not willing to take open positions against reform, and the legislation was unanimously approved after two strong speeches in its defense. Despite pleas from the plenary for a second vote (mandated in the Constitution) during the extraordinary legislative sessions that were about to start, President Arias did not allow it (Martínez Franzoni, Mora, and Voorend 2010, 58). This held up approval by half a year. A second vote was held on June 3, 2009, and the president signed the bill into law in July.[59]

Enforcement of Labor Rights

Costa Rica has stronger state capacity than any other country in Central America and much of South America. It has historically been more advanced with regard to labor rights and has a strong Ministry of Labor (Schrank and Piore 2007). It also has higher social security rates and a more extensive welfare state in general compared to other countries at a similar level of development.

Within this context, domestic workers have remained a neglected constituency. The path to reform—initiated by legislators without executive support—has influenced the enforcement of the legal reform to date (although it was still early to fully assess this at the end of 2010). In the late 2000s, the executive's concern to promote labor flexibility under the auspices of CAFTA reduced its commitment to labor law enforcement more generally. For example, the number of labor inspectors for San José actually declined from one hundred in the late 1990s to eighty-five in 2008.[60]

To enforce the labor rights of domestic workers, the Ministry of Labor relies on denunciations of individual workers to labor inspectors. While workers can submit complaints regardless of their legal status—and according to a Ministry of Labor official, about 20 to 25 percent of complaints come from foreigners (perhaps indicating a general lack of fear among foreigners about reporting violations)—the ministry engages in a conciliation process that is only advisory. A legally binding decision must be obtained through the courts, where workers must be able to document their legal status and where the process takes two to three years.[61] An additional hindrance is that labor inspectors cannot enter the household unless the head of household permits them to do so.

In this context, the state has not sought to proactively implement the new legal rights of domestic workers. Several officials at the Ministry of Labor acknowledged that many domestic workers did not know their rights and that the ministry did not seek to reach this sector through special offices or programs. In addition, not everyone in the Ministry of Labor supported legal reform—with adverse implications for enforcement.[62]

Pension protections currently reach less than one-quarter of the domestic worker labor force, lower than for the workforce in general. While a law passed in March 2010 that obligates employers to register foreign workers for social security may improve social security protections for Nicaraguan domestic workers, other barriers maintain low registration rates. One problem is the difficulty for workers with more than one employer to register for social security (Martínez Franzoni, Mora, and Voorend 2010, 66–67).

Improvement in the enforcement of labor rights and in social security rates requires a concerted, proactive effort on the part of executive agencies. Other measures involve media and outreach campaigns to inform employers and employees of their rights and obligations under the new law. Finally, more executive programs to professionalize the workforce are needed (Martínez Franzoni, Mora, and Voorend 2010, 67–69).

In sum, the long and arduous process of equalizing rights in Costa Rica is a testament to the persistence of leadership. Acosta kept up pressure through the years with every mechanism available to her. Over time, she succeeded in building a network of well-placed allies who pushed for reform from the inside. An institutional opening and the pressure to live up to Costa Rica's reputation as a leader in human rights finally brought the domestic worker bill to a vote and a unanimous approval. Enforcement, on the other hand, has thus far lagged. The executive's lack of support for reform is reflected in the low priority that executive agencies have so far placed on reaching this sector of workers.

Conclusion

In Bolivia and Costa Rica, domestic workers' organizations faced an uphill battle to make their cause visible, while the majority of political elites were uninterested in supporting reform or actively opposed to it. In both countries, we see the impact of strong leadership, as well as the ability of organization leaders to recruit social and political allies and to frame the issue in a broader way to build more support for the cause. In Bolivia, leaders and allies framed their demands for equality as an issue of indigenous revindication in the context of the political rise of the indigenous movement. In Costa Rica, they framed it as an issue of human rights in the context of the country's reputation.

The political process in both countries illustrates the difficulties faced by multiply disadvantaged groups, while at the same time showing that reform, even if difficult, is possible. In both countries, organization leaders and their political allies were savvy and prepared enough to take advantage of political windows of opportunity when they finally arose. In neither country did the executive actively support reform, although in both countries ombudsmen's offices did. For years, major parties did not take up the cause as a programmatic goal in either country, although in Bolivia the left-wing MAS finally helped force legal reform upon gaining seats in the Senate in 2002.

Effective implementation, on the other hand, has lagged in both countries. This requires both strong state capacity and executive commitment, with the latter being more likely under left-leaning governments. In neither Bolivia nor Costa Rica have both conditions been in place. Bolivia lacks state capacity and a stably committed executive despite its left-leaning stance, and in Costa Rica, despite stronger state capacity, the center-right executive has not prioritized this issue to date.

5

URUGUAY AND CHILE

Basic Universalism Versus Top-Down Incrementalism

Uruguay and Chile are similar in several ways. They have higher levels of economic and human development from a regional perspective. Both have had stable democratic politics since their transitions to democracy (Uruguay in 1985, Chile in 1990), and both have had recent left-wing or center-left governments. They also have stronger state capacity, reflected in higher social security rates for workers in general and domestic workers in particular. Within this context, Uruguay has succeeded in equalizing domestic workers' rights, and Chile has instituted piecemeal reforms but maintains unequal work hours. These differences are reflective of more general differences in the political dynamics of the two countries, as well as issue-specific characteristics such as domestic workers' mobilization and coalition-building capacities. Uruguay's "basic universalism" under the participatory left-wing government has extended to the most marginalized groups, while Chile's incrementalism within the context of lower mobilization up until 2010 and strong conservative opposition have improved the absolute conditions of domestic workers but without delivering equal rights.[1]

Uruguay: Solidarity and Equal Rights for Everyone

Uruguay stands out for its higher levels of development in the region and for its more extensive social policies. As table 2.3 indicates, the GDP per capita of Uruguay in 2000, prior to reform, was almost US$10,000 in PPP dollars. In addition, Uruguay has one of the lowest income inequalities in Latin America, high levels of human development, and historically more developed social policies and labor rights. Until 2006, however, domestic workers were excluded from labor rights granted to other workers. Attempts at legislative reform by political advocates in the 1990s were hampered by lack of visibility and any organized social pressure, allowing elite resistance to block reform. The window of opportunity came when the left-wing Frente Amplio gained the presidency and an absolute majority in Congress in 2005. The government encouraged collective organization in the sector and initiated equal rights reform. Full executive support allowed for rapid reform in 2006 that confronted no organized opposition. Enforcement has reflected the reform path: the executive took ownership of the reform, and the Ministry of Labor promoted extensive enforcement campaigns.

Social and Legal Context

It is estimated that there are around 109,000 domestic workers in Uruguay, over 99 percent of whom are female (Amarante and Espino 2007, 68–69). Many come from the interior of the country and work in Montevideo, where 1 million of the country's 3.5 million people live. While Uruguay does not have an indigenous minority, 9 percent of its population is (at least partly) of African descent, and these individuals are disproportionately represented among paid domestic workers. Seventeen percent of all Uruguayan women in urban areas worked in domestic service in 2006; the corresponding figure for Afro-Uruguayan women was 29 percent (73). In addition, almost one-third (31 percent) of domestic workers were heads of households, indicating that their economic situation was particularly vulnerable (71–72). Finally, over half of domestic workers in 2006 had only a primary education (70).

Uruguay does not have a specific labor code as other Latin American countries do, but rather a series of laws that regulate the labor rights of workers in general and in particular sectors. Until the legal reform of 2006, there was no legal statute that regulated the rights of domestic workers. In 1915, an eight-hour workday was established in Uruguay, but decrees, most recently in 1980, excluded domestic and rural workers from this limit.[2] Even though a limited workday is enshrined in the Uruguayan Constitution in Article 54, the daily work hours of domestics were not regulated, and they had the right to only one day off per week (Trezza de Piñeyro 2001, 93–104). While they received the right to be included in social security pensions in 1950, they were excluded from health and unemployment insurance (117–27). This also reduced their incentives to register for and contribute to social security, as their contribution levels (in terms of percentages) were the same as those of other workers yet they received lower benefits.[3]

Indeed, prior to the legal reform, social security coverage for domestic workers was much below the average for other workers, as indicated by the International Labour Organization (ILO) data given in table 3.1. In 2001, 31.1 percent of domestic workers had pension protections; this actually declined to 26.5 percent in 2005.[4] In addition, the minimum wage for domestic workers was established by executive decree and allowed for up to a 20 percent discount from this wage for payment in kind (that is, food and lodging).

The Political Process

Before 2005 and with the exception of military rule between 1973 and 1985, Uruguay was governed throughout its independent history by two catchall parties, the Colorado Party and the Blanco Party. These two parties contain many ideological factions and have largely operated through patronage and clientelism rather than through ideological competition. They were nonetheless relatively inclusionary in comparison to other elite-organized parties in Latin America (Luna 2006). Historically, the lack of ethnic cleavages, the weakness of the church and conservative forces (Uruguay never had a strong conservative coalition), rapid suffrage extension at the turn of the century, and the incorporation of the lower classes all contributed to both solidifying the dominance of the two parties and achieving a relatively inclusive political and social system (Luna 2006, 113–14). During the early twentieth century, under the presidency of José Batlle y Ordóñez, Uruguay instituted a set of uniquely progressive laws (including, for example, legalization of divorce at the behest of the woman in 1914), leaving a legacy of progressive policies that have influenced the country's social fabric to this day.

Uruguay was not immune to the socioeconomic and political unrest in Latin America, however. The democratic system broke down in the early 1970s, and the country was ruled by a military regime from 1973 until 1985. While the regime had a high incarceration rate of political prisoners, it did not become the kind of killing machine that its counterparts in Argentina and Chile were. Moreover, unlike the Pinochet regime in Chile (1973–90), it did not dismantle the extant social welfare system (Castiglioni 2005).

At democratization, both the Blancos and the Colorados reemerged as the two dominant parties. Although the Blancos had some neoliberal strands, no strong conservative party, or a strong advocate for neoliberal reform, emerged (Luna 2006, 115). On the other hand, a programmatic left-wing party, the Frente Amplio, which had been founded in 1971, gained importance as an opposition party. It appealed to voters primarily on the basis of ideology and programmatic issue positions, and it was also highly participatory in its organizational structure (Pribble 2011). While both of the dominant parties tried to implement neoliberal reforms when in office, many of these were halted by the Frente Amplio's increasing use of popular referenda to block such policies, an option that is allowed for in the Constitution. Overall, Uruguayan citizens and elites have remained "loyal to a statist ideology and opposed to market-oriented solutions that dismantle universal social services and privatize public utility companies" (Luna 2006, 174).

During the 1980s and 1990s, the Frente Amplio gradually increased its voter share from just over 20 percent in 1984 to a historic absolute majority of just under 52 percent for the presidency as well as for Congress in 2005 (Luna 2006, 367). During its time in opposition and in municipal governance, the party had fostered strong ties to civil society and labor unions (Luna 2006). Pribble (2011) characterizes the Frente Amplio as a "constituency-coordinating party" that, while dispersing power and thereby slowing the policy-making process, at the same time generates a setting in which outputs are likely to be more universalistic in scope.

Since the democratic transition and prior to 2005, individual legislators submitted four reform bills on different aspects of domestic workers' rights to Congress. One project, initially submitted in 1990, worked slowly through the legislative process and actually made it quite far; it was approved in the Chamber but repeatedly postponed in the Senate, where it finally died.[5] The victory of the Frente Amplio in 2005 was the key catalyst for reform on domestic workers' rights. The government initiated equal rights reform and set up an executive commission to draft a bill that was then unanimously approved in Congress. The executive put its full weight behind enforcement efforts as well.

ORGANIZATIONS, COALITION BUILDING, AND AGENDA SETTING

The first association of domestic workers in Uruguay, the Asociación Nacional de Empleadas de Casa Particular (National Association of Household Workers, ANECAP), was founded in the early 1960s by the left-leaning Juventud Obrera Católica (Catholic Young Workers' Organization) as a grassroots organization. ANECAP joined the labor movement in 1967 but then split due to ideological divisions between more conservative and more left-wing members (Prates 1989, 281–83). During the military regime, all union activity was disbanded and ANECAP was reorganized as a more top-down, assistentialist organization with financing from Catholic organizations abroad. It remained as such in the

1980s (283–85). After the transition to democracy, the domestic workers' union from the 1960s (Sindicato Único de Trabajadoras Domésticas, SUTD) was reconstituted in 1986.[6] However, it functioned actively for only a few years due to the workers' "fear of organizing themselves" and "employer repression," according to a Uruguayan labor union leader.[7] During the 1990s, domestic workers' organizations became virtually defunct.[8]

Two left-wing legislators submitted a reform bill on domestic workers in 1990 and pursued it throughout the decade. Daisy Tourné in the House and Helios Sarthou in the Senate—both of them from the Frente Amplio—acted without organized backing and with little visibility. They tried to push the project through for years, despite indifference and at times strong opposition. Although support for and opposition to the project did not strictly follow party lines, stronger support came from politicians on the left and opposition tended to come from more conservative legislators.

The process itself was very slow. The bill was discussed and revised several times in the House Labor Commission over the years, but it did not make it out of the commission.[9] Finally, a revised project, unanimously approved by the Labor Commission in 1996, went to the plenary for debate that year. This project sought to guarantee domestic workers the same labor rights as other workers, including an eight-hour workday, one and a half days off per week, the right to overtime, and social security.[10] The presentation of the bill to the plenary for debate was reflective of the indifference the issue faced at the time. The Labor Commission representative, Tourné, argued that the legal reform was needed because women in this sector were invisible and unrecognized and worked with a "complete lack of legal protection." At the time of voting, thirty-seven out of ninety-nine deputies—just over one-third—were present. Tourné lamented the frequent delays the project had experienced and criticized the legislators for the low importance they appeared to give to it. During Tourné's presentation, the president of the plenary had to intervene to get legislators to stop talking and pay attention to her, after which Tourné commented that "perhaps the behavior that we have in this moment as we analyze this project demonstrates how the Uruguayan Congress views domestic workers."[11]

The plenary debate itself was very brief, and all of the public declarations, save two, were in favor of approval. This was reflected in the vote: thirty-four out of thirty-seven deputies approved the bill in general.[12] Two left-wing deputies referred to the need to protect the weaker member of the labor relation and called it a "delayed" and "very important" project. A conservative deputy from the Partido Nacional also voiced his support and lamented the indifference of his colleagues. One deputy justified his negative vote by stating that, with the reform, lower-income families would have a harder time contracting domestic workers, and workers would be denied the employment they needed.[13]

During this process, there was no organized pressure from domestic workers. Indeed, during the plenary debate, Tourné referred to the lack of pressure: "Due to this, this project is buried in congress after congress. If we were dealing with a group of workers who were better organized and with more influence, the legislators would have felt compelled to approve this project earlier."[14]

The project was sent to the Labor Commission in the Senate the same year, where it confronted active opposition as well as indifference. The strongest opposition came from Senator Luis Brezzo of the Colorado Party, who disliked the project and succeeded in getting it derailed over the years. Senator Helios Sarthou, its most vocal supporter, repeatedly urged the commission to vote speedily and affirmatively on the Chamber bill so as to avoid additional veto points. All of the senators except one were male.

Overall, the senators' substantive comments reflect a lack of information about the parameters of paid domestic work and an inclination to view the issue solely from the employers' point of view. Discussion relied on personal feelings and impressions, with little systematic information about the sector. During the many discussions of the bill, there were no attempts to solicit input from domestic workers or their representatives, and it is unclear whether there were attempts by any domestic workers to get audiences.

Over the years, Brezzo provided the most articulate and staunch opposition, to which several senators who had not thought much about the issue were inclined to lend their support. The opposition to the bill stemmed from the senators' views of the exceptional nature of domestic work as an occupation, with the issue of work hour limits generating the most conflict. First was the nature of the work itself, which to Brezzo was distinct because it "is a type of work where rest, interruptions, moments of distraction, carrying out a schedule are totally different."[15] The "Uruguayan reality of today" was such that "normally the domestic worker does not suffer the same pressure at work as, for example, a factory worker who must constantly work for eight hours." If an eight-hour workday was approved, he argued, employers would "apply more pressure on the worker during the work hours," creating an "unimaginable situation inside a home."[16] Another senator, this time from the left, was concerned that legislating an eight-hour workday with overtime would provoke a lot of legal cases against employers for back pay.[17]

Second, the labor relation within the privacy of a home was perceived as distinct as well. Reference was made constantly to "families" rather than "employers," and several of the senators who expressed their opposition did not perceive the status quo as abusive. Brezzo argued that there were no intermediaries in this relation but rather "a mother who asks another one to help her in certain tasks. Normal people do not abuse these types of situations, and I would not like to provoke tensions in this labor relation by legislating it."[18] He also opposed the right of labor inspectors to enter "people's homes." Another senator commented that "these are not employers or businessmen but regular people who need the help of a domestic worker."[19] A senator from the conservative Partido Nacional linked this issue to women's increased labor force participation: "Everything should be very flexible because we must adapt to the changing conditions of the woman who in addition to being a worker is a mother and who many times needs that flexibility for her own work. . . . I have doubts about who is . . . the weaker one in a contract of this nature. Many times it is the employee, but at other times it is the employer."[20]

Several senators argued that legal reform was unnecessary or harmful, since permanent employers already granted their employees all the necessary legal rights and since "rigid legislation will make domestic workers lose" nonsalary benefits.[21] Some senators, including Brezzo, argued that with increased legal rights, many lower-middle-class employers would not be able to hire domestic workers. Providing more legal rights was thus unfair to lower-income families who hired domestic help, and it would also end up harming the intended beneficiaries by increasing informality and unemployment.[22] According to one senator, "There are forms of protection that will result in a 'boomerang' for those people whom we are reasonably trying to defend."[23]

The president of the Labor Commission, the left-wing Sarthou, was strongly in favor of the project. He argued, over the course of many meetings, that domestic service was like any other wage relation and thus should have the same legal limits, that legislation should protect the more vulnerable party in a labor relation, and that the Constitution granted workday limits to all workers and domestic workers should therefore not be excluded and discriminated against. Several other senators expressed concern about the low rates of social security registration among domestic workers and the need to increase formalization.

The two opposing views, based also in different perceptions of the relationship between laws and reality, were crystallized when the commission discussed limits on work hours for adolescent domestic workers. For Brezzo, who was opposed to such limits, "the problem lies in legislating over an imaginary situation.

The norms are not followed now, nor will they be followed in the future. I think we are committing an error. I repeat that it is not my intention to leave people unprotected but to legislate in a way that functions better for the worker, not by taking away the possibility to gain employment or by creating a relation of great tension."[24] For Sarthou, who was in favor of limits, "the law exists in tension with reality, to correct it and improve upon it. If the argument is not to legislate because reality demonstrates that the norm is very difficult to follow, we would not pass laws.... Historically, some people worked between twelve and sixteen hours, and there was a struggle to reduce the workday.... Reality... must go through a process of adaptation to the legislation." He also noted that "the argument that an improvement will produce prejudices and lead to workers being fired has always been made since an eight-hour workday was established."[25]

The project kept being postponed, and finally several substitute clauses were proposed by those opposed to the House bill but amenable to legislating on the issue in principle. The key revision centered on work hours. In the revised clause, a distinction was made between live-out domestic workers (referred to as "part-time workers"), who worked up to eight hours, and "full-time" live-in domestic workers with no daily or weekly limits on their work hours or guaranteed rest. The proponents of the revised clause argued that workday limits allowed for the possibility of judicial claims for overtime by live-in domestic workers, which was unfair to families who employed them.[26] Given that any limits on work hours could be grounds for legal claims, the senators felt that no limits could thus be imposed, leaving the issue up to the employer and employee. The situation, one senator argued, would regulate itself: "Live-in domestic work must be without work hour limits. In practice, this aspect regulates itself, since no one can treat badly or not allow rest to the person who one then asks to take care of one's children."[27]

The support for no limits went further than this, however. There was a sense that live-in workers had the duty to be on call at all times. For example, another senator argued that there might be instances in which the family had a sick child or an accident, and in these instances there existed "naturally the right of the [patron] to decide that he/she needs [a domestic worker's] services during this period."[28] The primary concern was very much to guarantee the interests of and legal protection (from overtime claims) to the employers.

Two senators expressed outrage at the revised clause. Sarthou stated that "we are in 1999 admitting the possibility that a workday extends to sixteen or seventeen hours," which, according to him, was unconstitutional and dangerous. The sole female senator, who was from the Frente Amplio, stated, "What we are saying is that one can work for twenty-four hours . . . and [we are] effectively doing everything possible so that one cannot present any kind of complaint against [the employers]."[29] She stated that she could not support such a law. Yet the revised clause was approved in the Labor Commission a month later with only one vote against it.[30] Nevertheless, the revised project never made it out of the commission. In October 2000, with new members in the commission, several senators stated that they were not ready to bring the project to the plenary for debate.[31] It was archived.

The victory of the Frente Amplio in 2005 brought a clearly different view on this issue into the government. The party campaigned on a political platform based on equity, universalistic programs, and social justice. Once it won the elections and assumed power under the leadership of President Tabaré Vázquez, the Frente Amplio's strong ties to civil society and the labor unions gave them significant consultative and decision-making power in party platforms and policies. The Plenario Intersindical de Trabajadores–Convención Nacional de Trabajadores (PIT-CNT), the central union confederation of Uruguay, gained significant policy access, and several of the government's ministers had tight union ties (Pribble 2011).

While the PIT-CNT has been relatively strong in comparative perspective, prior to 2005 its policy influence was largely reactive; the confederation was able to block unpopular reforms but not set the agenda. While it did not actively push for reform on domestic workers' rights in the 1990s, according to one PIT-CNT official, the legal discrimination against domestic workers had constituted a long-standing concern among the female union officials responsible for gender issues within the confederation.[32]

When the Frente Amplio took over the government, it immediately set about strengthening the country's labor unions and extended collective negotiation rights (Ermida Uriarte 2009, 42). It passed a law protecting union activity, and union membership rates increased by two and a half times during the first years of the party's government under the umbrella of the PIT-CNT (53). The government also reconvened national-level sectoral salary negotiation committees, which had existed in Uruguay after the democratic transition until 1992. These tripartite committees include the government, unions, and employers'/business associations, and they negotiate wages for the different sectors of the economy. Since 2008, their negotiations have encompassed twenty-four sectors and more than two hundred subsectors.

The Frente Amplio's broad participatory platform and its goal of social justice were also key catalysts for reform on domestic workers' rights. The government encouraged collective organization among domestic workers, drawing their perspective directly into the policy process. The contrast to the political process in the 1990s, in which the reform bill had been debated behind closed doors, was dramatic.

In March 2005, President Tabaré Vázquez announced his government's intention to include domestic workers in the collective salary negotiations, with the stated idea to collectively establish a salary "floor"—that is, a minimum wage—for that sector.[33] This would eliminate the executive decrees establishing the minimum wage and presumably reduce or prohibit in-kind deductions from the wage.

The government also declared its intention to regulate domestic work with a new law that established equal rights. It was framed as part of a broader attack on both labor and gender-based discrimination. The government reconvened the Tripartite Commission on Equality of Opportunity and Employment, which was established in 1997 but had lost much of its clout. The commission was given the mandate to draft a proposal to regulate domestic work, and this task was delegated to a subcommission.[34]

The president's decision to promote these policy reforms, especially collective negotiation, made it necessary to reconvene the domestic workers' union. Giving the union the opportunity to articulate its demands was a precondition for engaging in salary negotiations.[35] Thus, the PIT-CNT rapidly initiated the reconstitution of the defunct SUTD. The PIT-CNT sought out the leadership and provided both advice and the physical space in which the new union could be formed. This willingness to embrace and work with outsiders in order to extend them labor rights stands out in a comparative regional context, as many unions in other countries have functioned more intently to preserve insider privileges rather than seeking to recruit new, less organized members.

Strong leadership from within also drove the successful reconstitution of the SUTD. Two women with union backgrounds took over the organization. They had been textile workers in a large factory for many years and became union organizers during this time. When the textile factory closed in 2002 and they lost their jobs, the only employment they were able to find was domestic work. With the call of the PIT-CNT in 2005, they took their organizing know-how over to this sector and reconstituted the SUTD. Their view was that paid domestic work was like any other wage relation and should be treated as such; one of the leaders noted that women who worked in domestic service had often internalized elements of the more submissive master-servant dynamic that had historically characterized this relationship. Part of the struggle for her was making women in this sector more aware of their dignity and rights. The leaders' aggressive organizing efforts paid off: when the union was reconstituted in April 2005, it initially had twenty-five members; in June 2007, a national meeting attracted more than four hundred people.[36] By 2009, around one thousand domestic workers belonged to the union.[37] While these numbers are still small compared to the total number of domestic workers, they are impressive given the generally very low levels of organization among domestic workers.

When the government subcommission convened in 2005 to discuss several projects, a general consensus emerged that a law regulating domestic work should be a priority.[38] At this point, there was no discussion of the substance of the issue—that is, *whether* domestic workers' rights should be equalized with those of other workers—as there had so extensively been in the Senate less than ten years before. Now the focus was on the technicalities of writing the most appropriate law. The subcommission included the Women's Executive Agency (Instituto Nacional de las Mujeres, INAMU), the Ministry of Labor, the Social Security Bank (Banco de Previsión Social, BPS), the PIT-CNT, and employers'/business associations. The ILO participated in some sessions.[39] The SUTD was also invited to share its views with the subcommission. During the process of drafting the new law, the only opposition came from the employers' and business associations that did not agree with the proposed eight-hour workday limit or the right to household inspections with judicial authorization. However, their objections were not vehement, and in the end, instead of active opposition, these associations simply decided not to pronounce themselves in favor of the project.[40] All others supported the final bill.

The government gave the bill priority status and submitted it to Congress, where it was unanimously approved with no modifications. The executive signed it into law, and domestic workers finally received the same rights that had been granted to other workers in Uruguay much earlier—in the case of work hours, almost a century earlier. The law granted an eight-hour workday and forty-four-hour workweek, with overtime pay for any additional hours.[41] It also extended domestic workers any rights that other workers already had—for example, the right to unemployment insurance. Finally, it allowed for in-home inspections with a judicial order if the employer's authorization could not be gained.

Enforcement of Labor Rights

For Uruguay, legal reform is only half of the story. After legal reform, the executive moved quite rapidly to enforce equal rights. This involved initiating social security registration campaigns by the BPS within the Ministry of Labor, including the SUTD in salary negotiations, and instituting mechanisms for processing labor violations.

The BPS had been included in the tripartite subcommission and was supportive of legally extending all social security benefits to domestic workers, including unemployment insurance.[42] This ensured that the agency would be on board with enforcement. Immediately following legal reform, it began a broad and effective campaign to register domestic workers for social security.[43] The BPS was innovative in its strategies to ensure compliance, including door-to-door campaigns with informational fliers and personal contact with employers as well as domestic workers. It also used three award-winning thirty-second television ads shown in 2007 and 2008 to remind employers to register their workers for social security. The campaign was proactive yet positive; it reminded employers of their responsibility by appealing to their sense of integrity and to their sense of shame if they failed to register their workers. Only after repeated, more positive attempts were punitive actions considered.[44] The campaigns have been very effective, and fifty-five thousand domestic workers were registered for social security by March 2009—about 50 percent of the total number of domestic workers.[45]

At the same time, the government convened the SUTD and other unions and employers' associations to collectively negotiate sectoral minimum wages. The key problem in this process was that there was no obvious organized employer counterpart with whom the SUTD could negotiate salaries. Employers of domestic workers, as individual households, were not organized into business associations, nor did they tend to see themselves primarily as employers. The challenge was to find an appropriate negotiating partner for the union, and the government finally settled on a small organization called the Liga de Amas de Casa, Consumidores y Usuarios del Uruguay (League of Homemakers and Consumers of Uruguay, LACCUU). The league, with ten to fifteen active members, somewhat reluctantly took on this role. Ironically, some of the members of the LACCUU actually worked themselves for private households.

Despite the seemingly difficult setup, the bargaining process has so far functioned according to plan. As a result of the process, a minimum wage was established by collective bargaining in 2008 for the first time. While the final amount was much less than was originally demanded by the SUTD, its leaders—in an interview prior to the start of the salary commissions—had recognized that they would most likely have to compromise.[46] In December 2010, after many months of negotiations, the counterparts signed a collective agreement on salaries effective until the end of 2012, with a wage increase for domestic workers.[47]

Continued union-building efforts are crucial for the success of future negotiations and enforcement efforts overall. As Alma Fernández, the official in charge of the gender and equity department in the PIT-CNT, said, "The law will not enforce itself; the SUTD exists to make sure that happens."[48]

Finally, the government institutionalized mechanisms by which labor complaints could be processed. The law allows for home inspections when there is a "presumed violation" taking place. This inspection can be authorized either by the employer or by a labor judge on a case-by-case basis (ILO 2010a, 74). The law is considered a reasonable balance between the constitutional guarantee of the home as "sacred and inviolable" and the need to guarantee labor rights of domestic workers. These mechanisms are, of course, a last resort and have been combined with preventive awareness campaigns on domestic workers' rights and obligations.

In sum, Uruguay's legal and policy reforms since 2005 have been progressive and comprehensive. While they were initiated by the left-wing executive, a ready and willing base of union officials supported comprehensive reform. Once the intention to enact reform was articulated, support among relevant actors was public and strong, while opposition was fragmented and muted. By 2005—and unlike just a decade earlier, behind closed doors—very few felt comfortable speaking publicly against reform in Uruguayan society.

Chile

Chile has enjoyed twenty years of democratic politics since the end of the seventeen-year dictatorship of Augusto Pinochet. From 1990 until March 2010, the country was governed by a center-left coalition that presided over stable economic growth and was also able to incrementally improve the conditions of its most disadvantaged citizens with targeted social policies. Thus, while inequalities in Chile remain high even by regional standards, the country has been remarkably successful in reducing levels of absolute poverty. Legal reforms on domestic workers' rights reflect similar top-down incrementalism.

At the time of the democratic transition in 1990, domestic workers had few rights. Their workdays extended to twelve hours (and live-in domestics only got half a day off on national holidays), and they were legally entitled to only 75 percent of the national minimum wage. They had no severance pay and no maternity leave. Since then, two reforms have provided domestic workers with severance pay and maternity leave, in 1990 and 1998, respectively, and in 2008 the executive introduced a scale to equalize domestic workers' minimum wage with the national minimum wage by 2011. Finally, in 2003, live-in domestic workers were granted the same national holidays that other workers had. However, longer work hours remain unreformed.

Social and Legal Context

Chile had just over 360,000 domestic workers in 2006 (Ministerio del Trabajo y Previsión Social 2008). While the absolute number of domestic workers has almost doubled since 1980 (Gálvez and Todaro 1984, 13), domestic workers as a percentage of the total economically active female population declined from 18.3 percent in 1990 to 12.9 percent in 2006.[49] The share of women working as live-in domestics substantially declined during this time period as well, from 39 percent of domestic workers in 1990 to 14 percent in 2006 (Ministerio del Trabajo y Previsión Social 2008).

Educational levels among this sector are, unsurprisingly, lower. The average number of years of formal education completed by a domestic worker is 5.6 years, while the average for all economically active women is 7.5 years (Ministerio del Trabajo y Previsión Social 2008). Traditionally, many of the domestic workers in the urban areas—most importantly Santiago, where the majority work—have come from the rural areas of Chile, many of them from the south, with a higher representation of women of Mapuche heritage among the domestic worker labor force (SINTRACAP 1992). Increasingly, Peruvian women have also migrated to Santiago to work in domestic service, given the economic differences between the two countries (Maher and Staab 2006; Stefoni 2003, 2009).

As table 3.1 indicates, in 2006 about 42 percent of domestic workers had pension protections. It is also estimated that roughly half of domestic workers have a written contract, which is obligatory in Chile.[50] These figures are higher than those in other Latin American countries with the exception of Uruguay, indicating a generally stronger state and enforcement of the rule of law in Chile. However, even in Chile legal rights are often not respected when it comes to domestic workers—contract or no contract—particularly in the case of live-in domestic workers. According to one survey, they work on average seventy to ninety-four hours a week, although the legal limit is seventy-two hours a week (twelve hours a day, six days a week).[51]

The Political Process

During the twentieth century, Chile gradually developed democratic, multiparty politics, culminating in the introduction of the secret ballot in 1957. The state also expanded its reach by providing social security, education, and health care to a growing share of the population. Increased polarization in the 1960s led to the election of Socialist Salvador Allende to the presidency in 1970, with a staunch conservative opposition. In the context of the Cold War and U.S. support, the military staged a coup in 1973, leading to the seventeen-year dictatorship of Augusto Pinochet. The Pinochet regime dismantled many of the elements of the Chilean welfare state by privatizing pensions and health care and by deregulating labor, and it reconstituted the political system by writing up a new constitution in 1980. The 1980s witnessed the emergence of broad-based, prodemocracy protest movements, and a referendum in 1988 paved the way for elections. In 1989, the center-left Concertación coalition won the presidency and gained a majority in the Chamber.

Chile has, since 1990, remained stable with relatively programmatic political parties compared to other Latin American countries. Since 1989, the left (Party for Democracy, PPD; Socialist Party, PS) and the center (Christian Democratic Party, PDC; minor Radical Social Democratic Party, PRSD) have joined forces in the Concertación coalition. Meanwhile, the two right-wing parties—the Independent Democratic Union (UDI), most closely identified with the previous authoritarian regime, and the National Renovation (RN), right-wing but less identified with Pinochet—have formed the Alianza por Chile. The first four post-Pinochet presidents (1990–2010) came from the Concertación. Chile is governed by the 1980 constitution of the military regime and, until 2005, appointed (nondemocratically elected) senators tipped the balance of power in favor of the political right.

Chilean politics during the successive center-left administrations was characterized by stability and incrementality in the face of a well-organized and powerful right-wing opposition. The same dynamics have characterized the politics of domestic workers' rights; they have incrementally improved their economic and legal conditions over these two decades. To a large extent, these dynamics are reflective of the broader Chilean political dynamics of consensus building, top-down incremental reforms, and avoidance of the most controversial economic and sociomoral issues in the face of conservative opposition (Barrett 2001; Blofield 2006; Boeninger 1997; Drake and Jakšić 1999; Fuentes 2005; Garretón 2003; Haas 2010; Htun 2003; Pribble 2011; Siavelis 2009).

The first post-transition president, Patricio Aylwin, came from the PDC. After inauguration in March 1990, given pent-up social demands and its mandate of "the social debt of democracy," the center-left government set out to repeal some of the most radical Pinochet-era labor laws. This was challenging due to the strength of the economic elites and the political right in Chile. The executive proposed a bill on labor rights that overturned the ability of employers to fire workers at will and gave them some, if weak, protections. It initially excluded domestic workers from labor protections, including severance pay (Biblioteca del Congreso Nacional 1997, 6). The bill was sent to the Senate with the expectation that the staunchest opposition would be there and whatever passed the Senate was likely to pass the House. The final law was a compromise and included domestic workers in severance pay.

The second reform, under the administration of President Eduardo Frei, also from the PDC, took place during consideration of an executive bill on women's labor rights, specifically the rights of pregnant workers. It was introduced in 1995 and passed in 1998. While other Chilean female workers (with permanent positions) already had legal maternity leave, a law from 1981 explicitly excluded domestic workers from it (Jiménez and Parodi Macías 2003, 228). A left-leaning Christian Democratic senator inserted a clause extending maternity leave to domestic workers into the labor reform, and after strong opposition and heated debate in the Senate the bill was narrowly approved. In the Chamber, coincidentally, the vote took place right after Pinochet's arrest in London in late October 1998, and conservative legislators had all rushed off to protest the detainment and were not present for the vote.[52] This resulted in no votes against the bill, as the Concertación voted in favor of it (Biblioteca del Congreso Nacional 1998, 211–12).

These legal advances addressed the explicit exclusion of domestic workers from rights that other workers had. In both cases, the initiative came from left-leaning legislators who, in the face of executive reticence or disinterest, added clauses to larger executive-initiated labor reform bills in order to force the issue onto the political agenda and to debate.

In 2000, left-wing Ricardo Lagos won the presidential election. He pushed for more pro-poor reforms (see Pribble 2011), although none were specifically targeted at domestic workers. In 2006, left-wing Michelle Bachelet became the first female to be elected president in Chile. She campaigned on a platform to promote gender equity, and two legal reforms on domestic workers were passed during her administration. In the national minimum wage adjustment negotiations for 2008, her administration proposed a gradual equalization of the legal minimum wage for domestic workers, increasing it from 75 percent to 100 percent of the national minimum wage by 2011. In 2007, a group of left-wing legislators introduced a bill in the Chamber of Deputies that would grant live-in domestic workers the same national holidays off as other workers. This was approved and became law in 2009. The work hours of domestic workers, however, are still legally longer than those of other workers at twelve hours a day and seventy-two hours a week. They remained unchanged even when an executive-initiated reform by the Lagos administration that reduced the workweek for workers in general from forty-eight to forty-five hours was approved in 2001. In March 2010, for the first time since 1958, a right-wing president, Sebastián Piñera, democratically assumed power in Chile.

Organizations, Coalition Building, and Agenda Setting

There are two main organizations of domestic workers in Chile: the Asociación Nacional de Empleadas de Casa Particular (ANECAP, a national organization affiliated with the Catholic Church) and the Sindicato de Trabajadoras de Casas Particulares (SINTRACAP, a domestic workers' union). Both were founded by the late 1940s. While the 1973 military coup put an end to political organization, domestic workers' organizations regained momentum during the 1980s prodemocracy protest movements and peaked in their membership levels at this time. They even organized street marches in 1988, spearheaded by Aida Moreno, to demand equal rights from the military government and submitted an unsuccessful petition to the Ministry of Labor (SINTRACAP 1989, 1992). In all, the late 1980s witnessed a high level of social mobilization that diminished with the return to democracy.

Domestic workers' organizations brought the explicit exclusion of this sector from severance pay in the 1990 labor reform to the attention of legislators (Biblioteca del Congreso Nacional 1997, 6). They found a political ally in Laura Rodríguez, a left-wing legislator. The bill was introduced for debate in the Senate, and with Rodríguez's lobbying (she was in the Chamber), two left-leaning senators (José Ruiz de Giorgio and Ronaldo Calderón, both former union leaders) recommended the inclusion of domestic workers with a 4.11 percent flat-rate severance pay. Given that inclusion of domestic workers was a relatively minor, noncostly measure, the clause was accepted by both the executive and the right-wing opposition and no public arguments were made against it.

While the left had put the severance pay clause on the agenda, the right sought appropriate ownership of it, given that it was one of the measures that the right had been willing to accept. In the thirteen speeches by senators regarding the bill in general, domestic workers were mentioned by only three, all of them right-wing. One right-wing senator claimed personal credit for introducing the severance pay clause (while his support helped break right-wing opposition to the clause, he was not the author of it). Another congratulated his institution for passing "an extraordinarily important advance and a grand element of social justice," while a third senator expressed his "personal joy" at its passage (Biblioteca del Congreso Nacional 1997, 130–58). Senators on the left and center-left, dissatisfied with the compromises they had had to make with the right, focused in their speeches on the remaining challenges regarding labor rights that had not, in their view, been adequately addressed.

With the 1998 labor reform, Moreno unsuccessfully requested that the executive include maternity leave for domestic workers in the bill.[53] One of the senators involved in the prior reform, Ruiz de Giorgio, took up the cause in the Senate Labor Commission. He claimed that he had no contact with domestic workers' organizations at the time but was rather acting out of personal conviction to "defend labor rights." He inserted a clause to extend maternity leave to domestic workers during a Senate Labor Commission meeting on the broader project, with the goal of thus making it harder to turn down.[54]

This clause, unlike the other, divided the commission and the Senate along party lines and even within the governing coalition. It became the subject of heated debate. Ruiz de Giorgio took it upon himself to first convince reticent members of his own coalition to vote favorably, followed by members of the opposition. According to Ruiz de Giorgio, private opposition was quite strong and personal; one Christian Democratic legislator opposed the clause because his daughter said that it would adversely affect her relationship with her domestic worker.[55]

Once the issue was on the agenda of the Senate plenary, public positions followed party lines and right-wing senators had to publicly articulate their opposition. The arguments of the opposition centered on the adverse (if unintended) economic effects of maternity leave on the middle-class employers of domestic workers. Many referred to personal examples and connections. In effect, several senators argued, maternity leave would either "terminate" domestic employment as a source of work altogether or lead to a massive informalization, as employers would no longer want to contract employees with so many legal rights. Improved legal rights would thus end up hurting their intended beneficiaries. One senator argued that employers made almost the same amount of money as their employees and hence could not afford maternity leave (although it would come from a separate social security account). The second type of argument focused on the exceptionalism of domestic work, which takes place within a family and which makes it very uncomfortable to "maintain a labor relationship after the worker has broken the employer's trust [by becoming pregnant]" (Biblioteca del Congreso Nacional 1998, 153). Arguments in support of maternity leave focused on the need to promote equal rights for all, the injustice of discriminating against a group of workers who were already particularly vulnerable, and the need for Chile to legislate in accordance with the international treaties it had ratified (150–59, 179–210).

The final vote took two rounds. After the first round (16 in favor, 14 against, and 8 abstentions) some senators changed their minds, and the final result was 20 in favor and 15 against, with 1 abstention (Biblioteca del Congreso Nacional 1998, 158–59). At least one appointed (unelected) senator, a conservative Catholic, changed his vote after Ruiz de Giorgio argued that his position against maternity leave for domestic workers would force them to have abortions to retain their jobs and threatened to publicize his stance, thereby inviting criticism from the Catholic Church.[56] It may be that others also changed their minds given the potential negative publicity and the fact that their opposition had not killed the clause. In the Chamber, while support and opposition may also have coalesced along party lines, the arrest of Pinochet resulted in an unexpectedly speedy and unanimous vote in favor of extending maternity leave to domestic workers, as the right-wing opposition was not present.

Since the early 1990s, domestic workers' organizations gradually declined in terms of both their social base and their capacity to mobilize.[57] These problems are part of a broader defusion of social mobilization in Chile since the late 1980s up until 2010 (Blofield 2006; Franceschet 2005; Garretón 2003; Oxhorn 1995; Posner 2008), which has reduced potential social allies.[58] The same applies to labor unions: only 8 percent of workers in Chile are unionized, and only a small fraction of this 8 percent negotiate collectively.[59] Overall, it is difficult to unionize in Chile and the incentives are low; these dynamics are exacerbated in the case of domestic workers.[60]

Factors endogenous to domestic workers' organizations have reduced their influence as well. Since the 1990s, the organizations have suffered from a lack of unified and persistent leadership. Aida Moreno, who had been a key domestic workers' rights activist and advocated for both legal reforms in the 1990s, stepped down from her leadership position in the late 1990s due to internal divisions, and it has been difficult for the organizations to regain momentum in the 2000s. ANECAP's leadership has been hampered by its dependence on the Catholic Church, which has in recent years strongly discouraged militancy in favor of equal rights (e.g., street marches), while SINTRACAP's lack of resources (e.g., no full-time employees) has made it hard to build constructive alliances and to lobby politicians.[61]

These difficulties have fostered a general demoralization among the leadership of both organizations and reduced their ability to form constructive coalitions with labor unions and other groups. They have not been able to afford union dues or aggressively promote their interests to the Central Confederation of Workers (Central Unitaria de Trabajadores, CUT). While many of the domestic workers have traditionally been rural Chileans and of Mapuche or mixed heritage, ethnic discrimination is prevalent but not broadly and effectively politicized.[62] Since the 1990s, an increasing number of immigrants from Peru have become domestic workers in Chile, particularly among the upper classes.[63] This has also fostered negative media coverage of the Peruvian "invasion," which, according to the director of an immigrant organization, is more perception than reality, as a minimal fraction of domestic workers are actually foreigners.[64] Domestic workers' organizations have not, however, reached out to Peruvian domestics or their organizations. As of 2008, they had virtually no contact with feminist, indigenous, or immigrant organizations for Peruvian domestic workers. According to one of the former leaders, the organizations were simply "trying to survive," and according to officials in the Ministry of Labor, they were "totally collapsed" in 2008.[65] As the former leader herself pointed out, "Without a strong team to pressure politicians nothing gets accomplished."[66]

On the other hand, while their capacity to mobilize and to lobby politicians has not been strong, the shift to the left in the executive, especially under Bachelet, made officials more sensitive to the needs of this group of workers. During the administrations of the more conservative Christian Democratic presidents (1990–2000), individual legislators had tagged clauses onto broader labor reform bills, thus bypassing executive reticence and forcing a debate on the clauses. The left-wing executive under Bachelet—specifically officials in both the Ministry of Labor and the Women's Executive Agency (Servicio Nacional de la Mujer, SERNAM)[67]—has made an effort to promote social inclusion. The third initiative, which sought to gradually equalize the minimum wage for domestic workers, came from the executive. Sympathetic left-wing officials at the Ministry of Labor saw the minimum wage issue as one of a "historic debt" and of "social justice" for this group of workers and included them in the national minimum wage adjustment negotiations in July 2008.[68] This inclusion, which was approved by Congress without a fight, was largely viewed as a symbolic affirmation of equal rights since the current market wage for domestic workers was already above the national minimum wage.[69]

Finally, a group of left-wing legislators in the Chamber of Deputies introduced a bill in 2007 to grant live-in domestic workers the same national holidays off as other workers. It had gained executive backing with the claim that "there is no objective reason for such discrimination" (Biblioteca del Congreso Nacional 2009, 9). The vast majority of legislators agreed with the bill; the sole opposing vote came from a right-wing UDI legislator in the Chamber who claimed that "despite good intentions" the bill would increase unemployment (34). In the Senate, now without any appointed senators, there were no votes against it (87). In signing the bill into law, President Bachelet proclaimed, "I think it is just to recognize that without the help of [domestic workers], things would be much harder for many households, particularly for many mothers who work outside the home. We are talking about women who frequently . . . postpone or sacrifice their own families or personal development projects" (106).

These two reforms were top-down initiatives from well-meaning officials, not the result of significant lobbying capacity by the domestic workers' organizations. The difficulties that the organizations have had in actually getting their voices heard are reflected in their inability to get work hours onto the political agenda. While both ANECAP and SINTRACAP claimed that they had submitted petitions to politicians in the mid-2000s to equalize the work hours of domestics, they lacked effective strategies to follow up.[70] While the leaders of domestic workers' organizations claimed that they were ignored by politicians, Maria Antonieta Saa, one of the most sympathetic left-wing legislators in Congress, claimed that she had neither received a petition nor heard about a "campaign" to equalize labor rights when asked about it.[71] Whether politicians ignore them, as the leaders of domestic workers' organizations claim, or the organizations do not contact them, as politicians claim, the reality is that there has clearly been little visible social pressure to equalize the work hours of domestics. For example, when the 2001 labor reform was being debated in Congress during the Lagos government, at no point during the commission or plenary debates was the option of extending similar work hours to domestics even proposed. The final reform reduced the workweek from forty-eight to forty-five hours (after which overtime kicks in) but did not include domestic workers.

When Congress debated the 2007 bill, which would give live-in domestics national holidays off, the Labor Commission of the Chamber of Deputies invited one of the domestic workers' organizations to an audience. There the organization lamented the "semi-slavery" of the long work hours that prevented domestic workers from developing their personal lives. However, work hours were not introduced into the legal reform (Biblioteca del Congreso Nacional 2009, 10). A few politicians referred to the negative impact of extended work hours on domestics, but none actually introduced a clause to modify work hours in this legislative bill.

The less controversial, incremental reforms that have taken place are not negligible. However, low levels of social pressure from domestic workers' organizations to lobby for equal work hours and the knowledge among politicians that such a project would elicit strong (even if not open) opposition from other political elites have kept this issue off the agenda to date.

Enforcement of Labor Rights

In Chile, enforcement of laws in general is relatively strong in comparison to other Latin American countries, reflecting a stronger state capacity and a more rule-abiding political culture. Given this, new laws stand a better chance of actually being enforced. In addition, a core group of sympathetic officials in the executive, particularly during the Bachelet government, engaged in more proactive campaigns to reach domestic workers and enforce their rights.

In Chile, as mentioned earlier, a written contract is obligatory, and it is estimated that around 50 percent of domestic workers actually have such a contract.[72] Aside from the 4.11 percent severance pay, social security is paid from employees' salaries, reducing employer resistance to formalization, and 42 percent of domestic workers in 2006 had pension protections. Furthermore, as mentioned in chapter 3, a broader pension reform under President Bachelet, approved in 2008, has increased the access of low-income women to basic pensions. This is likely to also increase take-up rates for elderly domestic workers.

It appears that take-up rates for maternity leave are lower, at about 28 percent of eligible domestic workers. However, having the law on the books has given employees leverage to negotiate an informal "severance package" with their employers in the event of pregnancy. Thus, the law has had a positive effect on domestic workers' ability to achieve somewhat better working conditions.[73]

As in most of Latin America, labor inspectors cannot enter a private home, which makes it harder to investigate complaints by domestic workers. However, when a written contract does not exist, as long as a person can prove that she worked for a specific employer, the law will take her word over the employer's word, providing a safeguard for workers and an incentive for employers to establish a written contract.[74] If the labor relation cannot be established, or if a dispute with a written contract is not settled, the worker must take the complaint to the courts, where it may not be resolved for several years. Foreigners can also submit complaints.[75]

More broadly, the Ministry of Labor was particularly proactive during the Bachelet government (2006–10). In 2008, the ministry conducted a campaign to promote the professionalization and rights of domestic workers. This was a national-level campaign involving both the Ministry of Labor and SERNAM. The goal was to encourage the formalization of the labor force through written contracts, increased social security registration, better knowledge of rights, and more professionalization. The campaign used press conferences, fliers, radio programs, television advertisements, and newspaper advertisements to reach domestic workers as well as their employers. Programs included meetings with domestic workers and their organizations, seminars, training classes on different skills, and classes on labor rights.[76] For example, in Santiago, the ministry provided driving courses and first aid courses to nannies, which increase their marketable skills. Given the weakness of domestic workers' organizations, the campaign also sought to strengthen the organizations themselves.[77]

In sum, incremental legal reforms by sympathetic left-wing politicians have improved the rights of domestic workers in Chile. In addition, a left-wing executive from 2000 to 2010, particularly under the Bachelet administration, combined with stronger state capacity, has resulted in proactive campaigns and better enforcement of extant rights. However, the lack of social pressure from domestic workers themselves has kept the issue of equal work hours off the political agenda, despite some ostensible windows of opportunity during the 2001 and 2009 reforms. Equalizing work hours will remain a challenge, especially under a right-wing government.

Conclusion

Uruguay and Chile have both improved the legal rights and working conditions of domestic workers over the past two decades. In Uruguay, legal equality has been achieved, while in Chile work hours remain legally longer.

The reform paths of the two countries reflect broader political differences. Pribble (2011) characterizes Uruguay's left government as "constituency-coordinating" and Chile's as "professional-electoral." This is evidenced in the paths to reform on domestic workers' rights: the extension of equal rights has been pursued through a participatory, inclusive decision-making process under

Uruguay's left-wing government, while in Chile a well-intentioned center-left technocratic elite has pushed for less controversial reforms but with less policy-making input from the weak organizations, which themselves have also had little capacity to mobilize and pressure politicians. In Chile, three of the four piecemeal reforms were initiated by legislators, the first two without executive support. In those first two, senators were able to tag clauses onto broader labor reform bills, thus forcing a political debate on them. However, the social pressure to push for equal work hours—the most controversial issue—has not to date existed to counter elite indifference or opposition. While equal work hours may be even less well received under a right-wing government, the approval of the ILO convention may help bring it onto the political agenda in the future.

On enforcement, the interactive effect of strong state capacity and a left or center-left executive in both countries has resulted in proactive efforts by their governments to implement extant labor rights. Thus, while in both countries the absolute conditions of domestic workers have improved and both can serve as models for most other Latin American countries, Uruguay stands out in the regional vanguard by extending equal rights to a group of its most unprotected citizens and by making a concerted effort to enforce these equal rights.

CONCLUSION

While most states in the region have made significant strides in eliminating discriminatory statutes on women's rights and human and labor rights in general, equal rights for domestic workers have lagged despite constitutions that enshrine equality. Until recently, all states maintained discriminatory statutes toward this sector, mandating longer work hours and lower benefits with the assumption that the servant should basically always be available to serve her employers. The private lives and needs of domestic workers did not factor into these laws, exemplifying the social distance between elites—economic and political—and the lower classes. This has, in effect, subsidized a cheap labor force to meet the needs of well-off families, and those who benefit from this status quo have, over decades and centuries, come to view it as natural.

Within this context, domestic workers' organizations across the region have increasingly vocally demanded equal rights and respect for their occupation. Change has to date been slow and obstacle ridden, illustrating the particularly marginalized status of this group of workers. By 2010, only four countries (Bolivia, Colombia, Costa Rica, and Uruguay) had equalized the rights of domestic workers, while others had instituted some reforms; a fifth country—Argentina—was slated to equalize rights by 2011. In the majority of countries in the region, the legal status quo remains discriminatory.

Arguments in favor of equal rights are powerful, and advocates in all countries have made straightforward appeals to equal rights in the context of extant discrimination. They have pointed to the discrepancy between labor code clauses on domestic workers, international conventions, and national constitutions that guarantee equality, in some cases quite specifically by mandating an eight-hour workday. They have also pointed out the gendered, class-based, and often ethnic or racial dimensions of the discriminatory status quo.

Opponents have, across countries, responded to these arguments with what could be considered "gut reactions," as privileges that have come to seem natural are contested. The majority tend not to publicly or openly voice opposition. Among those who have (behind closed doors as well as in more open fora such as plenary debates), opposition has taken two broad forms. First, opponents have drawn on what they consider the "exceptional nature" of domestic work, arguing that the dynamics of this occupation make it unique and distinct from any other wage labor relation. Second, they have made more pragmatic arguments, which can be somewhat contradictory. Many have argued that legal reform will have negative economic effects, as increased rights will lead to higher levels of unemployment, hurting the intended beneficiaries. Others have argued that the status quo is not abusive, often drawing on personal examples of employers treating their household workers like family; they have contended that "normal people" do not abuse this relation, making legal reform unnecessary and potentially harmful by aggravating domestic tensions.

The opposition has tended to be most vehement when workday limits are debated. The adverse reactions are often grounded in unrecognized and unproblematized privilege. There is a pervasive sense among some of the well-off who employ domestic workers that they are, in effect, doing their servants a favor by giving them a job and that part of the job description is to be on call for extended periods of time. The views of domestic workers as well as their need for and right to decent work and a private life for themselves and their own families (many have children themselves) have, until recently, remained invisible.

Thus, the first step to reform has been for domestic workers to organize and to forge allies in order to make their cause visible. However, organizing among this sector is uniquely challenging, given the constraints these workers face on their time, their lack of resources, and the isolated nature of their work. Reform has not constituted a priority for almost any major social or political actors. Most feminist organizations and labor unions have not mobilized on behalf of this group or demanded reform, and those who have, have tended to do so as individuals. The same applies to politicians; the advocates whom domestic workers have been able to gain to date have acted on their behalf as individuals without programmatic party backing, with the exception of the Frente Amplio in Uruguay in 2005–6 and the Movimiento al Socialismo (Movement Toward Socialism, MAS) in Bolivia in 2002–3.

On the other hand, domestic workers have, with persistence spanning years, succeeded in forging allies and making their cause more visible over time. As a result, it has become harder to sustain arguments based on exceptionalism, and opposition to reform has tended to become less open. Those opposed to reform have instead sought to slow down the political process through formal and informal veto points, and they have often been aided by a general indifference among a large group of political elites who may not be actively or strongly opposed but who do not see the issue as particularly important or urgent and have other priorities.

The key struggle for advocates has been to gain enough allies to force equal rights reform onto the political agenda when the opportunity arises. Once equal rights reform goes to a plenary debate and vote, it is very difficult for politicians to openly argue against equality and cast a vote opposing it. Despite private opposition, many of the plenary votes on domestic workers have passed with unanimity or near unanimity.

Court rulings, however, can go either way, perhaps because they are shielded from the same political pressures. Even in seemingly straightforward cases on constitutional grounds, courts in Costa Rica, Guatemala, and Panama ruled against eight-hour workdays for domestic workers, arguing that they constituted an "exceptional case" and were thus not subject to the same rights as other workers. In Colombia, on the other hand, the Constitutional Court has consistently upheld equal rights.

Up until 2010, what has explained equal rights reform, most broadly, is the interactive effect of organizing among domestic workers, their ability to gain social and political allies and to make their cause visible, and, finally, whether a political opening has been forthcoming to force the reform onto the political agenda. In addition, all equal rights reforms via Congress have resulted from issue-specific bills that have centrally focused on domestic workers, while partial reforms have in some cases been tagged onto broader labor reforms. The rapidity of legal reform once a bill is submitted, on the other hand, has been influenced by whether the executive has lent its support to reform.

In all three cases of equal rights reform, advocates sought to frame the issue within the salient political cleavages of the country. In Bolivia, they framed the cause as an example of the oppression of indigenous people—indigenous women in particular—in what was repeatedly referred to as a "colonial" relation. This was successful in a majority indigenous country with a history of stark exclusion combined with a rising indigenous movement. In Costa Rica, advocates appealed to the country's reputation as a leader in human rights and its responsibility to provide an example with regard to the treatment of one of the most vulnerable groups in society. In Uruguay, advocates framed the issue as an extension of labor rights to an unfairly excluded sector of poor women. Given that the left-wing executive in 2005 gave its full support to equal rights reform, approval was rapid. Had the bill stalled, advocates may have tried to frame the issue as an example of racial oppression as well, given the over-representation of Afro-Uruguayan women in domestic service and the need to engage in coalition building to break through political resistance.

In Chile, advocates have sought to invoke sympathy for the most vulnerable sectors in society and their need for protection with more paternalistic arguments. This may have more appeal to conservative elements in the Chilean political class: Chile's right-wing parties are strong and socially conservative, as is a sector of the Christian Democrats (see Blofield 2006; Haas 1999, 2010; Htun 2003). The one issue that elicited the more open opposition of right-wing senators—and did not elicit the support of the Christian Democrat–dominated executive—was the extension of maternity leave to domestic workers. Here, a paternalistic and moralistic framing by several senators was evident: by becoming pregnant, a domestic worker had "broken her employer's trust." While those in favor of reform argued that domestic workers also had the right to have children and receive the same protections as other female workers, the initiator of the reform strategically couched his appeal in moral tones as well: this discrimination forced domestic workers to have abortions to keep their jobs, and hence opposition could elicit the disapproval of the Catholic Church. In many countries, framing strategies have not combined with a political opportunity structure that has succeeded in forcing political reform on the agenda.

Within these broad parameters, the case studies reveal three paths to reform. The first is the bottom-up path, which has required extensive social mobilization and pressure. In this case, advocates have had to push reform through slow, unresponsive legislative channels due to executive disinterest or opposition. This was Bolivia's and Costa Rica's route to reform. The second is top-down reform, initiated by the executive but with a heavy participatory element. This was the case of Uruguay's reform. The third is also top-down reform, initiated by well-placed legislators or executive officials without heavy social pressure but also without reform of work hours, the most contentious issue. This was the case of Chile's piecemeal reforms spanning the past two decades. Advocates in other countries have tried to pursue strategies to achieve reform through any of these paths and in some cases have achieved partial reforms. To date, however, the path of "no reform" remains the most common.

As this book goes to press, a new variable has emerged that is impacting the political dynamics on this issue: the international level, specifically the

International Labour Organization (ILO). As discussed in chapter 2, the forging of an ILO convention on domestic workers has increased the visibility of the issue and, relatedly, both organizing among domestic workers and executive attention to the cause.

A group of advocates, with funding from a trade union in the Netherlands, organized a meeting in that country in 2006 to bring together domestic workers' organizations from around the world (IRENE and IUF 2008). With financial support from trade unions and advocacy organizations in developed countries, these organizations have been able to learn about one another, come together, and hold several regional meetings.[1] In 2007, a regional conference on women in Quito declared its support for the equalization of domestic workers' rights (Montaño 2010, 42). As mentioned in chapter 2, the issue of domestic workers' rights has been present in the ILO since 1936 but had not made it onto the agenda (Valenzuela and Mora 2009a, 290–94). Lobbying by domestic workers' organizations and their advocates, with support from the Bureau for Workers' Activities (ACTRAV) in the ILO and with the expertise of other ILO officials, fostered more visibility for the issue, and in 2008 the ILO governing body decided to put a potential convention on the agenda. In 2009, domestic workers' organizations and advocates founded the International Domestic Workers' Network to push for this convention.[2]

The tripartite process of negotiating the terms of a potential convention or nonbinding recommendation and its approval includes the ILO, member governments, and employers' and employees' associations. The approval of a convention is a two-stage process. First, a simple majority decides whether to pursue a convention or a nonbinding recommendation. Following this, a two-thirds vote, with a quorum, is needed to approve the convention (ILO 2010a, 2010b, 2011a, 2011b).

In anticipation of the ILO votes, domestic workers' organizations and their advocates mobilized to push for a convention rather than a recommendation and to influence the substance of such a convention. While there was more consistent opposition from employers' associations, extensive lobbying efforts by the organizations and their advocates increased the receptiveness of many governments that were initially opposed to the idea of a convention, preferring a recommendation instead.[3] Indeed, the majority of governments ended up supporting a convention, and in June 2010 the ILO voted to approve a vote on a convention the following year.

Over the course of negotiating the convention, domestic workers' rights came to be framed as an issue of human rights, not just labor rights. The negotiations and attendant lobbying gave the cause visibility, and even employers' associations became divided in their opposition to a convention (and in support of a recommendation), as the hard-line stance of some made others uncomfortable given that it was well known that domestic workers were particularly prone to mistreatment around the world.[4] Even work hours, which, unsurprisingly, had been one of the most contentious issues and elicited the especially vehement opposition of the employers' associations, made it into the convention.[5]

The vote on the convention was held in June 2011 at the 100th session of the ILO, with many domestic workers' organizations in attendance. The final vote, which required a two-thirds majority and included governments and employers' and employees' associations, was 396 in favor and 16 against, with 63 abstentions.[6] The approved convention includes clauses to ensure the freedom to form unions, the elimination of discrimination in national laws (including work hours), protections for migrant workers, and employer responsibility in informing workers of the agreed terms and conditions of work.[7] Even some of the employers' associations ended up supporting the convention, and the total number of affirmative votes was higher than advocates had expected.[8] Once it became clear that the convention would pass regardless, some may have felt that they were better off with a recorded vote in favor than against.

The convention must now go to individual governments for the ratification process. With the increased visibility of the issue, and the ostensibly binding steps that such a convention provides for, domestic workers' organizations and their advocates may be well placed to push this issue onto the political agenda of national governments. The overall process has revitalized domestic workers' organizations in many countries (CEMyT 2010). For example, as of 2010, the Sindicato de Trabajadoras de Casas Particulares (SINTRACAP) had set up an informative, well-maintained web page to promote awareness of the working conditions of domestic workers in Chile as well as to promote attention to the ILO convention and its implications for Chile. The Brazilian government announced its intention in 2011 to consider the equalization of rights for domestic workers (Secretaria 2011), and The Paraguayan government announced a little over a month after the convention was approved that it planned to be the first Latin American country to ratify it.[9] In essence, this convention can provide a political window of opportunity for domestic workers' rights.

The reform currently under consideration in Argentina illustrates the changing dynamics of legal reform on this issue. One of the main domestic workers' unions in Argentina had been attempting for years to push for legal reform, without success.[10] The Argentine president's decision to initiate equal rights reform in March 2010 was made in anticipation of the upcoming ILO meetings in Geneva in June of that year. The tripartite commission in the Ministry of Labor, with its extensive contacts in the ILO, was involved in drafting the bill. Government officials as well as the president of the Labor Commission in the Chamber of Deputies mentioned the importance of ILO attention to the issue and noted that Argentina's reform places the country in the regional "vanguard" in protecting the rights of the most vulnerable members of society.[11] The bill, which equalizes the labor rights of domestic workers, was unanimously approved by the Chamber in March 2011 (before the ILO vote in June 2011) and now awaits Senate debate.

For those who won the initial reforms, the struggle was long and arduous. In most countries, extensive organization, mobilization, and coalition-building efforts have yet to pay off. In the countries that retain discriminatory statutes, governments may feel the pressure to reform their laws as Argentina is doing. Whether they act on it remains to be seen, but as the ILO provides more visibility for this issue, it may well become harder for politicians and governments to oppose reform or to ignore the issue, especially if they have active domestic workers' organizations and advocates putting pressure on them. Where equal rights reforms pass, the efforts and time of advocacy organizations will be freed up to focus on the equally important task of enforcement.

Drawing attention to and promoting equal rights for domestic workers have been uniquely challenging given the interaction of class, gender, and often ethnicity or race, which make this group disadvantaged from multiple perspectives. On the other hand, we can also observe similarities with other marginalized groups and issue areas. For example, the politicization of domestic workers' rights is similar to the politicization of violence against women in several ways. With both, the issue was invisible although substantively relevant to a sizeable share of women. Advocates had to organize, often alone, to fight against opposition and indifference to the issue, and to advocate for legal and policy reform. In both cases, the key struggle has been to make the problem more visible, as it has been harder for opponents to openly argue against equal rights or in favor of condoning violence against women. This also distinguishes both issues from reproductive rights, where the Catholic Church and conservatives have promoted a strong opposing moral discourse (Blofield and Haas 2011; Htun and Weldon 2010b; L. M. Morgan 2011). With domestic workers, as well as with violence against women, *any* attention tends to work in their favor.

With policies on violence against women (VAW), initial policy reforms in advanced industrialized countries date to the 1970s and 1980s and were often the result of years of organizing and mobilization by feminist groups. In Latin America, they date to the early 1990s (Weldon 2002a, 2002b). As international attention to the cause grew by the 1990s, especially in the United Nations, there was a shift in the scope and speed of policy reform cross-nationally. With the creation of international treaties on VAW since the 1990s, domestic governments have been more likely to speed up policy reform on the issue (Htun and Weldon 2010a). We may see a similar diffusion of international norms and the speeding up of policy reforms on domestic workers' rights as the ILO takes on a more prominent role.

One clear difference between these two issues, which is also linked to the delay in the politicization of domestic workers' rights in comparison to VAW policies, is that the effects of discrimination against domestic workers are so clearly stratified by class and often by ethnicity or race. Domestic and sexual violence can affect women regardless of their class status or ethnicity, and organizing for it has transcended class divisions among women and been a priority of women's movements (Blofield and Haas 2011; Weldon 2002a, 2002b). The issue of domestic workers' rights highlights class and racial or ethnic divisions, which has made it much harder to forge broader coalitions with women's groups and feminists.

From a class perspective, many of the problems that domestic workers confront are similar to the problems confronted by labor market outsiders in general. Almost half of Latin America's economically active population is employed in the informal sector, and most labor unions have been less willing or less able to engage in extensive labor organizing among these informal workers—and that applies to the domestic service sector, where most people work in "chronic informality" (Estévez and Esper 2009, 14). On the other hand, the explicit legal discrimination against this group distinguishes it from many other informal sector occupations, where the problem is not the law itself as much as it is the lack of access to it. In addition, domestic workers are not self-employed as, for example, streets sellers tend to be, but are rather in a dependent wage relation, especially if they work for only one employer. They also exhibit differences from other wage laborers, whether in the formal or informal sector. Their isolation and relationship with individual employers who often do not see themselves as employers, or give adequate recognition for the kind of labor performed, make it particularly difficult to organize and formalize this sector. Relatedly, the gender dimension of the occupation—the vast majority of these workers are women, doing "women's work"—has also kept it under the radar of more male-dominated labor unions.

As discussed in chapter 3, legal reform is a necessary but not sufficient condition for guaranteeing equal rights. Overall, enforcement across the region has been weak, as evidenced by the low coverage of domestic workers in pension programs, the prevalence of labor violations, and the low visibility of this group to the ministries of labor in the region. Enforcement cannot rely simply on the goodwill of individual employers in registering their employees for social security or on complaints of violations filed by individual domestic workers; given the invisibility of this sector, it must also involve proactive campaigns by the executive to diffuse these rights and to encourage formalization.

Enforcement is explained by a slightly different, although related, set of dynamics. State capacity and executive ideology interact to influence enforcement efforts toward this sector. Proactive campaigns are most likely to take place under left-wing governments where the executive has taken ownership of legal reform. They involve stronger state capacity and a core group of committed officials open to technical advice and policy input from the ILO, with links to strong domestic workers' organizations in civil society. Here, Uruguay again stands out as a model of comprehensive reform, followed by Chile, Brazil, and Argentina, where left governments have sought to include domestic workers in programs and campaigns.

With the increased involvement of the ILO, countries are likely to feel more pressure to reform their laws over the coming years, and the dynamics of reform could be different than they were prior to 2010, as explained by my theory. Even with the passage of equal rights laws, however, understanding and explaining implementation will remain relevant. With the international diffusion of norms, there is a risk that governments worldwide—of weaker states especially—will pay lip service to human rights in order to appease and look good in front of the international community, while doing little to follow up and actually implement any reforms. This could be a risk in some of the Latin American countries as well. Given that the ILO's attention has been directed not only at legal reform but also at the enforcement of labor rights and at strengthening domestic workers' unions and associations, cooperation between the ILO and ministries of labor, combined with union-strengthening efforts, is likely to encourage governments, especially those on the center-left or left, to follow up on any legal reforms.

Returning to the broader context of the politics of care work, the problems that surround paid domestic work, and the reforms that are needed, are not only those of laws and enforcement; they are also structural. As discussed in chapter 1, the continued prevalence of paid domestic work in Latin America is driven by the dependent care needs of a modernizing but highly unequal society. As more well-off families have dual-earner couples, child care and often elderly care are (or continue to be) outsourced to individual, often full-time wageworkers. High levels of poverty and inequality have ensured the ready supply of this workforce, which has been convenient for the well-to-do as the workers contract their labor out to just one household, come to employers' homes, often work long hours, and cook and clean in addition to taking care of dependents. Indeed, the elite in Latin America often hire both nannies and cleaning ladies.

While elites around the world tend to be able to hire full-time domestic workers, the professional classes in advanced industrialized countries, in contrast to Latin America, rarely have the purchasing power to hire a full-time worker exclusively dedicated to serving their care and housework needs. In less unequal societies, the dominant option of professionals has been to place their children in day care and the elderly in elderly care facilities, hire cleaning services on, for example, a weekly basis, and cook their own food, go to restaurants or buy take-out. This also reflects a specialization in the three services that in Latin America are performed by domestic workers. While early childhood education and care provision and cleaning jobs tend to be less prestigious and less well remunerated in most advanced industrialized countries as well, these occupations do tend to be more professionalized and formalized.

In addition to equal rights and enforcement of these rights, what is required over the medium and long term in Latin America is the professionalization of the services provided by domestic workers. To date, most domestic workers in Latin America are hired to perform any and all of the three main household tasks—cooking, cleaning, and dependent care—at the discretion of the employer. As discussed in chapters 4 and 5, some of the ministries of labor in the region have established programs to promote the professionalization of this sector—for example, training in first aid, driving lessons, and classes on child pedagogy. This increases the marketable skills of employees and benefits their employers.

Economic changes are impacting some of these dynamics already. If poverty and inequalities decline—as they recently have in many Latin American countries—especially the middle and upper middle classes will find it harder to afford to hire fully available, around-the-clock domestic workers. Much has recently been made in the media of Brazil's economic boom and growing middle class, and the resultant higher prices for nannies in that country, especially in the major urban centers, such as São Paulo and Rio de Janeiro.[12]

The long-term solution to the higher costs of paid domestic workers is more specialization and more collective forms of service provision. This can carry benefits for employers as well. Specialization can increase skills, and collective service provision spreads risks on both sides. A one-to-one relationship can create problems in the event of work interruptions (e.g., pregnancy or illness).[13] However, contracting the services of a cleaning co-op or cleaning company and/or a day care center can spread this risk among a larger group on both sides and enable the uninterrupted provision of services and employment. There have been recent examples of (former) domestic workers starting their own microenterprise cleaning companies to offer cleaning services to households (Valenzuela and Mora 2009a, 287).

Another challenge for Latin American states is finding adequate solutions to the dependent care needs of domestic workers themselves, as well as lower-income families in general. While important strides have been made in reducing extreme poverty and extending coverage of primary education through policies such as conditional cash transfer programs, the "crisis" of care among lower-income families has largely passed below the radar (CEPAL 2009; Heymann 2006). Working families in poverty face tremendous challenges with regard to the care needs of their dependents, and these challenges are exacerbated among the increasing share (30 percent) of female-headed households in the region (UNDP and ILO 2009). In many cases, these mothers struggle at the margin of survival and are employed as domestic workers or in other forms of precarious employment in the informal sector. They have little time off of work and few resources to attend to the needs of their own dependents in a satisfactory way. To address these problems, equalizing legal rights and enforcing them is, again, necessary but not sufficient. States must also provide these families with affordable services, especially early childhood education and care (ECEC). Provision to date is very limited in most countries, and demand for public ECEC services tends to far outstrip supply. Furthermore, as mentioned in chapter 1, when provided, this service tends to be seen as an educational service, which is, of course, very important in its own right. But services tend to be limited, especially for zero- to three-year-olds, and opening hours for both ECEC and schools are often narrow and do not correspond to work hours (see Filgueira 2011; Filgueira et al. 2011; UNESCO 2006, 2010).

The political challenge in the region is convincing political and economic elites that such services are in the interest of the long-term economic and social development of their countries and are hence in their own interests as well. Multiple arguments can be made in their favor. First, ECEC has positive effects on human capital and on equality of opportunities. One much-cited longitudinal study conducted in the United States found that one dollar invested in a preschool education program generated seventeen dollars in future benefits (UNESCO 2007, 125). Second, with adequate hours, ECEC would provide de facto day care to families, especially women. Third, extending such services would provide decent formal-sector employment for many women who now work in paid domestic work or other precarious forms of employment (Filgueira 2011). It would also keep children off the streets, where they can become targets of, and involved in, gangs and crime. Finally, it would help older girls, who are often caretakers of younger siblings, stay in school.

The relationship between the employer and domestic worker in Latin America has exemplified the deep social distance between classes as well as the undervaluation of what is traditionally considered "women's work." Often, the relationship has also been laced with ethnic and racial discrimination. This relationship, albeit slowly, has begun to change as democratic political contexts have allowed domestic workers to organize collectively and to demand equal rights and respect. The increased attention of the ILO is likely to bolster these demands and help force equal rights onto the political agenda of the majority of countries in the region where laws remain discriminatory. Once equal rights reform is achieved, the policy challenge becomes enforcement. Over the medium term, the challenge is also a broader, structural one rooted in the deep socioeconomic inequalities in the region. What is needed is both the professionalization of the workforce and the services that this sector provides, as well as more extensive state involvement in providing some of these services, especially child care, at affordable rates to these same workers and to lower-income families in general. Ultimately, what this implies is the reduction, even if slight, of the deep inequalities and social distance in Latin America.

The familiar phrasing used by employers in claiming that they treat their domestic workers as "part of the family" is no doubt often well meaning. However, such a relationship, even if it develops strong affective ties, must be based on a more equal standing that allows these workers, in addition to holding decent jobs, to live fulfilling private lives and have their own families.

Notes

Throughout the notes, I have cited numerous untitled transcripts of the proceedings of various legislative bodies and commissions. Page numbers are provided when they appeared in the original. Transcripts from the Congreso de Perú were printed in Lima by the Cámara de Representantes. Those from the Comisión Permanente de Asuntos Sociales in Costa Rica's Asamblea Legislativa were printed in San José by the Cámara de Representantes. Those from Uruguay's Comisión de Asuntos Laborales y Seguridad Social were printed in Montevideo by the Dirección General de Comisiones in the Senado. Those from the Senado de Bolivia were printed in La Paz. Those from the Cámara de Representantes in Uruguay were printed in Montevideo. Finally, the "Dictamen" of Guatemala's Comisión de Trabajo was printed in Guatemala City by the Congreso de la República de Guatemala.

INTRODUCTION

1. See the New York State Division of Human Rights brochure *Protection of Domestic Workers from Harassment Under the NYS Human Rights Law,* available at http://www.labor.ny.gov/legal/laws/pdf/domestic-workers/human-rights-trifold-domestic-workers.pdf.

2. The regional average, according to the ILO, is 16.8 percent, with figures ranging from 3.7 percent in Venezuela to 18.2 percent in Brazil and Paraguay (see table 1.1). These figures tend to include full-time workers of one employer.

3. The middle class is a broad concept, and can be defined in numerous ways. For example, the Fundacão Getulio Vargas defines the "new middle class" in Brazil according to a relatively low income floor (Classe C, in government statistics) (see Neri 2011). With this definition, over 60 percent of the Brazilian population was middle class or above by 2009, and most did not have full-time domestic workers as employees. In fact, some domestic workers in the large urban centers could themselves be classified as middle class. Occupational definitions or ones with a higher income floor narrow the size of the middle classes and exclude domestic workers from the definition. On the other hand, Portes and Hoffman (2003), in their discussion of changing class structures in Latin America, do not use "middle class" as a category. Given the differences in meaning I use terms such as "well-off" and "professionals and elites" for the rest of the analysis to characterize the sectors from which the vast majority of employers of domestic workers are drawn.

4. For a recent empirical study of intersectionality, see Ewig 2010 on health care reform in Peru.

5. Much of the extant literature on domestic workers in Latin America is sociological, anthropological, and historical. Some of the main published works are Bunster and Chaney's (1985) book on domestic workers in Peru; Chaney and Garcia Castro's (1989) edited volume on domestic workers across the region; Lauderdale Graham's (1992) historical book on nineteenth-century domestic workers in Rio de Janeiro; Lesley Gill's (1994) anthropological investigation of domestic workers and their employers in Bolivia; and, more recently, de

Santana Pinho and Silva's (2010) anthropological investigation of domestic relations in Brazil, and Valenzuela and Mora's (2009) edited volume on domestic workers in Latin America, published by the ILO. Maher and Staab (2006) and Blum (2004) have published sociological and historical journal articles, respectively. More generally, much of the social scientific literature has focused on domestic workers as immigrants who move from less to more developed countries.

6. Through the Colombian Constitutional Court.

CHAPTER 1

1. For a sample of the literature, see Daly and Lewis 2000; Esping-Andersen 1990, 1999, 2002, 2009; Fraser 1994; Gornick and Meyers 2003; Jenson 1997; Lewis 1997; K. J. Morgan 2009; O'Connor, Orloff, and Shaver 1999; Orloff 1993; Sainsbury 1994, 1996, 1999, 2008.

2. Similar options apply to elderly care.

3. The gini index is bound from zero to one; zero indicates complete equality, and one indicates that all income is received by one household.

4. Kofman (2005, 18), writing of the UK, notes that the trend of hiring foreign nannies may increase given the government's desire to keep child care costs down in general, which makes this type of work increasingly unattractive to national workers.

5. López-Calva and Lustig find that most of the decline can be attributed to a decline in labor income inequality (linked to increases in the coverage of basic education) and an increase in cash transfer programs.

6. See, for example, Díaz-Cayeros and Magaloni 2010; Filgueira 2011; Huber, Pribble, and Stephens 2009; Lindert, Skoufias, and Shapiro 2006; Martínez Franzoni and Voorend 2011.

7. See Chant 2003, chap. 8, for a theoretical discussion of women's increased labor force participation rates in Latin America.

8. Often the employer-employee relationship is between two females, given that household work is viewed as the realm of women: the female head of household, often referred to as a *patrona* in Latin America, and the domestic worker. Writing about the United States, Rollins stated in 1985 that domestic service "is unique because in no other labor arrangement is it typical for both employer and employee to be female, both members of the subordinate gender of all societies" (6–7). While this has been changing over the last quarter century, the direct female-to-female relation does tend to characterize domestic service around the world, including in Latin America.

9. See Hutchison 2001 and Salazar 2007 on some of these dynamics in nineteenth- and early twentieth-century Chile.

10. Some organizations for domestics were run by the orthodox Catholic, anti–liberation theology organization Opus Dei (e.g., in Colombia, Mexico, and Peru). These were very conservative and actually sought to serve the employers. Others were more welfarist and sought to provide for the needs of domestic workers, especially in their roles as mothers (e.g., in Uruguay). The third kind were those that became more radicalized and were linked to liberation theology (e.g., Juventud de Obreras Católicas in Mexico, Peru, and Uruguay). These groups sought to organize domestic workers and fostered more links with autonomous organizations, if they existed. In some countries, domestic workers also created autonomous organizations (see the contributions by Duarte, Goldsmith, Prates, Schellekens and Van Der Schoot, Pereira de Melo, Gálvez and Todaro, Moreno Valenzuela, and others in Chaney and Garcia Castro 1989).

11. Sindicato Nacional de Trabajadores/as del Hogar del Perú (SINTRAHOGARP), "Datos generales," http://www.sintrahogarlima.com/index.php?option=com_content&view=article&id=17&Itemid=36.

12. See the country-specific chapters in Chaney and Garcia Castro 1989 for a discussion of the working conditions of domestic workers in different Latin American countries in the 1980s.

13. ILO statistician, personal communication with author, June 20, 2011.

14. See chapter 4.

15. The percentage for Chile comes from the director of the immigrant organization Programa Andino para la Dignidad Humana (Andean Program for Human Dignity, PROANDES), interview by author, Santiago, August 10, 2006. The percentage for Costa Rica is from Martínez Franzoni, Mora, and Voorend 2010, 20.

16. See J. Anderson 2009 for an analysis of child domestics in Colombia, Paraguay, and Peru, and Human Rights Watch 2002 for an analysis of child domestics in El Salvador.

17. CEPAL and UNICEF, "Tareas domésticas no remuneradas: El dado o culto del trabajo infantil en América Latina," *Comunicados de Prensa*, 2005.

18. Mario Osava, "Pequeñas 'esclavas' del hogar," Inter-Press Service, May 5, 2003.

19. "Denuncian esclavitud entre las 1.8 millones de empleadas domésticas mexicanas," *El Periódico de México*, July 22, 2008.

20. "Que reforma diversas disposiciones de la Ley Federal del Trabajo, a cargo de la Diputada Rosario Ignacia Ortiz Magallón, del Grupo Parlamentario del PRD," *Gaceta Parlamentaria* (año 10, no. 2379-I), November 8, 2007, p. 82.

21. Sindicato Nacional de Trabajadores/as del Hogar del Perú (SINTRAHOGARP), "Propuesta programática SINTRAHOGARP: Documento de discusión," December 2008, p. 8, http://www.sintrahogarlima.com/images/leyes/propuesta_prog_th.pdf

22. Organización Panamericana de la Salud–Bolivia, "Trabajadoras del hogar son víctimas de maltrato y discriminación," *Centro de Noticias*, January 2, 2011.

23. The total number of domestic workers surveyed was 2,786, averaging about 400 per country (COMMCA 2010, 29).

24. The exception is Uruguay, which does not have a labor code per se but rather a set of laws passed over time defining the rights and obligations of workers. The practical effect of the legislation in Uruguay is similar to that in other countries—there were explicit and implicit exclusions of domestic workers from some labor rights until the 2006 legal reform.

25. The quote is from Decreto Ley 326/56, which is still in effect. The current (2011) legal reform project is discussed in chapter 2 and in the conclusion.

26. The legal reform under consideration in Argentina since 2010 would change this.

27. ILO, "Decent Work Agenda," http://www.ilo.org/global/about-the-ilo/decent-work-agenda/lang--en/index.htm.

CHAPTER 2

1. See, for example, Alvarez, Dagnino, and Escobar 1998; Blofield 2006; Escobar and Alvarez 1992; Franceschet 2005; Haas 2010; Htun 2003; Jaquette 1991, 1994; Richards 2004; Van Cott 2005; Yashar 2005.

2. See n. 47 below on the shift to the left.

3. For example, since the 1990s, political debate on abortion in many countries has moved in a more conservative direction (Blofield 2006, 2008; Haas 1999; L. M. Morgan 2011). Nicaragua, El Salvador, the Dominican Republic, and several Mexican states recently outlawed therapeutic abortion.

4. In Bolivia and Colombia, the workday for live-in domestic workers was established at ten hours, which is two hours more than for live-out domestic workers. While their legal work hours are therefore not fully equal, I categorize both as cases of full reform in the analysis since the difference is only two hours and live-in domestics do not have to spend time traveling to and from work. Of course, this legal regime may be contested at some point in the future.

5. Corte Constitucional de Colombia, Sentencia C-372/1998.
6. Corte Constitucional de Colombia, Sentencia C-310/2007.
7. Corte Constitucional de Colombia, Tutela T-552/2008.
8. Sala Constitucional de la Corte Suprema de Justicia, Resolución 3043-2007.
9. Ley 25.239, September 12, 2005.
10. Honorable Cámara de Diputados de la Nación, Mensaje 0327/10, Expediente 0001-PE-2010, Trámite Parlamentario 10, March 9, 2010. The president submitted the project on March 8, International Women's Day, and also called for a change of the title "domestic"—which, in the president's words, "refers to animals"—to "workers in private households" (*casas particulares*). See "Buscan rápida sanción del nuevo régimen para empleadas domésticas," *La Capital*, March 19, 2010; "Empleadas con más derechos," *Página12*, March 9, 2010. The legal project is not listed in table 2.1 as it is not yet law.
11. Hector Recalde, president of the Labor Commission and legislator in the Chamber of Deputies, interview by author, Buenos Aires, March 29, 2011.
12. Lei 10.208, March 23, 2001; Lei 11.324, July 19, 2006. See Sanches 2009, 126–28, for a discussion of the legislative process and the latter law.
13. Sindicato Nacional de Trabajadores/as del Hogar del Perú (SINTRAHOGARP), "Datos generales," http://www.sintrahogarlima.com/index.php?option=com_content&view=article&id=17&Itemid=36.
14. Ibid.; Congreso de Perú, legislative session 25, May 6, 2003, pp. 11–12.
15. The vote was 88 to 2.
16. Congreso de Perú, legislative session 25a, May 6, 2003, p. 11.
17. Proyecto de Ley 02911/2008-CR (Ley Que Modifica la Ley 27986, Ley de los Trabajadores del Hogar).
18. See Ministerio de Trabajo y Promoción del Empleo, "Preguntas frecuentes," http://www.mintra.gob.pe/mostrarContenido.php?id=365&tip=358.
19. Ley 666, September 22, 2008. The twelve-hour workday and one weekly day of rest remained the same, even though the Labor Code mandates an eight-hour workday and forty-eight hour workweek (Palacios, Tinoco, and Centeno 2008, 52–56). Hence, I do not classify this even as a case of partial reform. More broadly, my analysis does not include changes to child and adolescent labor laws in Latin America, which may also affect underage domestic workers.
20. Marcelina Bautista, general secretary of the Latin American and Caribbean Confederation of Domestic Workers (Confederación Latinoamericana y del Caribe de Trabajadoras del Hogar, CONLACTRAHO), interview by the International Trade Union Confederation, October 20, 2009, http://www.ituc-csi.org/primer-plano-de-marcelina-bautista.html.
21. "Que reforma diversas disposiciones de la Ley Federal del Trabajo, a cargo de la Diputada Rosario Ignacia Ortiz Magallón, del Grupo Parlamentario del PRD," *Gaceta Parlamentaria* (año 10, no. 2379-I), November 8, 2007, p. 83.
22. Cámara de Diputados, Boletín No. 0914, March 18, 2007; Judith Garcia, "Trabajo doméstico, un sector con más violaciones en derechos humanos," *El Sol de México*, March 31, 2008; "Persisten abusos contra trabajadoras domésticas en México," *El Financiero*, March 26, 2010.
23. "Trabajadoras del hogar en la indefensión," *El Universal*, March 30, 2010.
24. Guadalupe Cruz Jaimes, "Reformas para prohibir discriminación a trabajadoras del hogar," *Cimac*, April 9, 2010.
25. Guadalupe Cruz Jaimes, "A comisiones iniciativa perredista para regular trabajo doméstico," *Cimac*, April 23, 2010; Marcelina Bautista, president of CONLACTRAHO, personal communication with author, January 14, 2011.
26. Social and Economic Agreement, Article 13(e)(iv), quoted in Human Rights Watch 2002, 24.
27. Nineth Montenegro submitted the bill. Congreso de la República de Guatemala, Registro No. 1591, August 14, 1996.

28. Congreso de la República de Guatemala, Registro No. 2131, January 1, 1999; Registro No. 3243, May 31, 2005; Registro No. 3467, May 25, 2006.
29. Comisión de Trabajo, "Dictamen," October 6, 2005.
30. Corte de Constitucionalidad de la República de Guatemala, Expediente 549-2006.
31. See "El jurado y el público escogieron las decisiones ganadoras," April 16, 2009, http://uncovered.womenslinkworldwide.org/es/nominations/2009.
32. Melissa Pinel, "Empleadas domésticas: Interminable historia de poco salario y largas jornadas," *Unifem Noticias,* March 23, 2010.
33. Corte Suprema de Justicia, "Acción de inconstitucionalidad interpuesta por el Lcdo. Rafael Murgas Torraza en contra de las primeras frases del numeral 2 del Artículo 231 del Código de Trabajo," August 10, 1994, *Registro Judicial Agosto 1994,* 115–19.
34. "Gobierno proyecta mejora para empleadas domésticas," *Vistazo.com,* August 16, 2009; "Trabajadoras domésticas se informan sobre sus derechos," *El Mercurio de Cuenca,* March 24, 2010.
35. Tribunal Supremo de Justicia de Venezuela, Sala de Despacho de la Sala de Casación Social, R.I. No. AA60-S-2005-00034C, April 14, 2009.
36. Advocates of reform referred to a lack of "political will" over and over again in conversations and in newspapers and reports. Lack of political will can refer to both of these dynamics: it can be active opposition, or it can be indifference and an issue of priorities. I would like to thank Jonathan Hartlyn for this observation.
37. I would like to thank Jennifer Pribble for this observation.
38. Congreso de Perú, legislative session 25a, May 6, 2003, p. 16.
39. Senado de Bolivia, extraordinary legislative session 56, April 2, 2003, p. 25.
40. Asamblea Legislativa, Comisión Permanente de Asuntos Sociales, session 80, December 7, 1999, p. 10.
41. Comisión de Asuntos Laborales y Seguridad Social, June 30, 1997, p. 18. Also quoted by Trezza de Piñeyro 2001, 93–94.
42. Congreso de Perú, legislative session 25, May 6, 2003, p. 14.
43. Corte Suprema de Justicia, "Acción de inconstitucionalidad interpuesta por el Lcdo. Rafael Murgas Torraza en contra de las primeras frases del numeral 2 del artículo 231 del Código de Trabajo." The court also noted that the "availability" of domestic workers during their fifteen-hour day should be interpreted "with caution" (*cuidadosamente*).
44. Corte de Constitucionalidad de la República de Guatemala, Expediente 549-2006.
45. Sala Constitucional de la Corte Suprema de Justicia, Resolución 3150-1994.
46. For a discussion of the historical evolution of organized labor and its political influence in Latin America, see Collier and Collier 1991 and Schrank and Murillo 2010.
47. There is an extensive literature examining this shift to the left. See, for example, Cameron and Hershberg 2010; Filgueira et al. 2011; Natanson 2008; Roberts 2007; Weyland 2010.
48. See Haas 2010, chap. 1, for a concise discussion of the literature on feminist movements in Latin America.
49. However, women who migrate to become domestic workers in wealthier countries often can be more highly educated.
50. This point was emphasized by Marcelina Bautista, president of CONLACTRAHO, in personal communication with the author, December 17, 2010.
51. Olga Méndez, quoted in "Entre deficiencias y conflictos," *El Universo,* June 11, 2006.
52. "Qué dicen las autoridades?" *BBC Mundo,* March 16, 2006.
53. See Isaacs 2010 for a succinct overview of the flaws of Guatemala's democracy.
54. Several authors have pointed to the lower legal protections of noncitizen domestic workers and to the difficulties in enshrining minimal legal rights as well as enforcing extant rights for this group. See Kofman 2005, Piper 2004, and the discussion on immigration in chapter 1. I have also made this argument previously (Blofield 2009).

55. One study in Buenos Aires found that of the hundreds of labor complaints made by domestic workers, only one was from a non-Argentine citizen—although it is estimated that about 13 percent of domestic workers are non-Argentine (Birgin 2009). On the other hand, according to a Ministry of Labor official in Costa Rica, there is not a significant difference in the share of labor denunciations made by Nicaraguans compared to their prevalence in the domestic worker labor force overall. See chapter 4.

56. Karin Pape, coordinator of the International Domestic Workers' Network, Skype interview by author, June 20, 2011.

57. Ibid. For more information, see the website of the International Domestic Workers' Network, http://www.domesticworkerrights.org/.

58. See IADB 2006 for a discussion of the role of the executive regionwide. See Haas 2010 on the executive and women's rights in Chile, and Siavelis 2000 on Chile.

59. Marcelina Bautista, personal communication, December 17, 2010.

60. SINTRAHOGARP, "Datos generales."

61. This may be due to the fact that judges can be more shielded from public criticism and are not electorally accountable; however, this is speculation and more research is required to examine this claim in the case of Latin American countries.

CHAPTER 3

1. The Colombian Constitutional Court rulings affirming domestic workers' right to unemployment insurance in 2007 and social security in 2008 may have encouraged higher social security rates among domestic workers since then, but this remains to be seen.

2. Silvana Silveira, "'Just Like a Daughter'—Until You Exert Your Rights," Inter-Press Service, June 8, 2009.

3. "Tomada: Esta norma ayudará a blanquera a trabajadores," *Diario Norte,* March 9, 2010.

4. "Menos del 1% de las empleadas domésticas cuenta con cobertura social,"
La Hora, April 19, 2010.

5. "Demandan asegurar a trabajadores domésticos en Honduras," *La Gente,* March 15, 2007.

6. Roberto Fonseca, "Trabajadoras domésticas siguen marginadas en INSS," *Confidencial,* no. 697, April 25–May 1, 2010.

7. Bendeck 2004; "Concederán seguridad médica a empleadas domésticas en El Salvador," *Nacion.com,* April 30, 2010.

8. The total number of domestic workers surveyed was 2,786, averaging about 400 per country (COMMCA 2010, 29).

9. These surveys included several hundred women in each country, but it is not clear how the data were collected, so this should be kept in mind when assessing the results.

10. Diego Rubinzal, "Blanquer a la mucama," *Página12,* July 9, 2006.

11. Legislative bill submitted to Congress. See "Que reforma diversas disposiciones de la Ley Federal del Trabajo, a cargo de la Diputada Rosario Ignacia Ortiz Magallón, del Grupo Parlamentario del PRD," *Gaceta Parlamentaria* (año 10, no. 2379-I), November 8, 2007, p. 81.

12. Sindicato Nacional de Trabajadores/as del Hogar del Perú (SINTRAHOGARP), "Propuesta programática SINTRAHOGARP: Documento de discusión," December 2008, p. 9, http://www.sintrahogarlima.com/images/leyes/propuesta_prog_th.pdf.

13. See Schrank and Piore 2007 for a discussion of the "Latin model" in labor law enforcement.

14. Such capacity can be assessed by resources—inspectors per worker—as well as the number of inspections and their "proactive" and "reactive" nature; see Schrank and Piore 2007. See also Schrank 2009 for an excellent study of labor law enforcement in the Dominican Republic.

15. Birgin also found that of the one hundred complaints she analyzed, only one was made by a non-Argentine domestic worker—a Peruvian with permanent residency. On the other hand, 13 percent of domestic workers in Argentina are foreigners (and this percentage could be higher in Buenos Aires), indicating that non-Argentines may be less likely to file complaints (Ministerio de Trabajo, Empleo y Seguridad Social 2005, 180).

16. For Paraguay, see López, Soto, and Valiente 2005, 205–8.

17. See Collier and Collier 1991; Filgueira 1998, 2011; Martínez Franzoni and Voorend 2009; Pribble 2011; Rueschemeyer, Stephens, and Stephens 1992; Schrank and Piore 2007; Segura-Ubiergo 2007.

18. Here I have focused on the political factors that influence enforcement. Sociological factors, such as the regionwide increase in female-headed households, may also have played a role in incentivizing domestic workers to register for social security (ILO 2010a, 57–58; Valenzuela and Mora 2009a).

19. Ley 25.239, September 12, 2005.

20. *Editora El Sol*, January 4, 2006

21. Lei 11.324, July 19, 2006.

22. "Salario de domésticas crea debate tras su alza," *El Universo*, January 7, 2010. An increase over the national minimum wage raised fears even among some leaders of the domestic workers' organizations that it could increase unemployment.

23. "Empleadas domésticas exigen afiliación al IESS," *El Universo*, June 11, 2009.

24. Sindicato Nacional de Trabajadores/as del Hogar del Perú (SINTRAHOGARP), "Derechos laborales de las y los trabajadores del hogar," December 2008, p. 8, http://www.sintrahogarlima.com/images/leyes/derecho_laboral_th.pdf.

25. Decreto Supremo 015-2003-TR (Reglamento de la Ley de los Trabajadores del Hogar), November 11, 2003. See also SINTRAHOGARP, "Derechos laborales de las y los trabajadores del hogar," pp. 8–9.

26. SINTRAHOGARP, "Propuesta programática SINTRAHOGARP: Documento de discusión," p. 9.

27. Ibid., p. 14.

28. Corte Constitucional de Colombia, Tutela T-552/2008. The case referred to a domestic worker who had worked for the same family for twenty-seven years without the legal minimum wage, with seventeen-hour workdays, and without adequate social security registration. When her employers fired her in 2003, they promised to pay her pension. The promise was neglected, and the court ruled in favor of the worker.

29. Guadalupe Cruz Jaimes, "Condiciones adversas para Mexicanas en el trabajo doméstico," *Cimac*, January 8, 2010.

30. Guadalupe Cruz Jaimes, "Reformas para prohibir discriminación a trabajadoras del hogar," *Cimac*, April 9, 2010.

31. "Concederán seguridad médica a empleadas domésticas en El Salvador," *Nacion.com*, April 30, 2010.

CHAPTER 4

1. Rodríguez went on to head the regional confederation and then served as minister of justice in 2006. Basilia Catari, domestic worker and former president of FENATRAHOB, interview by author, La Paz, July 24, 2006; L. Gill 1994, chap. 7.

2. Catari, interview by author; L. Gill 1994.

3. Lisette Dávalos, researcher at Fundación Ebert, interview by author, La Paz, July 25, 2006; leaders of FENATRAHOB, interviews by author, La Paz, July 24, 2006; CONLACTRAHO 2003, 17.

4. Elizabeth Peredo, president of Fundación Solón, quoted in FENATRAHOB, TAHIPAMU, and Fundación Solón 1998, 29.

5. Legislator Clara Flores, quoted in ibid., 37.

6. Dávalos, interview by author; Betty Pinto, Defensoría del Pueblo (Ombudsman's Office), interview by author, La Paz, July 26, 2006; Fundación Solón 2001a; Fundación Solón 2001b, 41; Cook 2007; L. Gill 1994, chap. 7.

7. Plenary debates are not transcribed and are unavailable.

8. Mabel Cruz, MIR deputy from 1998 to 2002, interview by author, La Paz, July 19, 2006.

9. See, for instance, journalist Gloria Luz Eyzaguirre in FENATRAHOB, TAHIPAMU, and Fundación Solón 1998, 22.

10. Cruz, interview by author.

11. One senator told Brockman that if domestic workers are given more rights, they will "get educated; they'll be ungrateful and leave." Erika Brockman, former senator for MIR (1997–2002) and feminist activist, interview by author, La Paz, July 16, 2006.

12. Quoted in Fundación Solón 2001a, 15.

13. Waldo Albarracín, Asamblea Permanente de Derechos Humanos de Bolivia, quoted in ibid., 25, 27.

14. Ana María Romero de Campero, quoted in ibid., 9.

15. Brockman, interview by author.

16. Senado de Bolivia, extraordinary legislative session 56a, April 2, 2003, pp. 3, 10, 21–25.

17. Ibid., 25.

18. Official at the Dirección del Empleo, Ministry of Labor, interview by author, La Paz, October 15, 2008.

19. Official at the Defensoría del Pueblo, interview by author, La Paz, October 18, 2008.

20. Miguelina Colque, president of FENATRAHOB, interview by author, La Paz, October 20, 2008; official at the Dirección del Empleo, interview by author.

21. Colque, interview by author.

22. Official at the Dirección del Empleo, interview by author.

23. Ruth Barrón, director of the Unidad de Derechos Fundamentales (Unit of Fundamental Rights), Ministry of Labor, interview by author, La Paz, October 16, 2008.

24. "Trabajo se alarma por sueldos de empleadas y anuncia sanciones," *La Prensa*, November 15, 2010.

25. Organización Panamericana de la Salud–Bolivia, "Trabajadoras del hogar son víctimas de maltrato y discriminación," *Centro de Noticias*, January 2, 2011.

26. Dávalos, interview by author.

27. Draft of the Proyecto Decreto Supremo, October 2008. Colque, interview by author; Betty Pinto, interview by author, La Paz, October 17, 2008.

28. Director of immigration and employment, Ministry of Labor, interview by author, San José, October 2, 2008.

29. The survey was not published until 2004. It surveyed 314 domestic workers and was funded by the ILO and conducted by the Domestic Workers' Association (Asociación de Trabajadoras Domésticas, ASTRADOMES). It encompassed Costa Rica's central region, which includes the capital city and most of the country's population. Twenty percent of the respondents were Nicaraguan. The publication does not indicate how the sample was collected, so any findings must be taken with caution.

30. The sample consisted of 250 domestic workers.

31. Sala Constitucional de la Corte Suprema de Justicia, Resolución 3150-1994 and Resolución 3043-2007. There was another ruling relevant to domestic workers—and wage laborers in general—in 1993. The Constitutional Court ruled that workers could reclaim compensation for the violation of their labor rights after the labor relation with employers was over. The

specific case was that of a domestic worker who had worked for one man for twenty-seven years without ever receiving a salary or any benefits (only food and lodging). The court ruled that the employer owed her all of the back pay and benefits (Martínez Franzoni, Mora, and Voorend 2010, 51–52).

32. Rosita Acosta, president of ASTRADOMES, interview by author, San José, October 2, 2008.

33. Sala Constitucional de la Corte Suprema de Justicia, Resolución 3150-1994.

34. Asamblea Legislativa, Expediente 13.413, p. 25.

35. Virginia Aguiluz, Asamblea Legislativa, Comisión Permanente de Asuntos Sociales, act 33, August 10, 1999, p. 12.

36. Ibid.

37. Asamblea Legislativa, Comisión Permanente de Asuntos Sociales, session 80, December 7, 1999, p. 10.

38. Ibid., pp. 10–11. Also cited in Martínez Franzoni, Mora, and Voorend 2010, 49.

39. Asamblea Legislativa, Comisión Permanente de Asuntos Sociales, session 80, December 7, 1999, p. 11.

40. Ibid., pp. 15–16.

41. Asamblea Legislativa, Comisión Permanente de Asuntos Sociales, session 85, February 8, 2000, pp. 4–6.

42. Ibid., pp. 8–13. Víctor Morales Mora was the minister of labor and Sandra Piszk the ombudswoman.

43. Joycelyn Sawyers, ibid., pp. 9–11.

44. Marisol Clachar, ibid., p. 15.

45. Graciela Cruz, Asamblea Legislativa, Comisión Permanente de Asuntos Sociales, session 86, February 8, 2000, p. 4.

46. Asamblea Legislativa, Comisión Permanente de Asuntos Sociales, session 87, February 9, 2000, pp. 5–9.

47. Esmeralda Britton González, president of INAMU, "Criterio emitido sobre el Proyecto de Ley No. 15.417 (Reforma del Capítulo VIII del Código de Trabajo)," June 8, 2004.

48. Peter Guevara, Asamblea Legislativa, Comisión Permanente de Asuntos Sociales, "Dictamen negativo de minoria, Expediente 15.417 (Reforma del Capítulo VIII del Código de Trabajo)," December 13, 2004.

49. Sala Constitucional de la Corte Suprema de Justicia, Resolución 3043-2007.

50. Acosta, interview by author; official at the Ministry of Labor, interview by author, San José, October 2, 2008.

51. Acosta, interview by author; Sandra Arce, legislative assistant to Movimiento Libertario, interview by author, San José, October 2, 2008; Ana Helena Chacón, PAC deputy, interview by author, San José, October 1, 2008.

52. Chacón, interview by author.

53. Official at INAMU, interview by author, San José, October 3, 2008.

54. Carlos Gutiérrez, Movimiento Libertario deputy, interview by author, San José, October 6, 2008.

55. In civil society, ASTRADOMES has been quite successful in reaching Nicaraguans; according to Acosta, more Nicaraguans than Costa Ricans come to its meetings and workshops.

56. "Para que legislar para unas nicas que no votan?" Arce, interview by author; Chacón, interview by author; Patricia Romero, PAC deputy, interview by author, San José, October 6, 2008.

57. Romero, interview by author.

58. I was a personal witness to this. While I was in the halls of Congress interviewing Patricia Romero on October 6, 2008, she spotted the president of the plenary and decided to

make strategic use of my presence. She pulled him over and introduced me as an academic at a U.S. university "who is writing a book about how backward Costa Rica is on domestic workers' rights." She exhorted him to consider Costa Rica's reputation on human rights and reminded him yet again of the need to get the domestic worker bill on the agenda. He smiled and said, "We'll see."

59. Ley 8726 (Reforma del Capítulo Octavo del Título Segundo de Código de Trabajo, Ley 2, Ley del Trabajo Doméstico Remunerado), February 2, 2009.

60. Official at the Ministry of Labor, interview by author.

61. Director of immigration and employment, interview by author.

62. Officials at the Ministry of Labor, interview by author, San José, October 2, 2008; official at INAMU, interview by author.

CHAPTER 5

1. The term "basic universalism" was coined by Filgueira and his co-authors (see Filgueira et al. 2006 and Molina 2006) and refers to developing social protection for all citizens on essential services and a set of transfers. Tokman (2006) and Huber (2006) extend the concept to employment and social security. Here I use the concept slightly more broadly to denote the effort of Uruguay's government to provide domestic workers with access to social security as well as equal rights. On general political differences between Chile and Uruguay, see Luna 2006 and Pribble 2011.

2. Decreto 611/1980.

3. Lawyer and official at the Ministry of Labor and member of the tripartite subcommission, interview by author, Montevideo, August 18, 2008.

4. The decline is probably related to the 2001 economic crisis in Argentina, which had significant spillover effects in Uruguay.

5. Poder Legislativo de la República Oriental del Uruguay, Proyecto de Ley, Asunto no. 81062.

6. Cristina Otero, leader of the SUTD, interview by author, Montevideo, August 18, 2008.

7. Sonia Martínez, a leader of the Plenario Intersindical de Trabajadores–Convención Nacional de Trabajadores (PIT-CNT), interviewed in "Se conforma el Sindicato de Trabajadoras Domésticas," *Diario El País,* April 19, 2005.

8. Ofelia Ogara, PIT-CNT union official responsible for gender issues, interview by author, Montevideo, August 19, 2008.

9. The commission debates are unavailable.

10. Cámara de Representantes, October 8, 1996, pp. 49–50.

11. Ibid., p. 52.

12. Cámara de Representantes, October 9, 1996, p. 22.

13. Ibid., pp. 19–23.

14. Cámara de Representantes, October 8, 1996, p. 53.

15. Comisión de Asuntos Laborales y Seguridad Social, June 30, 1997, p. 18. Also quoted by Trezza de Piñeyro 2001, 93–94.

16. Comisión de Asuntos Laborales y Seguridad Social, September 8, 1997, pp. 22–23.

17. Comisión de Asuntos Laborales y Seguridad Social, July 7, 1997, p. 17.

18. Comisión de Asuntos Laborales y Seguridad Social, September 8, 1997, p. 24.

19. Comisión de Asuntos Laborales y Seguridad Social, June 28, 1999, p. 13.

20. Comisión de Asuntos Laborales y Seguridad Social, September 8, 1997, p. 17.

21. Comisión de Asuntos Laborales y Seguridad Social, August 11, 1997, p. 19; September 8, 1997, p. 20.

22. Comisión de Asuntos Laborales y Seguridad Social, July 7, 1997, p. 13.

23. Comisión de Asuntos Laborales y Seguridad Social, June 28, 1999, p. 22.

24. Comisión de Asuntos Laborales y Seguridad Social, June 21, 1999, p. 15.
25. Comisión de Asuntos Laborales y Seguridad Social, June 28, 1999, pp. 16, 23.
26. Comisión de Asuntos Laborales y Seguridad Social, June 21, 1999, pp. 4–6.
27. Jorge Gandini, Comisión de Asuntos Laborales y Seguridad Social, June 29, 1999, p. 14.
28. Edgardo Carvalho, Comisión de Asuntos Laborales y Seguridad Social, June 28, 1999, p. 13.
29. Marina Arismendi, ibid., pp. 16–17.
30. Comisión de Asuntos Laborales y Seguridad Social, July 26, 1999, p. 3.
31. Comisión de Asuntos Laborales y Seguridad Social, October 12, 2000.
32. Ogara, interview by author.
33. Martínez interview in "Se conforma el Sindicato de Trabajadoras Domésticas."
34. "Ministerio de Trabajo convocara a públicos y privados para negociación colectiva," *La Republica*, March 4, 2005.
35. Ogara, interview by author.
36. Otero, interview by author.
37. Silvana Silveira, "'Just Like a Daughter'—Until You Exert Your Rights," Inter-Press Service, June 8, 2009.
38. Official at the Instituto Nacional de las Mujeres (Women's Executive Agency, INAMU) and member of the tripartite subcommission, interview by author, Montevideo, August 15, 2008.
39. Ibid.
40. Lawyer and official at the Ministry of Labor, interview by author.
41. Ley 18.065, November 27, 2006. This law does not apply to rural domestic workers, as there is another law that covers rural workers. Marta Marquez, law professor at the Universidad de la República, interview by author, Montevideo, August 15, 2008. For an analysis of the legal implications of the law in the Uruguayan context, see Trezza de Piñeyro 2006.
42. Ariel Ferrari, in "Empleadas domésticas negociarán condiciones laborales en Consejos de Salarios," *El Espectador*, March 6, 2006.
43. In Uruguay, workers pay 15 percent and employers pay 7.5 percent of social security contributions.
44. Ariel Ferrari, director of the BFS, interview by author, Montevideo, August 20, 2008.
45. Silveira, "'Just Like a Daughter'"
46. Otero, interview by author.
47. "Costó pero salió: Acuerdo salarial en grupo de servicio doméstico," *La Diaria*, December 20, 2010.
48. Silveira, "'Just Like a Daughter.'"
49. During a 2008 legal reform, legislators constantly referred to 14.3 percent of the economically active female population, based on the same government household survey (CASEN 2006, cited in Ministerio del Trabajo y Previsión Social 2008). It is unclear why this discrepancy exists. The ILO data for 2009 is 10.8 percent (see table 1.1).
50. Official at the Servicio Nacional de la Mujer (Women's Executive Agency, SERNAM), interview by author, Santiago, August 12, 2006.
51. Results from a study of three thousand domestic workers conducted by Rosario Corcoll, reported in "Quieren nana las 24 horas," *BBC Mundo*, August 1, 2006.
52. Maria Antonieta Saa, legislator for the Partido por la Democracia (Party for Democracy, PPD), interview by author, Santiago, August 10, 2006.
53. Aida Moreno, former president of SINTRACAP and longtime activist, interview by author, Santiago, August 14, 2006. By this time, Rodríguez's untimely death meant that advocates of domestic workers' rights had lost their ally in the Chamber.
54. José Ruiz de Giorgio, former PDC senator (1990–2006), interview by author, Valparaíso, August 3, 2008.

55. Ibid.

56. Ibid.

57. See SINTRACAP 1992. This was evident at the meeting of domestic workers' organizations, the Primer Congreso Nacional de Trabajadoras de Casa Particular, held in Santiago on August 12–15, 2000.

58. In recent years, and especially in 2011, student protests have rocked the country.

59. Official at the Labor Relations Office (Dirección del Trabajo), Ministry of Labor, interview by author, Santiago, August 5, 2008.

60. Official at the Social Security Institute (Instituto de Previsión Social), interview by author, Santiago, August 2, 2008.

61. Maria Gloria Fernández, president of ANECAP, interview by author, Santiago, August 10, 2006; Elena Urrutia, president of SINTRACAP, interview by author, Santiago, August 6, 2006. For example, the president of SINTRACAP noted that she could only engage in union-related activities on Sundays, as she worked during the rest of the week, and pointed out that it was hard to call legislators on a Sunday.

62. For example, the Mapuche, constituting only 4 percent of the population, do not have national political representation in representative bodies; the government has somewhat half-heartedly set up national commissions instead (Richards 2004).

63. Maher and Staab (2006) argue that the elites prefer Peruvians because they consider them more submissive.

64. The director of the immigrant organization Programa Andino para la Dignidad Humana (Andean Program for Human Dignity, PROANDES) estimated that only around 4 percent of domestic workers in Chile are of Andean origin. However, 86 percent of these 4 percent work in the two most upper-class districts in Santiago (Las Condes and Vitacura), creating a popular and media-fostered perception of a "Peruvian takeover" there. Interview by author, Santiago, August 10, 2006.

65. Moreno, interview by author; gender specialist at the Ministry of Labor, interview by author, Santiago, July 29, 2008.

66. Moreno, interview by author.

67. In 1991, the center-left government set up SERNAM, which has become important in drafting and implementing legislation on many women's rights issues (Franceschet 2005; Haas 2010).

68. Gender specialist at the Ministry of Labor, interview by author; Ley 20.279, July 1, 2008.

69. Gender specialist at the Ministry of Labor, interview by author.

70. See ANECAP, "Carta a los candidatos(as) a la Presidencia de la República, al Senado y a la Cámara de Diputados," Santiago, November 24, 2005.

71. Saa, interview by author.

72. Official at the Labor Relations Office, interview by author.

73. Official at the Ministry of Labor, interview by author, Santiago, August 12, 2006.

74. Official at the Labor Relations Office, interview by author.

75. Official at the Social Security Institute (Instituto de Previsión Social), interview by author, Santiago, August 4, 2008.

76. Dirección del Trabajo, "Actividades campaña de capacitación y diffusion: Trabajadoras de casa particular," unpublished program, Ministry of Labor, Santiago, 2008.

77. Ibid.

CONCLUSION

1. Karin Pape, coordinator of the International Domestic Workers' Network, Skype interview by author, June 20, 2011.

2. Ibid.

3. IDWN 2010; ILO 2011a; Pape, interview by author.

4. Pape, interview by author.

5. Restrictions on work hours raised opposition especially from the national employers' associations. In this context, the comments of the Employers' Confederation of the Dominican Republic (Confederación Patronal de la República Dominicana, COPARDOM) stand out. The association opposed the article guaranteeing the right of domestic workers to leave their employer's residence during their time off, as it is "inappropriate considering the nature of the work. Domestic workers must be required to stay in the household during their rest periods to ensure, for example, that children under their care are not left unattended" (ILO 2011a, 43). Even during rest periods, domestic workers should "not leave the household, except under special authorized leave" (47).

6. International Labour Conference, "Final Record Vote on the Adoption of the Convention Concerning Decent Work for Domestic Workers," Provisional Record, 100th session, Geneva.

7. International Labour Conference, "Text of the Convention Concerning Decent Work for Domestic Workers," Provisional Record, 100th session, Geneva.

8. Pape, interview by author.

9. Ministerio de Justicia y Trabajo, "Viceministerio del Trabajo plantea ratificación del convenio de la OIT que protege a trabajadoras domésticas," *Gacetilla Oficial*, August 3, 2011.

10. Dr. Marta Roncoroni, official at the Argentine domestic workers' union UPAPC (Unión Personal Auxiliar de Casas Particulares), personal communication with author, April 5, 2011.

11. Hector Recalde, president of the Labor Commission and legislator in the Chamber of Deputies, interview by author, Buenos Aires, March 29, 2011; official in the tripartite commission of the Ministry of Labor, interview by author, Buenos Aires, March 28, 2011.

12. See, for example, Alexei Barricnuevo, "Upwardly Mobile Nannies Move into the Brazilian Middle Class," *New York Times*, May 19, 2011; Manuela Noguiera, "Domésticas passam a apitar as regras do jogo," *VEJA São Paulo*, May 11, 2011.

13. This point was also made by Nora Goren of the Centro de Mujer y Trabajo, interview by author, Buenos Aires, March 27, 2011.

References

Abramo, Laís, and María Elena Valenzuela. 2005. "Women's Labour Force Participation Rates in Latin America." *International Labour Review* 144 (4): 369–40:.
Albó, Xavier. 2002. "Bolivia: From Indian and Campesino Leaders to Councillors and Parliamentary Deputies." In *Multiculturalism in Latin America: Indigenous Rights, Diversity, and Democracy*, edited by Rachel Sieder, 74–102. New York: Palgrave Macmillan.
Alvarez, Sonia E. 1990. *Engendering Democracy in Brazil: Women's Movements in Transition Politics*. Princeton, N.J.: Princeton University Press.
Alvarez, Sonia E., Evelina Dagnino, and Arturo Escobar, eds. 1998. *Cultures of Politics, Politics of Cultures: Re-visioning Latin American Social Movements*. Boulder, Colo.: Westview Press.
Amarante, Verónica, and Alma Espino. 2007. "Situación del servicio doméstico en Uruguay." In *Uruguay: Ampliando las oportunidades laborales para las mujeres*, 60–83. Montevideo: Instituto Nacional de las Mujeres (INAMU) and Banco Mundial.
Anderson, Bridget. 2000. *Doing the Dirty Work? The Global Politics of Domestic Labour*. London: Zed Books.
Anderson, Jeanine. 2009. "Invertir en la familia: Factores preventivos y de vulnerabilidad frente al trabajo infantil doméstico en familias rurales y urbanas de Colombia, Paraguay y Perú." In Valenzuela and Mora 2009, 233–60.
ASTRADOMES (Asociación de Trabajadoras Domésticas). 2004. *Humanizando el trabajo doméstico: Hacer visible lo invisible. La realidad de las trabajadoras del hogar en América Latina y el Caribe: Costa Rica*. San José: ASTRADOMES.
Bachrach, Peter, and Morton S. Baratz. 1970. *Power and Poverty: Theory and Practice*. New York: Oxford University Press.
Baldez, Lisa. 2002. *Why Women Protest: Women's Movements in Chile*. New York: Cambridge University Press.
Barbagelata, Héctor Hugo. 2004. *Derecho del trabajo*. Vol. 2, *Especialidades y modalidades de los contratos de trabajo*. 2nd ed. Montevideo: Fundación de Cultura Universitaria.
Barrett, Patrick S. 2001. "Labour Policy, Labour-Business Relations, and the Transition to Democracy in Chile." *Journal of Latin American Studies* 33 (3): 561–97.
Bartley, Tim. 2003. "Certifying Forests and Factories: States, Social Movements, and the Rise of Private Regulation in the Apparel and Forest Products Fields." *Politics and Society* 31 (3): 433–64.
Bellman, Mary J. 2004. "Rationalism and Identity in the Participation Choices of Female Maquila Workers." *Comparative Political Studies* 37 (5): 563–89.
Bendeck, Xochitl. 2004. *Análisis legislativo sobre trabajo doméstico en El Salvador y propuesta de reforma legislativa*. El Salvador: Corte Suprema de Justicia, Centro de Documentación Judicial.
Bernardino-Costa, Joaze. 2007. "Sindicatos das trabalhadoras domésticas no Brasil: Teorias da descolonização e saberes subalternos." Ph.D. diss., Universidade de Brasília.

Biblioteca del Congreso Nacional de Chile. 1997. *Historia de la ley. Ley 19010 (D. Oficial 20 de noviembre 1990). Terminación de contrato y estabilidad en el empleo.* Valparaíso, Chile: Biblioteca del Congreso Nacional de Chile.
———. 1998. *Historia de la ley. Ley 19591 (D. Oficial 9 de noviembre 1998). Modifica el Código del Trabajo en material de protección a la maternidad.* Valparaíso, Chile: Biblioteca del Congreso Nacional de Chile.
———. 2009. *Historia de la ley. Ley 20336 (D. Oficial 3 de abril 2009). Modifica el Artículo 150 del Código del Trabajo, relativo al descanso semanal de los trabajadores de casa particular.* Valparaíso, Chile: Biblioteca del Congreso Nacional de Chile.
Birgin, Haydee. 2009. "Sin acceso a la justicia: El caso de las trabajadoras domésticas en Argentina." In Valenzuela and Mora 2009, 261–84.
Blofield, Merike. 2006. *The Politics of Moral Sin: Abortion and Divorce in Spain, Chile, and Argentina.* New York: Routledge.
———. 2008. "Women's Choices in Comparative Perspective: Abortion Policies in Late-Developing Catholic Countries." *Comparative Politics* 41 (4): 399–419.
———. 2009. "Feudal Enclaves and Political Reforms: Domestic Workers in Latin America." *Latin American Research Review* 44 (1): 158–90.
———. 2011a. "Conclusion: Inequality and the Politics of Redistribution." In Blofield 2011c, 377–90.
———. 2011b. "Desigualdad y política en América Latina." *Journal of Democracy en Español* 3 (July): 58–74.
———, ed. 2011c. *The Great Gap: Inequality and the Politics of Redistribution in Latin America.* University Park: Pennsylvania State University Press.
———. 2011d. "Introduction: Inequality and Politics in Latin America." In Blofield 2011c, 1–18.
Blofield, Merike, and Liesl Haas. 2005. "Defining a Democracy: Reforming the Laws on Women's Rights in Chile, 1990–2002." *Latin American Politics and Society* 47 (3): 35–68.
———. 2011. "Gender Equality Policies in Latin America." In Blofield 2011c, 278–309.
Blofield, Merike, and Juan Pablo Luna. 2011. "Public Opinion on Income Inequalities in Latin America." In Blofield 2011c, 147–81.
Blum, Ann S. 2004. "Cleaning the Revolutionary Household: Domestic Servants and Public Welfare in Mexico City, 1900–1935." *Journal of Women's History* 15 (4): 67–90.
Boeninger, Edgardo. 1997. *Democracia en Chile: Lecciones para la gobernabilidad.* Santiago: Editorial Andres Bello.
Boserup, Ester. 1970. *Woman's Role in Economic Development.* New York: St. Martin's Press.
Brysk, Alison. 2000. *From Tribal Village to Global Village: Indian Rights and International Relations in Latin America.* Stanford: Stanford University Press.
Bunster, Ximena, and Elsa M. Chaney. 1985. *Sellers and Servants: Working Women in Lima, Peru.* New York: Praeger.
Cameron, Maxwell A., and Eric Hershberg, eds. 2010. *Latin America's Left Turns: Politics, Policies, and Trajectories of Change.* Boulder, Colo.: Lynne Rienner.
Campello, Daniela. 2011. "The Politics of Redistribution in Less Developed Democracies: Evidence from Brazil, Ecuador, and Venezuela." In Blofield 2011c, 185–216.
Carnes, Matthew Edward. 2008. "The Politics of Labor Regulation in Latin America." Ph.D. diss., Stanford University.
Castiglioni, Rossana. 2005. *The Politics of Social Policy Change in Chile and Uruguay: Retrenchment Versus Maintenance, 1973–1998.* New York: Routledge.
Castillo, G., and A. Orsatti, eds. 2005. *Trabajo informal y sindicalismo en América Latina y el Caribe: Buenas prácticas formativas y organizativas.* Montevideo: CINTERFOR, OIT.

CBDHDD (Capítulo Boliviano de Derechos Humanos, Democracia y Desarrollo) and CDH (Comunidad de Derechos Humanos). 2005. *Estado de situación de los derechos económicos, sociales y culturales en Bolivia al año 2005*. La Paz: CBDHDD and CDH.

CEMyT (Centro de Mujer y Trabajo). 2010. *Situación del trabajo en casas particulares: Hacia el reconocimiento de los derechos laborales*. Informe No. 2. Buenos Aires: CEMyT.

Centeno, Miguel Angel, and Alejandro Portes. 2006. "The Informal Economy in the Shadow of the State." In *Out of the Shadows: Political Action and the Informal Economy in Latin America*, edited by Patricia Fernández-Kelly and Jon Shefner, 23–48. University Park: Pennsylvania State University Press.

Centro Nacional para el Desarrollo de la Mujer y la Familia. 1997. "El servicio doméstico en Costa Rica. Cuaderno de investigación no 1." Unpublished manuscript, San José.

CEPAL (Comisión Económica para América Latina y el Caribe). 2009. *Panorama social de América Latina*. Santiago: CEPAL.

Ceriani, Pablo, Corina Courtis, María Inés Pacecca, Pablo Asa, and Laura Pautassi. 2009. "Migración y trabajo doméstico en Argentina: Las precariedades en el marco global." In Valenzuela and Mora 2009, 147–90.

Chaney, Elsa M., and Mary Garcia Castro, eds. 1989. *Muchachas No More: Household Workers in Latin America and the Caribbean*. Philadelphia: Temple University Press.

Chang, Grace. 2000. *Disposable Domestics? Immigrant Women Workers in the Global Economy*. Cambridge, Mass.: South End Press.

Chant, Sylvia. 2003. *Gender in Latin America*. With Nikki Craske. New Brunswick: Rutgers University Press.

Cheng, Shu-Ju Ada. 2006. *Serving the Household and the Nation: Filipina Domestics and the Politics of Identity in Taiwan*. New York: Lexington Books.

Choque, Claudia. 2003. "Los retos para las trabajadoras del hogar." In *Mujeres en la Coyuntura Nacional* (conference proceedings), 73–81. La Paz: Articulación de Mujeres por la Equidad y la Igualdad (AMUPEI).

Collier, Ruth Berins, and David Collier. 1991. *Shaping the Political Arena: Critical Junctures, the Labor Movement, and Regime Dynamics in Latin America*. Princeton, N.J.: Princeton University Press.

COMMCA (Consejo de Ministras de la Mujer de Centroamérica). 2008. *Informe nacional: El trabajo doméstico remunerado en Guatemala*. Guatemala City: COMMCA, Agenda Económica de las Mujeres.

———. 2010. *La institucionalización sociocultural y jurídica de la desigualdad: El trabajo doméstico remunerado. Estudio regional de Centroamérica y República Dominicana*. La Libertad, El Salvador: COMMCA. Available at http://www.sica.int/commca.

CONLACTRAHO (Confederación Latinoamericana y del Caribe de Trabajadoras del Hogar). 2003. *Las condiciones de vida de las trabajadoras del hogar de la ciudad de La Paz, Bolivia*. La Paz: Organización Internacional del Trabajo.

———. 2004. *Humanizando el trabajo doméstico: Hacer visible lo invisible. La realidad de las trabajadoras del hogar en América Latina y el Caribe: Bolivia, Brasil, Costa Rica, Guatemala, México, Perú y República Dominicana*. Santiago: Alerce Talleres Gráficos.

Constable, Nicole. 2007. *Maid to Order in Hong Kong: Stories of Migrant Workers*. 2nd ed. Ithaca, N.Y.: Cornell University Press.

Cook, Maria Lorena. 2007. *The Politics of Labor Reform in Latin America: Between Flexibility and Rights*. University Park: Pennsylvania State University Press.

Coser, Lewis A. 1973. "Servants: The Obsolescence of an Occupational Role." *Social Forces* 52 (1): 31–39.

Daly, Mary, and Jane Lewis. 2000. "The Concept of Social Care and the Analysis of Contemporary Welfare States." *British Journal of Sociology* 51 (2): 281–98.

Defensa de Niñas y Niños Internacional–Sección Bolivia. 2004. *De criadas a obreras.* Cochabamba: Defensa de Niñas y Niños Internacional.
Defensoría del Pueblo. 2004. *Memoria: Derechos laborales de las trabajadoras del hogar.* La Paz: Encuentro Nacional con Jueces Laborales, Directores e Inspectores de Trabajo.
de Santana Pinho, Patricia, and Elizabeth B. Silva. 2010. "Domestic Relations in Brazil: Legacies and Horizons." *Latin American Research Review* 45 (2): 90–113.
de Soto, Hernando. 2000. *The Mystery of Capital: Why Capitalism Triumphs in the West and Fails Everywhere Else.* New York: Basic Books.
Díaz-Cayeros, Alberto, and Beatriz Magaloni. 2010. "La ayuda para los pobres de América Latina." *Journal of Democracy en Español* 2 (July): 185–200.
Dion, Michelle. 2010. *Workers and Welfare: Comparative Institutional Change in Twentieth-Century Mexico.* Pittsburgh, Pa.: Pittsburgh University Press.
Domínguez, Jorge I., and Alejandro Poiré. 1999. *Toward Mexico's Democratization: Parties, Campaigns, Elections, and Public Opinion.* London: Routledge.
Drake, Paul W., and Ivan Jakšić. 1999. *El modelo chileno.* Santiago: LOM Ediciones.
Duarte, Isis. 1989. "Household Workers in the Dominican Republic: A Question for the Feminist Movement." In Chaney and Garcia Castro 1989, 197–220.
Ermida Uriarte, Oscar. 2009. "La política laboral de los gobiernos progresistas, el posneoliberalismo y el movimiento syndical." In *Diálogo movimiento sindical—gobiernos progresistas: Un primer balance de las políticas progresistas en la región,* 35–54. Montevideo: Fundación Friedrich Ebert Stiftung.
Escobar, Arturo, and Sonia E. Alvarez, eds. 1992. *The Making of Social Movements in Latin America: Identity, Strategy, and Democracy.* Boulder, Colo.: Westview Press.
Esping-Andersen, Gøsta. 1990. *The Three Worlds of Welfare Capitalism.* Princeton, N.J.: Princeton University Press.
———. 1999. *The Social Foundations of Postindustrial Economies.* Oxford: Oxford University Press.
———. 2002. *Why We Need a New Welfare State.* With Duncan Gallie, Anton Hemerijck, and John Myles. New York: Oxford University Press.
———. 2009. *The Incomplete Revolution: Adapting to Women's New Roles.* Malden, Mass.: Polity Press.
Esquivel, Valeria. 2010. "Care Workers in Argentina: At the Crossroads of Labour Market Institutions and Care Services." *International Labour Review* 149 (4): 477–93.
Estévez, Alejandro M., and Susana C. Esper. 2009. "La relación entre el sistema impositivo y la desigualdad: El papel de la Administración Tributaria en la cohesión social." Working Paper 19, Observatory on Inequality in Latin America, University of Miami. Available at http://www.observatoryla.org/observatoryla/about/paper-series.
Ewig, Christina. 2010. *Second-Wave Neoliberalism: Gender, Race, and Health Sector Reform in Peru.* University Park: Pennsylvania State University Press.
FENATRAHOB (Federación Nacional de las Trabajadoras del Hogar de Bolivia), TAHIPAMU (Taller de Historia y Participación de la Mujer), and Fundación Solón. 1998. *Una Ley para las Trabajadoras del Hogar. 1998.* La Paz: FENATRAHOB, TAHIPAMU, Fundación Solón.
Fernández-Kelly, Patricia, and Jon Shefner. 2006. *Out of the Shadows: Political Action and Informal Economy in Latin America.* University Park: Pennsylvania State University Press.
Ferreira, Francisco H. G., and Martin Ravallion. 2008. "Global Poverty and Inequality: A Review of the Evidence." Policy Research Working Paper 4623, World Bank Development Research Group.
Filgueira, Fernando. 1998. "El nuevo modelo de prestaciones sociales en América Latina: Residualismo, eficiencia y ciudadanía estratificada." In *Ciudadanía y políticas sociales,* edited by Brian Roberts, 32–73. San José: FLACSO and SSRC.

———. 2011. "Fault Lines in Latin American Social Development and Welfare Regime Challenges." In Blofield 2011c, 21–57.
Filgueira, Fernando, Carlos Gerardo Molina, Jorge Papadópulos, and Federico Tobar. 2006. "Universalismo básico: Una alternativa posible y necesaria para mejorar las condiciones de vida." In Molina 2006, 19–58.
Filgueira, Fernando, Luis Reygadas, Juan Pablo Luna, and Pablo Alegre. 2011. "Shallow States, Deep Inequalities, and the Limits of Conservative Modernization: The Politics and Policies of Incorporation in Latin America." In Blofield 2011c, 245–77.
Fish, Jennifer Natalie. 2006. *Domestic Democracy: At Home in South Africa*. New York: Routledge.
Franceschet, Susan. 2005. *Women and Politics in Chile*. Boulder, Colo.: Lynne Rienner.
Franceschet, Susan, and Jennifer Piscopo. 2008. "Gender Quotas and Women's Substantive Representation: Lessons from Argentina." *Politics and Gender* 4 (3): 393–425.
Fraser, Nancy. 1994. "After the Family Wage: Gender Equity and the Welfare State." *Political Theory* 22 (4): 591–618.
Fuentes, Claudio. 2005. *Contesting the Iron Fist: Advocacy Networks and Police Violence in Democratic Argentina and Chile*. New York: Routledge.
Fundación Paniamor. 2002. *El trabajo infantil y adolescente doméstico en Costa Rica . . . yo no trabajo sólo ayudo!* San José: Oficina Internacional del Trabajo.
Fundación Solón. 2001a. *Memoria de la presentación del video "Para Sumar Derechos" (la lucha de las trabajadoras del hogar en Bolivia)*. La Paz: Fundación Solón.
———. 2001b. *Perspectivas de acción en la lucha de las trabajadoras del hogar por el derecho a la igualdad*. La Paz: Fundación Solón.
Gálvez, Thelma, and Rosalba Todaro. 1984. "Las trabajadoras de casa particular en la década 1970–1980: Empleo y características." Documento de Trabajo No. 2, Ediciones Centro de Estudios de la Mujer, Santiago.
———. 1989. "Housework for Pay in Chile: Not Just Another Job." In Chaney and Garcia Castro 1989, 307–22.
Gamson, William A. 1992. *Talking Politics*. New York: Cambridge University Press.
Garretón, Manuel Antonio. 2003. *Incomplete Democracy: Political Democratization in Chile and Latin America*. Chapel Hill: University of North Carolina Press.
Gaviria, Alejandro. 2007. "Social Mobility and Preferences for Redistribution in Latin America." *Economía* 8 (1): 55–96.
Gerring, John. 2007. *Case Study Research: Principles and Practices*. New York: Cambridge University Press.
Gill, Indermit S., Claudio E. Montenegro, and Dörte Dömeland. 2002. *Crafting Labor Policy: Techniques and Lessons from Latin America*. Washington, D.C.: World Bank; New York: Oxford University Press.
Gill, Lesley. 1994. *Precarious Dependencies: Gender, Class, and Domestic Service in Bolivia*. New York: Columbia University Press.
Godinho Delgado, Didice. 2007. "Sindicalismo y género: Experiencias y desafíos de la Central Única de los Trabajadores de Brasil." *Nueva Sociedad* 21:160–76.
Goertz, Gary, and Amy G. Mazur. 2008. *Politics, Gender, and Concepts*. New York: Cambridge University Press.
Goldsmith, Mary. 1989. "Politics and Programs of Domestic Workers' Organizations in Mexico." In Chaney and Garcia Castro 1989, 221–44.
Goñi, Edwin J., Humberto López, and Luis Servén. 2008. "Fiscal Redistribution and Income Inequality in Latin America." Policy Research Working Paper 4487, World Bank Development Research Group.
González de la Rocha, Mercedes. 2006. "Vanishing Assets: Cumulative Disadvantages Among the Urban Poor." In *Out of the Shadows*, edited by Patricia Fernández-Kelly and Jon Shefner, 97–124. University Park: Pennsylvania State University Press.

Gornick, Janet C., and Marcia K. Meyers. 2003. *Families that Work.* New York: Russell Sage Foundation.

Graham, Sandra Lauderdale. 1992. *House and Street: The Domestic World of Servants and Masters in Nineteenth-Century Rio de Janeiro.* Austin: University of Texas Press.

Gregson, Nicky, and Michelle Lowe. 1994. *Servicing the Middle Classes: Class, Gender, and Waged Domestic Labour in Contemporary Britain.* London: Routledge.

Guerrero, Elsa, Claribeth Terán, Claudia Tijerino, and Martha Mairena. 1993. *La empleada doméstica en Nicaragua: ¡Solo lava, cocina y limpia!* [Managua?]: Centro de Estudios y Analisis Socio-Laborales.

Haas, Liesl. 1999. "The Catholic Church in Chile: New Political Alliances." In *Latin American Religion in Motion,* edited by Christian Smith and Joshua Prokopy, 42–65. New York: Routledge.

———. 2010. *Feminist Policymaking in Chile.* University Park: Pennsylvania State University Press.

Heymann, Jody. 2006. *Forgotten Families: Ending the Growing Crisis Confronting Children and Working Parents in the Global Economy.* New York: Oxford University Press.

Hite, Amy Bellone, and Jocelyn S. Viterna. 2005. "Gendering Class in Latin America: How Women Effect and Experience Change in the Class Structure." *Latin American Research Review* 40 (2): 50–82.

Hondagneu-Sotelo, Pierrette. 2001. *Doméstica: Immigrant Workers Cleaning and Caring in the Shadows of Affluence.* Berkeley: University of California Press.

Htun, Mala N. 2003. *Sex and the State: Abortion, Divorce, and the Family Under Latin American Dictatorships and Democracies.* New York: Cambridge University Press.

———. 2004. "Is Gender Like Ethnicity? The Political Representation of Identity Groups." *Perspectives on Politics* 2 (3): 439–58.

Htun, Mala N., and Laurel Weldon. 2010a. "International Norms on Women's Human Rights: The Personal Becomes the International." Paper prepared for presentation to the American Political Science Association, Washington, D.C., August 20.

———. 2010b. "When Do Governments Promote Women's Rights? A Framework for the Comparative Analysis of Sex Equality Policy." *Perspectives on Politics* 8 (1): 207–16.

Huber, Evelyne. 2006. "Un nuevo enfoque para la seguridad social en la región." In Molina 2006, 169–88.

Huber, Evelyne, Jennifer Pribble, and John D. Stephens. 2009. "The Politics of Effective and Sustainable Redistribution." In *Stuck in the Middle: Is Fiscal Policy Failing the Middle Class?* edited by Antonio Estache and Danny Leipziger, 155–88. Washington, D.C.: Brookings Institution Press.

Huber, Evelyne, and John D. Stephens. 2001. *Development and Crisis of the Welfare State: Parties and Policies in Global Markets.* Chicago: University of Chicago Press.

Human Rights Watch. 2002. *From the Household to the Factory: Sex Discrimination in the Guatemalan Labor Force.* New York: Human Rights Watch.

———. 2004. *No Rest: Abuses Against Child Domestic Workers in El Salvador.* Vol. 16, no. 1 (B). New York: Human Rights Watch.

———. 2006. *Swept Under the Rug: Abuses Against Domestic Workers Around the World.* Vol. 18, no. 7 (C). New York: Human Rights Watch.

Hutchison, Elizabeth Quay. 2001. *Labors Appropriate to Their Sex: Gender, Labor, and Politics in Urban Chile, 1900–1930.* Durham: Duke University Press.

IADB (Inter-American Development Bank). 2006. *The Politics of Policies: Economic and Social Progress in Latin America.* Washington, D.C.: IADB; Cambridge, Mass.: David Rockefeller Center for Latin American Studies, Harvard University.

———. 2008. *Outsiders? The Changing Patterns of Exclusion in Latin America and the Caribbean.* Washington, D.C.: IADB.

IDWN (International Domestic Workers' Network). 2010. *Platform of Demands*. Prepared for the International Labour Conference, 99th sess., 2010. Geneva: International Union of Food, Agricultural, Hotel, Restaurant, Catering, Tobacco, and Allied Workers' Associations (IUF).
ILO (International Labour Organization). 2010a. *Decent Work for Domestic Workers*. International Labour Conference, 99th sess., 2010. Report IV (1). Geneva: International Labour Office.
———. 2010b. *Decent Work for Domestic Workers*. International Labour Conference, 99th sess., 2010. Report IV (2). Geneva: International Labour Office.
———. 2011a. *Decent Work for Domestic Workers*. International Labour Conference, 100th sess., 2011. Report IV (2a). Geneva: International Labour Office.
———. 2011b. *Decent Work for Domestic Workers*. International Labour Conference, 100th sess., 2011. Report IV (2b). Geneva: International Labour Office
INAMU (Instituto Nacional de las Mujeres). 2007. *Informe acerca de la aplicación de la Convención sobre la Eliminación de Todas las Formas de Discriminación contra la Mujer*. Montevideo: Ministerio de Desarrollo Social de la República Oriental de Uruguay.
IRENE (International Restructuring Education Network Europe) and IUF (International Union of Food, Agricultural Hotel, Restaurant, Catering, Tobacco, and Allied Workers' Associations). 2008. *Respect and Rights: Protection for Domestic/Household Workers!* Report of the international conference, Amsterdam, November 8–10, 2006. Tilburg, Netherlands: IRENE; Geneva: IUF. Available at http://www.domesticworkerrights.org/sites/en.domesticworkerrights.org/files/ENGtextRaR.pdf.
Isaacs, Anita. 2010. "Guatemala on the Brink." *Journal of Democracy* 21 (2): 108–22.
Jaquette, Jane, ed. 1991. *The Women's Movement in Latin America: Feminism and the Transition to Democracy*. Boulder, Colo.: Westview Press.
———, ed. 1994. *The Women's Movement in Latin America: Participation and Democracy*. 2nd ed. Boulder, Colo.: Westview Press.
Jelin, Elizabeth. 1977. "Migration and Labor Force Participation of Latin American Women: The Domestic Servants in the Cities." *Signs* 3 (1): 129–41.
Jenson, Jane. 1997. "Who Cares? Gender and Welfare Regimes." *Social Politics* 4 (2): 182–87.
Jiménez Mira, Alexis M., and Juan A. Parodi Macías. 2003. *La mujer y el contrato de trabajador de casa particular: Una visión actual*. Memoria de prueba, Licenciatura en Ciencias Jurídicas y Sociales. Santiago: Universidad de Chile.
Jones, Mark P. 1997. "Legislator Gender and Legislator Policy Priorities in the Argentine Chamber of Deputies and the United States House of Representatives." *Policy Studies Journal* 25 (4): 613–29.
Karl, Terry Lynn. 2000. "Economic Inequality and Democratic Instability." *Journal of Democracy* 11 (1): 149–56.
Kingdon, John W. 1995. *Agendas, Alternatives, and Public Policies*. 2nd ed. New York: HarperCollins.
Kitschelt, Herbert, Kirk A. Hawkins, Juan Pablo Luna, Guillermo Rosas, and Elizabeth J. Zechmeister. 2010. *Latin American Party Systems*. Cambridge: Cambridge University Press.
Kofman, Eleonore. 2005. "Citizenship, Migration, and the Reassertion of National Identity." *Citizenship Studies* 9 (5): 453–67.
Kuznesof, Elizabeth. 1989. "A History of Domestic Service in Spanish America, 1492–1980." In Chaney and Garcia Castro 1989, 17–36.
Lan, Pei-Chi. 2006. *Global Cinderellas: Migrant Domestics and Newly Rich Employers in Taiwan*. Durham: Duke University Press.
Langer, Erick D., ed. 2003. *Contemporary Indigenous Movements in Latin America*. With Elena Muñoz. Wilmington, Del.: Scholarly Resources.

Laurie, Nina, Robert Andolina, and Sarah Radcliffe. 2002. "The Excluded 'Indigenous'? The Implications of Multi-ethnic Policies for Water Reform in Bolivia." In *Multiculturalism in Latin America: Indigenous Rights, Diversity, and Democracy*, edited by Rachel Sieder, 252–76. New York: Palgrave Macmillan.

Levitsky, Steven. 2003. *Transforming Labor-Based Parties in Latin America: Argentine Peronism in Comparative Perspective*. New York: Cambridge University Press.

Lewis, Jane. 1997. "Gender and Welfare Regimes: Further Thoughts." *Social Politics* 4 (2): 160–77.

Lindert, K., E. Skoufias, and J. Shapiro. 2006. *Redistributing Income to the Poor and the Rich*. Washington, D.C.: World Bank.

López, Verónica, Lilian Soto, and Hugo Valiente. 2005. *Trabajo doméstico remunerado en Paraguay*. Lima: Oficina Internacional del Trabajo.

López-Calva, Luis F., and Nora Lustig, eds. 2010. *Declining Inequality in Latin America: A Decade of Progress?* Baltimore: Brookings Institution Press and the United Nations Development Programme.

Loyo, María Gabriela, and Mario D. Velásquez. 2009. "Aspectos jurídicos y económicos del trabajo doméstico remunerado en América Latina." In Valenzuela and Mora 2009, 21–70.

Luna, Juan Pablo. 2006. "Programmatic and Non-Programmatic Party-Voter Linkages in Two Institutionalized Party Systems: Chile and Uruguay in Comparative Perspective." Ph.D. diss., University of North Carolina at Chapel Hill.

Madalozzo, Regina, and Adriana Bortoluzzo. 2010. "The Impact of Tax Exemptions on Labor Registration: The Case of Brazilian Domestic Workers." Insper Working Paper WPE-232. Available at http://www.insper.edu.br/working-papers/2011/the-impact-of-tax-exemptions-on-labor-registration-the-case-of-brazilian-domestic-workers.

Madrid, Raúl L. 2005. "Indigenous Parties and Democracy in Latin America." *Latin American Politics and Society* 47 (4): 161–79.

Maher, Kristen Hill, and Silke Staab. 2006. "The Dual Discourse About Peruvian Domestic Workers in Santiago de Chile: Class, Gender, and a Nationalist Project." *Latin American Politics and Society* 48 (1): 87–116.

Mahon, James E., Jr. 2011. "Tax Reforms and Income Distribution in Latin America." In Blofield 2011c, 313–47.

Martínez Franzoni, Juliana. 2008. "Welfare Regimes in Latin America: Capturing Constellations of Markets, Families, and Policies." *Latin American Politics and Society* 50 (2): 67–100.

Martínez Franzoni, Juliana, Sindy Mora, and Koen Voorend. 2010. *El trabajo doméstico remunerado en Costa Rica: Entre ocupación y pilar de los cuidados*. San José: AGEM, UNIFEM, AECID, COMMCA, and SICA.

Martínez Franzoni, Juliana, and Koen Voorend. 2009. "Sistemas de patriarcado y regímenes de bienestar en América Latina: ¿Una cosa lleva a la otra?" Documento de Trabajo No. 27, Fundación Carolina, Madrid.

———. 2011. "Are Coalitions Equally Important for Redistribution in Latin America? The Intervening Role of Welfare Regimes." In Blofield 2011c, 348–75.

McAdam, Doug, John D. McCarthy, and Mayer N. Zald, eds. 1996. *Comparative Perspectives on Social Movements: Political Opportunities, Mobilizing Structures, and Cultural Framings*. New York: Cambridge University Press.

McAdam, Doug, Sidney Tarrow, and Charles Tilly. 2001. *Dynamics of Contention*. Cambridge: Cambridge University Press.

Ministerio de la Protección Social, República de Colombia. 2009. *Cartilla del servicio doméstico*. Bogotá: Ministerio de la Protección Social. Available at http://www.minproteccionsocial.gov.co/Documentos%20y%20Publicaciones/CARTILLA%20SERVICIO%20DOMESTICO.pdf.

Ministerio del Trabajo y Previsión Social de Chile. 2008. *Trabajadoras de casa particular.* Santiago: Ministerio del Trabajo y Previsión Social, Departamento de Estudios.

Ministerio de Trabajo, Empleo y Seguridad Social de Argentina. 2005. *Situación laboral del servicio doméstico en la Argentina.* Buenos Aires: Ministerio de Trabajo, Empleo y Seguridad Social, Subsecretaria de Programación Técnica y Estudios Laborales.

———. 2010. "Comisión Tripartita de Igualdad de Trato y Oportunidades entre Varones y Mujeres en el Mundo Laboral—Argentina. Encuentros regionales por la igualdad y la inclusión. Revalorización del trabajo doméstico en Argentina." Unpublished government document, Buenos Aires.

Mohanty, Chandra Talpade. 2003. "'Under Western Eyes' Revisited: Feminist Solidarity Through Anticapitalist Struggles." *Signs* 28 (2): 499–535.

Molina, Carlos Gerardo, ed. 2006. *Universalismo básico: Una nueva política social para América Latina.* Washington, D.C.: Inter-American Development Bank.

Montaño Virreira, Sonia. 2010. "El cuidado en acción." In *El cuidado en acción: Entre el derecho y el trabajo,* edited by Montaño and Coral Calderón Magaña, 13–68. Santiago, Chile: CEPAL.

Moreno Valenzuela, Aida. 1989. "History of the Household Workers' Movement in Chile, 1926–1983." In Chaney and Garcia Castro 1989, 407–16.

Morgan, Kimberly J. 2009. "Caring Time Policies in Western Europe: Trends and Implications." *Comparative European Politics* 7 (1): 37–55.

Morgan, Lynn M. 2011. "Claiming Rosa Parks: Strategic Secularism and Human Rights in Latin America." Paper presented at the international conference Global Flows, Human Rights, Sexual, and Reproductive Health: Ethnographies of Institutional Change in the Global South, University of Sussex, July 2011. Available at http://www.sxpolitics.org/wp-content/uploads/2009/02/morgan-claiming-rosa-parks-sussex-short-version.pdf.

Natanson, José. 2008. *La nueva izquierda: Triunfos y derrotas de los gobiernos de Argentina, Brasil, Bolivia, Venezuela, Chile, Uruguay y Ecuador.* Buenos Aires: Editorial Sudamericana.

Neri, Marcelo. 2011. *Os Emergentes dos Emergentes: Reflexões Globais e Ações Locais para a Nova Classe Média Brasileira.* Rio de Janeiro: Fundação Getulio Vargas.

Nett, Emily M. 1966. "The Servant Class in a Developing Country: Ecuador." *Journal of Interamerican Studies* 8 (3): 437–52.

O'Connor, Julia S., Ann Shola Orloff, and Sheila Shaver. 1999. *States, Markets, Families: Gender, Liberalism, and Social Policy in Australia, Canada, Great Britain, and the United States.* New York: Cambridge University Press.

O'Donnell, Guillermo. 1994. "Delegative Democracy." *Journal of Democracy* 5 (4): 55–69.

OIT (Oficina Internacional del Trabajo). 2007. *Panorama laboral 2007: América Latina y el Caribe.* Lima: OIT.

———. 2009. *Panorama laboral 2009: América Latina y el Caribe.* Lima: OIT.

———. 2010. *Panorama laboral 2010: América Latina y el Caribe.* Lima OIT.

Orloff, Ann Shola. 1993. "Gender and the Social Rights of Citizenship: The Comparative Analysis of State Policies and Gender Relations." *American Sociological Review* 58 (3): 303–28.

Orsatti, Alvaro. 2011. "Organización de trabajadoras del hogar." In *Procesos de autoreforma sindical en las Américas,* 74–85. São Paulo: Confederación Sindical de Trabajadores y Trabajadoras de las Américas. Available at http://www.csa-csi.org/index.php?option=com_content&view=section&id=38&Itemid=274&lang=es.

Oxhorn, Philip. 1995. *Organizing Civil Society: The Popular Sectors and the Struggle for Democracy in Chile.* University Park: Pennsylvania State University Press.

Palacios N., Martha C., Gilma Y. Tinoco F., and Rebeca D. Centeno O. 2008. *La institucionalización sociocultural y jurídica de la desigualdad: El trabajo doméstico remunerado*

en Nicaragua. Managua: Consejo de Ministras de la Mujer de Centroamérica, Agenda Económica de las Mujeres.
Pateman, Carole. 1989. *The Disorder of Women: Democracy, Feminism, and Political Theory.* Cambridge: Polity Press.
Pautassi, Laura C., Eleonor Faur, and Natalia Gherardi. 2004. *Legislación laboral en seis países latinoamericanos: Avances y omisiones para una mayor equidad.* Santiago: CEPAL, Unidad Mujer y Desarrollo.
Peñaranda Davezies, Katrina, Álvaro Fernando Arandia Davezies, and Ximena Flores Castro. 2005. *Con preferencia cholita: Representaciones sociales de la trabajadora del hogar asalariada en Sucre.* La Paz: Fundación PIEB.
Pereira, Milena, and Hugo Valiente. 2007. *Regímenes jurídicos sobre trabajo doméstico remunerado en los estados del Mercosur.* Montevideo: Cotidiano Mujer, Oxfam.
Pereira de Melo, Hildete. 1989. "Feminists and Domestic Workers in Rio de Janeiro." In Chaney and Garcia Castro 1989, 245–70.
Piper, Nicola. 2004. "Rights of Foreign Workers and the Politics of Migration in South-East and East Asia." *International Migration* 42 (5): 71–97.
Piven, Frances Fox, and Richard A. Cloward. 1977. *Poor People's Movements: Why They Succeed, How They Fail.* New York: Pantheon.
Portes, Alejandro, and Kelly Hoffman. 2003. "Latin American Class Structures: Their Composition and Change During the Neoliberal Era." *Latin American Research Review* 38 (1): 41–82.
Posner, Paul. 2008. *State, Market, and Democracy in Chile: The Constraint of Popular Participation.* New York: Palgrave Macmillan.
Postero, Nancy Grey, and Leon Zamosc, eds. 2004. *The Struggle for Indigenous Rights in Latin America.* Portland, Ore.: Sussex Academic Press.
Prates, Suzana. 1989. "Organizations for Domestic Workers in Montevideo: Reinforcing Marginality?" In Chaney and Garcia Castro 1989, 271–90.
Pribble, Jennifer. 2011. "Political Parties and Welfare Politics in Latin America: Between Elites and the Masses." Unpublished manuscript.
Razavi, Shahra, and Silke Staab. 2010. "Underpaid and Overworked: A Cross-national Perspective on Care Workers." *International Labour Review* 149 (4): 407–22.
Richards, Patricia. 2004. *Pobladoras, Indígenas, and the State: Conflicts over Women's Rights in Chile.* New Brunswick: Rutgers University Press.
Roberts, Kenneth M. 2002. "Social Inequalities Without Class Cleavages in Latin America's Neoliberal Era." *Studies in Comparative International Development* 36 (Winter): 3–33.
———. 2007. "Repoliticizing Latin America: The Revival of Populist and Leftist Alternatives." *Woodrow Wilson Center Update on the Americas,* November.
Rodgers, Janine. 2009. "Cambios en el servicio doméstico en América Latina." In Valenzuela and Mora 2009, 71–114.
Rodríguez, Casimira, and Aída Moreno. 2005. "CONLACTRAJO. La construcción de una estrategia de laborización de las trabajadoras del hogar." In *Trabajo informal y sindicalismo en América Latina y el Caribe: Buenas practicas formativas y organizativas,* edited by G. Castillo and A. Orsatti, 99–109. Montevideo: CINTERFOR, OIT.
Rodríguez, Victoria E. 2003. *Women in Contemporary Mexican Politics.* Austin: University of Texas Press.
Rodríguez-Garavito, César A. 2005. "Global Governance and Labor Rights: Codes of Conduct and Anti-sweatshop Struggles in Global Apparel Factories in Mexico and Guatemala." *Politics and Society* 33 (2): 203–33.
Rollins, Judith. 1985. *Between Women: Domestics and Their Employers.* Philadelphia: Temple University Press.

Rubbo, Anna, and Michael Taussig. 1983. "Up Off Their Knees: Servanthood in Southwest Colombia." *Latin American Perspectives* 10 (4): 5–23.
Rueschemeyer, Dietrich, Evelyne Huber Stephens, and John D. Stephens. 1992. *Capitalist Development and Democracy.* Chicago: University of Chicago Press.
Sainsbury, Diane, ed. 1994. *Gendering Welfare States.* London: Sage.
———. 1996. *Gender, Equality, and Welfare States.* New York: Cambridge University Press.
———, ed. 1999. *Gender and Welfare State Regimes.* New York: Oxford University Press.
———. 2008. "Gendering the Welfare State." In Goertz and Mazur 2008, 94–113.
Salazar, Gabriel. 2007. *Ser niño "huacho" en la historia de Chile.* Santiago: Lom Ediciones.
Salazar Parreñas, Rhacel. 2001. *Servants of Globalization: Women, Migration, and Domestic Work.* Stanford: Stanford University Press.
Sanches, Solange. 2009. "El trabajo doméstico en Brasil." In Valenzuela and Mora 2009, 115–46.
Scartascini, Carlos, Ernesto Stein, and Mariano Tommasi, eds. 2010. *How Democracy Works: Political Institutions, Arenas, and Actors in Latin American Policymaking.* Washington, D.C.: Inter-American Development Bank.
Schellekens, Thea, and Anja Van Der Schoot. 1989. "Household Workers in Peru: The Difficult Road to Organization." In Chaney and Garcia Castro 1989, 291–306.
Schrank, Andrew. 2009. "Professionalization and Probity in a Patrimonial State: Labor Inspectors in the Dominican Republic." *Latin American Politics and Society* 51 (2): 91–114.
Schrank, Andrew, and Victoria Murillo. 2005. "With a Little Help from My Friends: Partisan Politics, Transnational Alliances, and Labor Rights in Latin America." *Comparative Political Studies* 38 (8): 971–99.
———. 2010. "Labour Unions in the Policymaking Process in Latin America." In *How Democracy Works: Political Institutions, Arenas, and Actors in Latin American Policymaking,* edited by Carlos Scartascini, Ernesto Stein, and Mariano Tommasi, 247–68. Washington, D.C.: Inter-American Development Bank.
Schrank, Andrew, and Michael Piore. 2007. *Norms, Regulations, and Labor Standards in Central America.* Serie estudios y perspectivas 77. Mexico City: Sede Subregional de la CEPAL.
Schwindt-Bayer, Leslie A. 2006. "Still Supermadres? Gender and the Policy Priority of Latin American Legislators." *American Journal of Political Science* 50 (3): 570–85.
———. 2010. *Political Power and Women's Representation in Latin America.* New York: Oxford University Press.
Secretaria de Políticas para as Mulheres. 2011. "Trabalho Doméstico." Relatório do grupo de trabalho. Brasília: Presidênica da República do Brasil. April.
Segura-Ubiergo, Alex. 2007. *The Political Economy of the Welfare State in Latin America: Globalization, Democracy, and Development.* Cambridge: Cambridge University Press.
Siavelis, Peter M. 2000. *The President and Congress in Post-authoritarian Chile: Institutional Constraints to Democratic Consolidation.* University Park: Pennsylvania State University Press.
———. 2009. "Enclaves de la transicion y democracia chilena." *Revista de Ciencia Política* 29 (1): 3–21.
Sieder, Rachel, ed. 2002. *Multiculturalism in Latin America: Indigenous Rights, Diversity, and Democracy.* New York: Palgrave Macmillan.
Sindicato de Trabajadoras del Hogar. 1982. *Basta: Testimonios.* Cusco: Centro de Estudios Rurales Andinos "Bartolomé de Las Casas."
SINTRACAP (Sindicato de Trabajadoras de Casas Particulares). 1985. *Cuadernillo de antecedentes históricos de Sintracap, Area Metropolitana.* Santiago: SINTRACAP.
———. 1992. *Resumen ejecutivo: Realidad de las trabajadoras de casa particular en Chile.* Santiago: Servicios Investigaciones y Estudios Economico-Sociales.

Smith, Christian, and Joshua Prokopy, eds. 1999. *Latin American Religion in Motion*. New York: Routledge.
Stefoni E., Carolina. 2003. *Inmigración peruana en Chile: Una oportunidad a la integración*. Santiago: FLACSO.
———. 2009. "Migración, género y servicio doméstico: Mujeres peruanas en Chile." In Valenzuela and Mora 2009, 191–232.
Stetson, Dorothy McBride, and Amy Mazur, eds. 1995. *Comparative State Feminism*. London: Sage.
Stevenson, Linda S. 1999. "Gender Politics in the Mexican Democratization Process." In *Toward Mexico's Democratization: Parties, Campaigns, Elections, and Public Opinion*, edited by Jorge I. Domínguez and Alejandro Poiré, 57–87. London: Routledge.
Strolovitch, Dara Z. 2006. "Do Interest Groups Represent the Disadvantaged? Advocacy at the Intersections of Race, Class, and Gender." *Journal of Politics* 68 (4): 894–910.
Tarrow, Sidney G. 1994. *Power in Movement: Social Movements, Collective Action, and Politics*. New York: Cambridge University Press.
Todaro, Rosalba, and Thelma Gálvez. 1987. *Trabajo doméstico remunerado: Conceptos, hechos, datos*. Santiago: Centro de Estudios de la Mujer.
Tokman, Victor E. 2006. "Empleo y protección: Una vinculación necesaria." In Molina 2006, 115–68.
———. 2010. "Domestic Workers in Latin America: Statistics for New Policies." Paper prepared at the request of the International Union of Food, Agricultural, Hotel, Restaurant, Catering, Tobacco, and Allied Workers' Associations (IUF) and Women in the Informal Economy: Globalizing and Organizing (WIEGO). Available at http://www.wiego.org/pdf/Tokman-Domestic-Workers-Latin-America.pdf.
Trezza de Piñeyro, Alicia. 2001. *La relación de trabajo doméstico*. Montevideo: Facultad de Derecho, Universidad de la República.
———. 2006. "La Ley No 18 065 de Trabajo Doméstico y sus logros." *Derecho Laboral* 49 (224): 954–69.
UNDP (United Nations Development Programme) and ILO (International Labour Organization). 2009. *Trabajo y família: Hacia nuevas formas de conciliación con corresponsabilidad social*. Geneva: UNDP and ILO.
UNESCO (United Nations Educational, Scientific, and Cultural Organization). 2006. *Policy Review Report: Early Childhood Care and Education in Brazil*. Paris: UNESCO.
———. 2007. *Strong Foundations: Early Childhood Education and Care*. Paris: UNESCO.
———. 2010. *Early Childhood Education and Care Regional Report: Latin America and the Caribbean*. Report prepared for the World Conference on Early Childhood Care and Education, Moscow, September 2010. Santiago: UNESCO.
United Nations. 2007–8. *Human Development Report*. New York: United Nations.
United Nations Economic and Social Council. 2001. *Observaciones finales del Comité de Derechos Económicos, Sociales y Culturales: Bolivia*. E/C.12/1/Add.60. Geneva: United Nations Economic and Social Council.
Valenzuela, Maria Elena, and Claudia Mora. 2009a. "Esfuerzos concertados para la revaloración del trabajo doméstico remunerado en América Latina." In Valenzuela and Mora 2009b, 285–304.
———, eds. 2009b. *Trabajo doméstico: Un largo camino hacia el trabajo decente*. Santiago: Organización Internacional del Trabajo.
Van Cott, Donna Lee. 2000. "Party System Development and Indigenous Populations in Latin America: The Bolivian Case." *Party Politics* 6 (2): 155–74.
———. 2003. "From Exclusion to Inclusion: Bolivia's 2002 Election." *Journal of Latin American Studies* 34 (4): 751–75.

———. 2005. *From Movements to Parties in Latin America: The Evolution of Ethnic Politics.* New York: Cambridge University Press.

Wachendorfer, Achim. 2007. "¿Hacia una nueva arquitectura sindical en América Latina?" *Nueva Sociedad* 211:32–49.

Warren, Kay B., and Jean E. Jackson, eds. 2002. *Indigenous Movements, Self-Representation, and the State in Latin America.* Austin: University of Texas Press.

Weisberg, D. Kelly. 1996a. "Rape: Introduction." In *Applications of Feminist Legal Theory to Women's Lives: Sex, Violence, Work, and Reproduction,* edited by D. Kelly Weisburg, 405–13. Philadelphia: Temple University Press.

———. 1996b. "Violence: Introduction." In *Applications of Feminist Legal Theory to Women's Lives: Sex, Violence, Work, and Reproduction,* edited by D. Kelly Weisburg, 277–85. Philadelphia: Temple University Press.

Weldon, Laurel. 2002a. "Beyond Bodies: Institutional Sources of Representation for Women in Democratic Policymaking." *Journal of Politics* 64 (4): 1153–74.

———. 2002b. *Protest, Policy, and the Problem of Violence Against Women: A Cross-National Comparison.* Pittsburgh: University of Pittsburgh Press.

———. 2008. "The Concept of Intersectionality." In *Politics, Gender, and Concepts,* edited by Gary Goertz and Amy G. Mazur, 193–218. New York: Cambridge University Press.

Weyland, Kurt, ed. 2010. *Leftist Governments in Latin America.* New York: Cambridge University Press.

Yashar, Deborah. 2005. *Contesting Citizenship: The Rise of Indigenous Movements and the Postliberal Challenge.* New York: Cambridge University Press.

Index

Page numbers followed by "t" refer to tables; those followed by "n" refer to notes, with note number.

absent parenting, in immigrant domestic workers, 15
Acción Democrática Nacional (ADN), 85
Acosta, Rosita, 59, 96, 97, 98, 101, 104
ACTRAV. *See* Bureau for Workers' Activities
ADN. *See* Acción Democrática Nacional
agenda-setting, visibility of issue and, 40, 56–57, 59–60, 64, 131–32, 136
   in Bolivia, 86–90
   in Chile, 122–27
   in Costa Rica, 96–103
   in Uruguay, 109–16
age of domestic workers, 25–26. *See also* children as domestic workers
Alianza de Mujeres Costarricenses, 97
Alianza por Chile, 120
Allende, Salvador, 120
allies of domestic workers' organizations
   in Bolivia, 86–90
   in Chile, 122–27
   in Costa Rica, 96–103
   and enforcement of labor laws, 78
   as key to success, 56, 131–32
   potential allies, 59–64
   strategies for, 63–67
   in Uruguay, 109–16
amenities and household spaces, restrictions for domestic workers, 29
ANECAP. *See* Asociación Nacional de Empleadas de Casa Particular
Argentina
   enforcement of labor laws in, 76, 138
   exploitative working conditions for domestic workers in, 74
   immigrant domestic workers in, 13, 25
   laws on domestic worker rights, 3, 31, 32t
   legal reform efforts, 42, 42t, 43–44, 57, 130
      executive support, 43–44, 55, 79
      ILO convention and, 135
      immigrant workers and, 62
      political context, 54, 55
      women's rights organizations and, 60
   live-in domestic workers, percentage of, 27
   maternity leave laws, 31
   minimum wage laws, 31
   percentage of women employed in domestic work, 24, 24t
   social security enrollment for domestic workers, 70, 71t, 72–73
   vacation days for domestic workers, 30
   workday length laws, 29–30, 29t, 43–44
Arias, Óscar, 93, 96, 102, 103
Asociación Nacional de Empleadas de Casa Particular (ANECAP), 109–10, 122, 124–25, 126
Associación de Trabajadoras Domésticos (ASTRADOMES), 96, 97, 98
Aylwin, Patricio, 121

Bachelet, Michelle, 55, 80, 121, 125, 126, 127, 128
Barahona Streber, Oscar, 21–22
basic univeralism, in Uruguay, 106, 152 n. 1
Batlle y Ordóñez, José, 108
benefits. *See* laws on domestic work
Birgin, Haydee, 76
Black February, 89–90
Blanco Party, 108
Bolivia, 83–92
   and case selection criteria, 47–49
   domestic workers' organizations, activism of, 59, 85, 86–90, 104–5

Bolivia (*continued*)
  enforcement of labor laws, 86, 90–92, 105
  exploitative working conditions for domestic workers in, 74, 84
  income inequality in, 12, 48t, 49, 83
  indigenous majority in, 83
    as domestic workers, 84
    marginalization of, 83, 84
    political power, rise of, 85, 87
    solidarity in, 86
  laws on domestic worker rights, 3, 32t, 84
  legal reform efforts, 41, 42, 42t, 43, 48t, 57, 145 n. 4
    as bottom-up reforms, 133
    economic context, 83
    framing of issue, 61, 89, 104–5, 132
    as legislative effort, 65, 66
    obstacles to, 80
    opposition to, 51, 56, 88–89, 89–90
    political context, 54, 55, 83, 84–85, 86, 91
    political process, 84–86
    social context, 83
    success of, 83–84, 90
    women's rights organizations and, 60
  live-in domestic workers, percentage of, 27
  minimum wage laws, 30–31
  number of domestic workers in, 84
  percentage of women employed in domestic work, 24t
  restrictions on domestic workers in, 19
  social security enrollment for domestic workers, 70
  sociodemographic and political data, 48t, 49
  state capacity in, 90, 105
  vacation days for domestic workers, 30
  workday length laws, 28, 29t, 30, 84, 85
Brazil
  children as domestic workers in, 25
  domestic work in, history of, 21
  enforcement of labor laws in, 79, 138
  exploitative working conditions for domestic workers in, 74
  income inequality in, 12
  laws on domestic worker rights, 3, 28–29, 32t
  legal reform efforts, 42, 42t, 44
    executive support, 55, 79
    political context, 54, 55
  minimum wage laws, 30–31
  percentage of women employed in domestic work, 24, 24t
  social security enrollment for domestic workers, 70, 71t, 72
  taxation in, 13
  vacation days for domestic workers, 30
  workday length laws, 28–29, 29t, 44
Brezzo, Luis, 111–13
Brockman, Erika, 89
Bunster, Ximena, 19, 22, 23
Bureau for Workers' Activities (ACTRAV), 63, 134

CAFTA (Central American Free Trade Agreement), 102
Calderón, Felipe, 82
Calderón, Ronaldo, 122
Cárdenas, Victor Hugo, 85, 87
Cardoso, Fernando Enrique, 79
care work, private, traditional undervaluation of, 10
Carnes, Matthew Edward, 28, 52–53, 63
case selections, criteria for, 47–49
Castro, Mary Garcia, 5
Catari, Basilia, 59, 86
Catholic Church, and domestic workers' organizations, 22, 58, 96, 122, 124–25, 144 n. 8
Catholic Youth Workers' Organization, 109
CEDAW. *See* Convention to Eliminate All Forms of Discrimination Against Women
Central America
  exploitative working conditions for domestic workers in, 75
  laws on domestic worker rights, 36t–38t
  legal reform efforts, obstacles to, 82
  percentage of contract domestic workers, *vs.* full-time employees, 27
  percentage of domestic workers with children, 26
  social security enrollment for domestic workers, 73
  tasks of domestic workers in, 26
  vacation days for domestic workers, 30
Central American Free Trade Agreement (CAFTA), 102
Central Confederation of Workers (CUT), 125
Central Labor Union (Central Obrera Boliviana; COB), 88

Central Unitaria de Trabajadores (CUT), 125
Chacón, Ana Helena, 101
Chaney, Elsa M., 5, 19, 22, 23
Cheng, Shu-Ju Ada, 19–20
child care options, 10–11
   among poor, 4, 14–15
   in industrialized nations, 11–12
   in Latin America, 14–15
   professional early childhood education and care (ECEC), 140–41
   state-subsidized care, 4, 98, 140–41
children as domestic workers, 25–26
   in Costa Rica, 94
   as invisible problem, 77, 82
   in Uruguay, 112
children of domestic workers. *See* family of domestic workers
Chile, 118–28
   and case selection criteria, 47–49
   domestic workers' organizations, activism of, 59, 122–27, 128, 129
   enforcement of labor laws in, 76, 77, 127–28, 129, 138
   exploitative working conditions for domestic workers in, 118–19
   general labor law reforms in, 53, 65
   Gini coefficient, 48t, 49
   immigrant domestic workers in, 13, 20, 25
   income inequality in, 12
   laws on domestic worker rights, 3, 33t, 118–19
   legal reform efforts, 42, 42t, 44, 48t, 80, 128–29
      economic context, 49, 118
      ILO convention and, 135
      immigrant workers and, 62
      legal context, 119
      opposition to, 51, 80, 121, 123–24
      political context, 49, 54, 55, 106, 118, 120–22, 127, 128, 133
      political process in, 120–22
      social context, 119
      as top-down, 64, 126, 133
      women's rights organizations and, 60
   live-in domestic workers, percentage of, 27
   minimum wage laws, 30–31, 44, 48t, 64, 121–22, 125–26
   percentage of women employed in domestic work, 24t
   social security enrollment for domestic workers, 70, 71t, 72, 77, 119

   sociodemographic and political data, 48t, 49
   state capacity, 106, 127
   vacation days for domestic workers, 30
   workday length laws, 29t, 30, 44, 118, 122, 126–27, 128, 129
Chinchilla, Laura, 96
Christian Democratic Party (PDC) [Chile], 120
Citizen Action Party (PAC). *See* Partido Acción Ciudadana
class inequality, 12
   exacerbation of, by informal nature of domestic work, 17–18
   and history of domestic work in Latin America, 21
   as inherent feature of domestic work, 20
   and low status of domestic workers, 35
   mobility and, 12–13
   and "safe" intimacy with domestic workers, 18–19
   and social distance, 12–13
   state policies reinforcing, 13
   structural reforms needed in, 138–41
   and supply of domestic workers, 1, 2, 9–10, 138–39
   vs. industrialized nations, 11–12
class prejudice, and laws on domestic workers, 1, 3–4, 22, 136, 137
coalition building
   in Bolivia, 86–90
   in Chile, 122–27
   in Costa Rica, 96–103
   and enforcement of labor laws, 78
   as key to successful reform, 56, 131–32
   potential allies, 59–64
   strategies for, 63–67
   in Uruguay, 109–16
COB. *See* Central Labor Union
Colombia
   income inequality in, 12
   laws on domestic worker rights, 3, 33t
   legal reform efforts, 41, 42–43, 42t, 145 n. 4
      as court-driven, 42–43, 81–82
      general labor law reforms in, 53, 54
      opposition to, 50–51
   minimum wage laws, 30–31
   percentage of women employed in domestic work, 24t
   social security enrollment for domestic workers, 70, 71t, 72–73

Colombia (*continued*)
  vacation days for domestic workers, 30
  workday length laws, 29t, 30, 43
Colorado Party, 108, 111
Colque, Miguelina, 91, 92
Comité Impulsor, 87–88, 88–89
Concertación coalition, 120
Confederación Latinoamericana y del Caribe de Trabajadoras del Hogar (CONLACTRAHO), 58–59
Confederación Patronal de la República Dominicana (COPARDOM), 154–55 n. 5
CONLACTRAHO. *See* Confederación Latinoamericana y del Caribe de Trabajadoras del Hogar
constitutions, national
  conflict of domestic workers laws with, 28, 31, 42–44, 46, 50, 52, 66–67
  Costa Rican guarantees of labor rights
    exclusion of domestic workers from, 93, 94
    as frame for reform, 99
contract domestic workers
  exclusion from employment data, 25, 27
  percentage of, *vs.* full-time employees, 27
contracts for domestic workers
  relative scarcity of, 3, 16, 31, 74 (*See also* informal workers)
  as requirement, in Chile, 119, 127, 128
Contreras, Rina, 98–99
Convention to Eliminate All Forms of Discrimination Against Women (CEDAW), 50, 98, 100
COPARDOM. *See* Confederación Patronal de la República Dominicana
Correa, Rafael, 47, 80
corruption, and enforcement of labor laws, 78
Costa Rica, 92–104
  and case selection criteria, 47–49
  constitutional guarantees of labor rights
    exclusion of domestic workers from, 93, 94
    as frame for reform, 99
  domestic workers' organizations, 59, 94, 96–103, 105
  enforcement of labor laws, 96, 103–4, 105
  exploitative working conditions for domestic workers in, 74, 75, 94–95
  Gini coefficient, 48t, 49, 93
  immigrant domestic workers in, 13, 25, 94

  laws on domestic worker rights, 3, 31, 36t, 94
  legal reform efforts, 41, 42, 42t, 43, 48t, 57
    allies in, 64
    as bottom-up reforms, 133
    economic context, 92–93
    framing of issue, 61–62, 96, 101, 102–3, 105, 132, 151 n. 58
    immigrant workers and, 62
    judicial remedies, 93, 96, 97, 101, 132, 150 n. 31
    legal context, 94–95
    as legislative effort, 65, 66
    obstacles to, 81
    opposition to, 51, 52, 96, 98–100, 101–2
    political context, 54, 55, 92–93, 95
    political process, 95–96
    social context, 93–95
    women's rights organizations and, 60
  minimum wage laws, 30–31
  number of domestic workers, 93
  percentage of contract domestic workers, *vs.* full-time employees, 27
  percentage of women employed in domestic work, 24t, 25
  reputation as human rights leader, 93, 102–3, 151 n. 58
  social security enrollment for domestic workers, 70, 73, 94, 103, 104
  sociodemographic and political data, 48t, 49
  state capacity in, 103, 105
  tasks of domestic workers in, 26
  vacation days for domestic workers, 30
  workday length laws, 29t, 30, 43, 93, 94, 97–98, 100, 101
Costa Rican Women's Alliance, 97
CUT. *See* Central Confederation of Workers

day care centers, in Latin America, 15. *See also* child care; early childhood education and care
debt crises of 1980s, and supply of domestic workers, 23
Defensoría del Pueblo (Ombudsman's Office) [Costa Rica], 93, 95, 100–101
demand for domestic workers
  economic conditions and, 139
  income inequality and, 1, 2, 9–10

increase number of women in Latin American labor market and, 2, 9–10, 22, 35
strong worker rights and, 51, 99, 100, 111, 112, 113, 123, 131
democratic governments in Latin America
and demand for equal rights, 2–3, 23
and marginalized groups, rights of, 39, 50
and workers' ability to organization, 57
dependent care, percentage of domestic workers performing, 26
disadvantaged workers, domestic workers in Latin America as, 39, 136
domestic work
continued importance of, 3, 9
devaluation of as women's work, 10, 16, 35, 40, 52, 61, 89, 137, 141
inequality as inherent feature of, 20
informal labor relations, impact of, 16–20
in Latin America, history of, 20–23
Domestic Workers' Association (ASTRADOMES), 96, 97, 98
domestic workers in Latin America
as citizens, 2, 13, 25
as exemplary disadvantaged workers, 39, 136
political clout, limitations on, 50
domestic workers' organizations. *See also* allies of domestic workers' organizations
activism of, 39, 58–59, 130
in Bolivia, 59, 85, 86–90, 104–5
Catholic Church, and, 22, 58, 96, 122, 124–25, 144 n. 8
in Chile, 59, 122–27, 128, 129
in Costa Rica, 59, 94, 96–103, 105
and enforcement of labor laws, 79
in Guatemala, 46
as key to reform, 56, 131
leadership, importance of, 59
limited efficacy of, 47
in Mexico, 45
obstacles to organization, 57–58, 131
in Peru, 81
regional confederation, 58–59
resources, access to, 58
services offered by, 58
in Uruguay, 59, 109–10, 111
Dominican Republic
exploitative working conditions for domestic workers in, 74, 75

general labor law reforms in, 53
laws on domestic worker rights, 36t
percentage of contract domestic workers, *vs.* full-time employees, 27
percentage of domestic workers with children, 26
percentage of women employed in domestic work, 24t
social security enrollment for domestic workers, 73
tasks of domestic workers in, 26
workday length laws, 29, 29t
dual protection regimes, worker benefits in, 72

early childhood education and care (ECEC), universal availability of, as goal, 140–41
economic conditions
debt crises of 1980s, and supply of domestic workers, 23
and demand for domestic workers, 139
free market reforms, and laws protecting domestic workers, 23
Ecuador
general labor law reforms in, 53
laws on domestic worker rights, 33t
legal reform efforts, 46–47
executive support for, 80
political context, 54
women's rights organizations and, 60
percentage of women employed in domestic work, 24t
vacation days for domestic workers, 30
workday length laws, 29t, 46–47
education
of domestic workers, 25–26, 94–95, 119
early childhood, access to in Latin America, 15, 140–41
El Salvador
class structure in, 12
enforcement of labor laws in, 77
exploitative working conditions for domestic workers in, 75
laws on domestic worker rights, 31, 36t
legal reform efforts, 46, 54, 82
percentage of women employed in domestic work, 24t
social security enrollment for domestic workers, 73
vacation days for domestic workers, 30
workday length laws, 29t, 46

employers
  union negotiations with, 117
  women as, 144 n. 8
Employers' Confederation of the Dominican Republic (COPARDOM), 154–55 n. 5
enforcement of domestic work laws
  allies of domestic workers and, 78
  in Argentina, 76, 138
  in Bolivia, 86, 90–92, 105
  in Brazil, 79, 138
  in Chile, 76, 77, 127–28, 129, 138
  in Costa Rica, 96, 103–4, 105
  executive support for, 77–82, 89–90, 101–2, 104, 116–17, 138
  inadequacy of, 3, 18, 68, 76–77, 82
  inspection mechanisms and complaint procedures, 68, 76–77
  integration into formal economy and, 68
  labor inspections in home and, 18, 76, 112, 116, 118, 127
  leftist parties and, 78, 79, 80, 82, 138
  as low priority for government, 68–69, 74, 75–76, 77
  and marginalized groups' rights, 39
  necessary improvements in, 137–38
  in Peru, 76
  proactive, benefits of, 68, 78, 80, 82, 138
  skimping on, as risk, 138
  social security enrollment and, 68, 69–73
  state capacity and, 138
  technical advice and support in, 76
  in Uruguay, 76, 77, 116–18, 129, 138
  variations, causes of, 77–82
  in Venezuela, 76
  victims' reluctance to report, 74–75, 91, 103, 128, 148 n. 15
Esper, Susana C., 70
Estévez, Alejandro M., 70
Europe, Gini coefficient, 11
exclusive social protection systems, worker benefits in, 72, 73
executive
  support for enforcement of labor laws, 77–82, 89–90, 101–2, 104, 116–17, 138
  support of legal reforms of domestic worker rights
    in Argentina, 43–44, 55, 79
    in Brazil, 55, 79
    in Chile, 44, 55, 65, 66, 119, 125–26, 128
    in Ecuador, 80
    female executives and, 55
    importance of, 40, 57, 64, 65, 132, 133
    in Uruguay, 43, 57, 66, 79, 107, 115, 118
exploitative working conditions for domestic workers, 22, 74–75, 81, 84, 94–95, 118–19

family of domestic workers
  activist workers and, 59
  lack of consideration for, 99, 131
  percentage of domestic workers with children, 26
  poor care given to, 15–16
  and right to life outside of work, 52, 130
  work's interference with family life, 16, 22
family of employer, domestic workers as part of
  and exacerbation of inequalities in labor relation, 17–18, 21, 141
  and exceptional nature of domestic work, 51–52, 55, 97, 101, 111, 123–24, 131–32
  and "safe" intimacy, 18–19
  and strong worker rights, impact of, 51, 52–53, 88, 99, 100, 112, 124
Federación Nacional de las Trabajadoras del Hogar de Bolivia. *See* National Household Workers' Federation of Bolivia
FENATRAHOB. *See* National Household Workers' Federation of Bolivia
Fernández, Alma, 118
Fernández de Kirchner, Christina, 43–44, 55
Filgueira, Fernando, welfare state topologies of, 70–72
Fish, Jennifer Natalie, 19, 20
Fox, Vincente, 82
framing of domestic workers' cause
  in Bolivia, 61, 89, 104–5, 132
  in Chile, 133
  in Costa Rica, 61–62, 96, 101, 102–3, 105, 132, 151 n. 58
  as key to successful reform, 59–60, 61–62, 132–33
  in Uruguay, 62, 132–33
free market reforms, and laws protecting domestic workers, 23
Frei, Eduardo, 121
Frente Amplio, 63, 66, 107, 108–9, 110, 113–15, 131

Fujimori, Alberto, 44, 66
Funes, Mauricio, 82

gender discrimination
　and devaluation of domestic work, 10, 16,
　　35, 40, 52, 61, 89, 137, 141
　and laws on domestic workers, 3–4,
　　21–22, 23, 136, 137
　as policy concern in industrialized
　　nations, 11
　and salaries for domestic workers, 26
gender roles, traditional
　and double burden on working women,
　　13–14
　shift in, in industrialized nations, 11
　and undervaluation of care work, 10
Gill, Lesley, 19, 20
Gini coefficient
　Bolivia, 48t, 49, 83
　Chile, 48t, 49
　Costa Rica, 48t, 49, 93
　in Latin America vs. other regions,
　　11–12
　and taxation in Latin America, 13
　Uruguay, 48t, 49
González, Esmeralda Britton, 100
Graham, Sandra Lauderdale, 21
Guatemala
　children as domestic workers in, 25
　domestic workers' organizations in, 46
　exploitative working conditions for
　　domestic workers in, 74, 75
　laws on domestic work, 3, 21–22, 31, 36t
　legal reform efforts, 45–46
　　factors in failure of, 62
　　opposition to, 52
　　political context, 54
　social security enrollment for domestic
　　workers, 73
　status of domestic workers in, 16
　vacation days for domestic workers, 30
　workday length laws, 29, 29t, 46
Guatemalan Labor Code of 1947, 21–22
Gutiérrez, Carlos, 101

hacienda system, and women as domestic
　workers, 21
health care rights
　denial to domestic workers, 84
　in Mexico, 82
　reform efforts, 45
　in Uruguay, 107
Hoffman, Kelly, 12
Honduras
　children as domestic workers in, 25
　laws on domestic worker rights, 3, 31, 37t
　percentage of contract domestic workers,
　　vs. full-time employees, 27
　percentage of women employed in
　　domestic work, 24t
　social security enrollment for domestic
　　workers, 73
　vacation days for domestic workers, 30
　workday length laws, 29, 29t
household spaces and amenities, restric-
　tions for domestic workers, 19
Human Rights Watch, 16, 59, 74, 77, 82

immigrant domestic workers
　child care options for, 15
　in Chile, discrimination against, 125
　focus of scholarship on, 10, 19
　ILO convention and, 135
　increase in, 25
　and labor violations, willingness to
　　report, 128
　numbers of, and legal reform, 62
　obstacles to organization in, 57–58
　powerlessness of, 5
　precarious legal position of, 19–20
　prevalence of, 13
　protections for, difficulties of implement-
　　ing, 40, 62, 102, 147 n. 54, 147 n. 55
　subservience of, as attractive, 20
import-substitution industrialization, eco-
　nomic and political effects of, 50
INAMU. See Instituto Nacional de las
　Mujeres
income inequality. See also Gini coefficient
　in Bolivia, 12, 48t, 49, 83
　and demand for domestic workers, 1, 2,
　　9–10
　in Latin America vs. industrialized
　　nations, 11–12
Independent Democratic Union (UDI), 120
indigenous majority in Bolivia, 83
　as domestic workers, 84
　marginalization of, 83, 84
　political power, rise of, 85, 87
　solidarity in, 86

indigenous rights
  democratic governments and, 39
  and organizing of domestic workers, 61
industrialized nations
  child care options in, 11
  gender equality as policy concern in, 11
  income inequality in, 11–12
  legal status of, 2
inequality. *See* class inequality
informal workers, domestic workers as
  chronic informality, 70, 137
  consequences of, 16–20
  and enforcement of labor laws, 68
  and lack of benefits, 14
  and organized labor, 39, 54, 137
  as percentage of all workers, 12
  and power of employer, history of, 21
  unique aspects of, 137
Instituto Nacional de las Mujeres (INAMU), 97, 100, 101, 116
Inter-American Court of Human Rights, 95
International Domestic Workers' Network, 134
International Labour Organization (ILO)
  as ally in reform struggle, 59–60, 62–63, 116
  Bureau for Workers' Activities (ACTRAV), 63, 134
  convention on domestic workers' rights (2011), 4, 63
    negotiation of, 134–35
    ratification of, 135
    as tool for reform, 133–36, 138, 141
  data collection on pensions and health care, 69
  data on percentage of women employed in domestic work, 24–25, 24t
  on differential treatment of domestic workers, 17–18
  and enforcement of labor laws, 78–79, 138
  on invisibility of domestic work, 16–17
  standards for decent work, 31
  treaties, and discrimination against domestic workers, 31, 50, 98, 99, 100
international norms, diffusion of in Latin America, 136–37
international organizations, as allies in reform struggle, 59–60, 62–63. *See also* International Labour Organization (ILO)

international treaties, conflict of domestic worker laws with, 31, 42, 46, 66–67, 98
intimacy with domestic workers
  class inequality and, 18–19
  sexual harassment, 75, 84

judicial remedies, 42–43, 46, 66–67
  in Colombia, 42–43, 132
  in Costa Rica, 93, 96, 97, 101, 132, 150 n. 31
  in Guatemala, 46, 132
  limited effectiveness of, 132
  in Panama, 132
Juventud Obrera Católica, 109

Karl, Terry Lynn, 12
Kuznesof, Elizabeth, 21, 23

labor inspections for domestic work conditions
  in Chile, 127
  opposition to, 18, 76, 112
  in Uruguay, 116, 118
labor market, increase of women in, and supply and demand for domestic workers, 2, 9–10
labor unions
  as allies in reform struggle, 61, 88, 101, 114, 124–25, 131
  government responses to, 22
  ILO convention and, 135
  informal workers and, 39, 54, 137
  and marginalized groups, limited interest in, 53–54
  organizing among domestic workers (*See also* domestic workers' organizations)
    history of, 22
    immigrant domestic workers and, 57–58
    obstacles to, 22, 57–58
  power of, and employment law reforms, 53
labor violations. *See* enforcement of domestic work laws
LACCUU. *See* Liga de Amas de Casa Consumidores y Usuarios del Uruguay
Lagos, Richard, 121, 122, 126
Lan, Pei-Chi, 19–20

Latin American And Caribbean Confederation of Domestic Workers (CONLACTRAHO), 58–59
laws on domestic work, 27–31. *See also* enforcement of domestic work laws; legal reform of domestic work laws
  in Argentina, 3, 31, 32t
  in Bolivia, 3, 32t, 84
  in Brazil, 32t
  in Chile, 33t, 118–19
  class prejudice and, 1, 3–4, 22, 136, 137
  in Colombia, 33t
  in Costa Rica, 3, 31, 36t, 94
  in Dominican Republic, 36t
  in El Salvador, 31, 36t
  as employer-focused, 50
  as exception to general laws on labor rights, 18, 28, 31, 51–52, 55, 84, 94, 97, 101, 111, 123–24, 130, 131–32
  free market reforms and, 23
  gender discrimination and, 3–4, 21–22, 23, 136, 137
  in Guatemala, 3, 21–22, 31, 36t
  history of, 21–22, 28
  in Honduras, 31, 37t
  immigrant domestic workers and, 19–20
  informal nature of domestic work and, 16–20
  and international treaties, conflicts with, 31, 42, 46, 66–67, 98
  limited nature of, in United States, 2
  and national constitutions, conflicts with, 28, 31, 42–44, 46, 50, 52, 66–67
  racial and ethnic prejudice and, 3–4, 4–5, 21–22, 23, 136, 137
  reform, slow pace of, 3
  respect clauses in, 3, 31, 32t, 34t, 36t, 37t, 94, 98, 100
  in Uruguay, 3, 34t, 106, 107
  in Venezuela, 3, 31, 34t
laws on labor rights, general
  domestic work as exception to, 18, 28, 31, 51–52, 55, 84, 94, 97, 101, 111, 123–24, 130, 131–32
  neoliberal reforms and, 53
  reforms, as separate from reform of domestic worker rights, 52–54, 65
  and rights of weaker parties, 50
  as well-developed in Latin America, 50

leadership, importance to domestic workers' organizations, 59
  in Bolivia, 86, 92
  in Chile, 124–25
  in Costa Rica, 96, 104
  in Uruguay, 115–16
League of Homemakers and Consumers of Uruguay. *See* Liga de Amas de Casa Consumidores y Usuarios del Uruguay
leftist parties
  as allies in reform struggle, 53, 54, 55, 63–64, 66
  in Bolivia, 89–90
  in Chile, 118, 121–22, 125, 128
  in Uruguay, 107, 108–9, 110, 113–14, 118
  and enforcement of labor laws, 78, 79, 80, 82, 138
legal equality, vs. levels of social security enrollment, 70
legal reform of domestic work laws. *See also individual nations*
  agenda-setting, visibility of issue and, 40, 56–57, 59–60, 64, 131–32, 136
  in Bolivia, 86–90
  in Chile, 122–27
  in Costa Rica, 96–103
  in Uruguay, 109–16
  alliances and coalitions and, 56, 59–64
  and enforcement, renewed interest in, 78
  executive support
    in Argentina, 43–44, 55, 79
    in Brazil, 55, 79
    in Chile, 44, 55, 65, 66, 119, 125–26, 128
    in Ecuador, 80
    female executives and, 55
    importance of, 40, 57, 64, 65, 132, 133
    in Uruguay, 43, 57, 66, 79, 107, 115, 118
  framing of issue, 59–60, 61–62, 132–33
  general forward progress of, 41
  ILO conventions as tool for, 133–36
  and immigrant domestic workers, impact of, 62
  judicial remedies, 42–43, 46, 66–67
    in Colombia, 42–43, 132
    in Costa Rica, 93, 96, 97, 101, 132, 150 n. 31
    in Guatemala, 45, 132
    limited effectiveness of, 132
    in Panama, 132

legal reform of domestic work laws (*continued*)
   and leftist government, impact of, 53, 54, 55, 63–64, 66, 535
   legislative strategies, 64–66, 132
   measurement of, 41
   nations successful in, 3, 41–42, 42t, 47–48, 83–84, 90, 107, 116
   as ongoing process, 130, 136
   opposition to, 3–4
      opponents' arguments and strategies, 51–52, 55–56, 131
      by political elites, 3–4, 39–40
   parallels with campaign to end violence against women, 136–37
   paths to, 133
   persistence, necessity of, 65
   political and social contexts of, 40–41
   as separate from general labor reforms, 52–54, 65
   strategies for, 40, 55–67
   types of, 41
   unions and, 53–54
   women in government and, 54–55
   workers' organizations and unions in, 57–59
legislation, strategies for, 64–66, 132
legislative branches, and legal reform, 43, 44
leverage for domestic workers, strategies for, 20
liberation theology, and union organizing among domestic workers, 144 n. 8
Libertarian Movement (Costa Rica), 100–101
Liga de Amas de Casa Consumidores y Usuarios del Uruguay (LACCUU), 117
live-in domestic workers, percentage of, *vs.* live-out workers, 26–27
lower classes
   child care options for, 4, 14–15
   liberation of middle and upper class women at expense of, 2, 14
   and political action, difficulty of, 2
Lula da Silva, Luiz Inácio, 79–80

Maher, Kristen Hill, 20
male domestic workers, higher status of, 10, 26
marginalized groups, rights of
   in Bolivia, 83, 84

   democratic governments and, 39, 50
   enforcement of, 39
   organized labor's limited interest in, 53–54
Martínez Franzoni, Juliana, 94–95, 97
MAS. *See* Movimiento al Socialismo
maternity leave laws
   in Argentina, 43–44
   in Brazil, 44
   in Chile, 42t, 44, 48t, 51. 64, 53, 64, 119, 121, 123–24, 127, 133
   for domestic workers *vs.* others, 31, 32t, 33t
   in Ecuador, 47
   in Peru, 45
   violations of, 75
Mesa, Carlos, 85
Mexico
   children as domestic workers in, 25
   constitution, conflict with domestic workers laws, 28, 31
   domestic workers' organizations in, 45
   exploitative working conditions for domestic workers in, 74
   laws on domestic worker rights, 3, 31, 37t
   legal reform efforts, 45
      labor unions and, 61
      obstacles to, 82
   minimum wage laws, 31
   percentage of women employed in domestic work, 24, 24t
   social security enrollment for domestic workers, 70, 71t, 72–73
   workday length laws, 28, 29t
middle and upper classes
   child care options for, 4, 14, 139
   interests of, states' prioritization of, 4
   opposition to reform of domestic work laws, 40
middle and upper class women
   liberation of, at expense of lower-class women, 2, 14
   opposition to legal reforms, 60, 88
minimum wage laws, 30–31
   in Brazil, 30–31, 44
   in Chile, 30–31, 44, 48t, 64, 121–22, 125–26
   in Costa Rica, 94, 100
   and demand for domestic workers, 90
   in Ecuador, 80
   in Paraguay, 30, 46

in Uruguay, 31, 115, 117–18
violations of, 74, 95
MNR. *See* Movimiento Nacional Revolucionario
Mora, Sindy, 94–95, 97
Morales, Evo, 66, 85–86, 90, 91
Moreno, Aida, 59, 122, 123
Movimiento al Socialismo (MAS), 66, 85–86, 89–90, 131
Movimiento Nacional Revolucionario (MNR), 84
Muchachas No More (Chaney and Castro), 5
Murgas Torraza, Rafael, 46

National Association of Household Workers (ANECAP), 109–10, 122, 124–25, 126
National Household Workers' Federation of Bolivia (FENATRAHOB), 87, 89, 90, 92
National Liberation Party (PLN), 95
National Renovation (RN), 120
neoliberal reforms, and labor protection, 53
NGOs (nongovernmental organizations), advocacy for domestic workers, 58
Nicaragua
  children as domestic workers in, 25
  exploitative working conditions for domestic workers in, 75
  laws on domestic worker rights, 37t
  legal reform efforts, 45, 54, 146 n. 15
  percentage of contract domestic workers, vs. full-time employees, 27
  percentage of women employed in domestic work, 24t
  social security enrollment for domestic workers, 73
  workday length laws, 29t
noncitizen domestic workers. *See* immigrant domestic workers
nongovernmental organizations (NGOs), advocacy for domestic workers, 58

Observatory on Gender and Justice, 46
Ombudsman Office
  in Bolivia, 89, 90
  in Costa Rica, 93, 95, 100–101
organizations advocating for domestic workers, 58. *See also* domestic workers' organizations

organized labor. *See* labor unions
overtime laws
  for domestic workers vs. others, 28
  reform efforts, 110, 116

PAC. *See* Partido Acción Ciudadana
Pacheco, Abel, 98
PAN. *See* Partido Acción Nacional
Panama
  exploitative working conditions for domestic workers in, 75
  laws on domestic worker rights, 37t
  legal reform efforts, 46, 52, 132
  percentage of contract domestic workers, vs. full-time employees, 27
  percentage of women employed in domestic work, 24t
  social security enrollment for domestic workers, 73
  tasks of domestic workers in, 26
  vacation days for domestic workers, 30
  workday length laws, 29t, 46
Paraguay
  children as domestic workers in, 26
  income inequality in, 12
  laws on domestic worker rights, 31, 33t
  legal reform efforts, 46
    ILO convention and, 135
    political context, 54
  minimum wage laws, 30, 46
  percentage of women employed in domestic work, 24, 24t
  social security enrollment for domestic workers, 70, 71t, 73
  vacation days for domestic workers, 30
  workday length laws, 29t, 30
parenting, absent, in immigrant domestic workers, 15
Parreñas, Salazar, 19–20
Partido Acción Ciudadana (PAC), 95
Partido Acción Nacional (PAN), 45
Partido de Liberación Nacional (PLN), 95
Partido de Revolución Democrática (PRD), 45
Partido Movimiento Libertario, 100–101
Partido Nacional, 112
Partido Unidad Social Cristiana (PUSC), 95
Party for Democracy (PPD), 120
PDC. *See* Christian Democratic Party
pension rights. *See* social security benefits for domestic workers

personal life outside work, right to, 52, 130
Peru
　children as domestic workers in, 26
　enforcement of labor laws in, 76
　exploitative working conditions for domestic workers in, 22, 74, 81
　general labor law reforms in, 53, 54
　laws on domestic worker rights, 34t
　legal reform efforts, 42, 42t, 44–45
　　as legislative effort, 65, 66
　　obstacles to, 81
　　opposition to, 51–52
　percentage of women employed in domestic work, 24t
　restrictions on domestic workers in, 19
　social security enrollment for domestic workers, 70, 71t, 73
　and union organizing among domestic workers, response to, 22
　vacation days for domestic workers, 30
　workday length laws, 28, 29t, 44–45
Piñera, Sebastián, 122
Pinochet, Augusto, 118, 120, 124
Plenario Intersindical de Trabajadores-Convención Nacional de Trabajadores (PIT-CNT), 113–14, 115
PLN. *See* Partido de Liberación Nacional
political action, difficulty of for low income workers, 2
politicians, opposition to reform of domestic work laws, 3–4, 39–40, 131
Portes, Alejandro, 12
poverty rates among domestic workers, 26
power mobilization theory, and legal reform, 53
PPD. *See* Party for Democracy
PRD. *See* Partido de Revolución Democrática
Pribble, Jennifer, 108–9, 128
proactive enforcement, benefits of, 68, 78, 80, 82
professionalization of domestic work
　among male workers, 10
　in Bolivia, 91
　in Chile, 80, 128
　as goal, 78, 104, 139–41
protest, violent, as counterproductive, 59
PRSD. *See* Radical Social Democratic Party
PS. *See* Socialist Party [Chile]
PUSC. *See* Partido Unidad Social Cristiana

racial and ethnic identity, and organizing of domestic workers, 61
racial and ethnic prejudice
　in Chile, 125
　and laws on domestic workers, 3–4, 4–5, 21–22, 23, 136, 137
　and opposition to legal reforms, 40
　and salaries of domestic workers, 26
racial minorities in Latin America, as domestic workers, history of, 21
Radical Social Democratic Party (PRSD), 120
reforms
　legal. *See* legal reform of domestic work laws
　structural, need for, 138–41
research on domestic workers, 5, 9, 143 n. 4
　focus on immigration, 10, 19
rights of domestic workers, arguments for and against, 50–52, 130–31
RN. *See* National Renovation
Rodgers, Janine, 20
Rodríguez, Casimira, 59, 86, 89, 90–91
Rodríguez, Laura, 122
Rollins, Judith, 17, 18–19, 20, 144 n. 8
Romero, Patricia, 101, 102, 151 n. 58
Ruiz de Giorgio, José, 122–23, 124

Saa, Maria Antonieta, 126
"safe" intimacy with domestic workers, class inequality and, 18–19
salaries for domestic workers, discrimination in, 26
Sánchez de Lozada, Gonzalo, 85, 89
Sarthou, Helios, 110, 111, 112–13
service economies, and women in work force, 10
severance notice laws, 84
severance pay, reform efforts, 44, 53, 119, 121, 122–23
sexual harassment of domestic workers, 75, 84
Sindicato de Trabajadoras de Casas Particulares (SINTRACAP), 122, 125, 126, 135
Sindicato Único de Trabajadoras Domésticas (SUTD), 109, 115, 117, 118
single-parent families
　child care options for, 15
　employment options for female head of, 15

SINTRACAP. *See* Sindicato de Trabajadoras de Casas Particulares
Social and Economic Agreement (Guatemala), 45–46
Social Christian Unity Party. *See* Partido Unidad Social Cristiana
Social Commission (Costa Rica), 96, 97–100
social distance
  in Latin America, 12–13
  and "safe" intimacy with domestic workers, 18–19
Socialist Party (PS) [Chile], 120
social movements, and cycles of protest, 57
social security benefits for domestic workers. *See also individual nations*
  correlation with legal equality, 70
  employers' failure to pay, 18
  enforcement of, 117, 127
  enrollment
    as indication of labor law enforcement levels, 68, 69
    poor efforts toward, 137
    vs. general population, by nation, 69–73, 71t
  reduction of by law, 18, 110
  reform efforts, 43, 44, 45, 46, 79–82, 85, 100
social status of domestic workers, class inequality and, 20, 35
social transfer programs in Latin America, privileging of upper classes in, 13
South Africa, domestic workers in, 19, 20
Staab, Silke, 20
state capacity, and enforcement of labor laws, 77–78
state policies in Latin America
  and class structure, reinforcement of, 13
  prioritization of middle and upper class interests, 4
stratified universal countries, benefits in, 70–72
structural reforms, need for, 138–41
subservience
  employers' view of as natural, 130, 131
  of immigrants, as attractive to employers, 20
supply of domestic workers
  class inequality and, 1, 2, 9–10, 138–39

debt crises of 1980s and, 23
increase number of women in Latin American labor market and, 2, 9–10
SUTD. *See* Sindicato Único de Trabajadoras Domésticas

Taiwan, domestic workers in, 20
taxation in Latin America, and class inequality, 13
Toledo, Alejandro, 66
Tourné, Daisy, 110, 111
training classes for domestic workers, 128
Tripartite Commission on Equality of Opportunity and Employment, 115

UDI. *See* Independent Democratic Union
UNDP (United Nations Development Programme), 13–14
unemployment insurance
  lack of, in Uruguay, 107
  reform efforts, 43, 44, 116
unions. *See* labor unions
United Nations
  Development Programme (UNDP), 13–14
  Economic and Social Council, 88
  treaties, discrimination against domestic workers and, 31, 50
United States
  childhood education and care in, 11
  domestic workers in, as foreign born, 2
  laws on domestic work, 2
  number of domestic workers in, 2
  preference for immigrant domestic workers in, 20
urbanization, and women in work force, 10
Uruguay, 106–18
  and case selection criteria, 47–49
  domestic workers' organizations in, 59, 109–10, 111
  enforcement of labor laws in, 76, 77, 116–18, 129, 138
  Gini coefficient, 48t, 49
  income inequality in, 12
  laws on domestic worker rights, 3, 34t, 106, 107
  legal reform efforts, 41, 42, 42t, 48t, 128–29
    economic context, 106

Uruguay (*continued*)
  executive support, 43, 57, 66, 79, 107, 115, 118
  framing of issue, 62, 132–33
  labor unions and, 61, 114, 115–16, 117–18
  legal context, 107–8
  as legislative effort, 65
  opposition to, 51, 111–14, 118
  political context, 54, 55, 106, 108–9, 128
  political process, 43, 49, 108–16
  social context, 107–8
  success of, 107, 116
  as top-down reform, 133
  minimum wage laws, 31, 115, 117–18
  national salary negotiation committees, 114
  number of domestic workers in, 107
  percentage of women employed in domestic work, 24t
  social security enrollment for domestic workers, 70, 71t, 72, 77, 107–8
  sociodemographic and political data, 48t, 49
  state capacity, 106
  vacation days for domestic workers, 30
  workday length laws, 29t, 30, 107, 110, 113–14, 116

vacation days and holidays, laws on
  in Chile, 118
  for domestic workers *vs.* others, 30, 84
  legal requirements for, failure to meet, 74
  reform efforts, 43, 44, 45, 93, 94, 101, 119, 122, 126
Vázquez, Tabaré, 79, 113–14, 115
Venezuela
  class structure in, 12
  enforcement of labor laws in, 76
  laws on domestic worker rights, 3, 31, 34t
  legal reform efforts, 47
    general labor law reforms in, 53
    political context, 54
  percentage of women employed in domestic work, 24, 24t
  vacation days for domestic workers, 30
  workday length laws, 29, 29t, 47
violence against women, campaign against, parallels with domestic work law reforms, 136–37

visibility of issue
  agenda-setting and, 40, 56–57, 59–60, 64, 131–32, 136
  in Bolivia, 86–90
  in Chile, 122–27
  in Costa Rica, 96–103
  in Uruguay, 109–16
  and effective enforcement, 78
Voorend, Koen, 94–95, 97

Weldon, Laurel, 5
welfare regimes, global, and childhood education and care, 11
women
  domestic work as historically important employment for, 21
  domestic workers
    as percent of all domestic workers, 10
    as percent of working women in Latin America, 1, 3, 9, 24–25, 24t
    salaries *vs.* male domestic workers, 26
  as employers, 144 n. 8
  in government, and pace of legal reforms, 54–55
  increase of in labor market, 13
    and child care options, 4
    and demand for domestic workers, 2, 9–10, 22, 35
    traditional gender roles and, 13–14
  middle and upper class
    liberation of, at expense of lower-class women, 2, 14
    opposition to legal reforms, 60, 88
Women's Executive Agency (INAMU), 97, 100, 101, 116
women's rights
  democratic governments and, 39
  in Guatemala, 45–46
women's rights groups, as allies in reform struggle, 59–60, 101, 131
women's work, devaluation of domestic work as, 10, 16, 35, 40, 52, 61, 89, 137, 141
workday/workweek length laws
  in Argentina, 29–30, 29t, 43–44
  in Bolivia, 28, 29t, 30, 84, 85
  in Brazil, 28–29, 44
  in Chile, 29t, 30, 44, 118, 122, 126–27, 128, 129
  in Colombia, 29t, 30, 43

in Costa Rica, 29t, 30, 43, 93, 94, 97–98, 100, 101
in Dominican Republic, 29
in Ecuador, 29t, 46–47
in El Salvador, 29t, 46
in Guatemala, 29, 29t, 46
in Honduras, 29, 29t
ILO convention and, 135
longer workday for domestic workers, 18, 28, 29t
in Mexico, 28, 29t
in Nicaragua, 29t
opposition to charges in, 51–52, 65, 99, 111, 131, 154–55 n. 5
in Panama, 29t, 46
in Paraguay, 29t, 30
in Peru, 28, 29t, 44–45
in Uruguay, 29t, 3c, 107, 110, 113–14, 116
in Venezuela, 29, 29t, 47
violations of, 74, 75

Yashar, Deborah, 61

www.ingramcontent.com/pod-product-compliance
Lightning Source LLC
Chambersburg PA
CBHW021406290426
44108CB00010B/405